SOUL WISDOM

MASTER SHA'S TAO HEALING CENTER
885 Queen Street, Second Floor
Honolulu, Hawaii 96813
808.988.8090
*Please use this blessed book to serve your healing, transformation
and enlightenment. Hold it to your heart and make a request for
any aspect of your life or anyone that needs healing. To learn and
experience more, please visit or call us. Many blessings!*
MasterShaSHCH@gmail.com
drsha.com/soulhealingcenters/hawaii

SOUL WISDOM

Practical Soul Treasures
to Transform Your Life

Dr. Zhi Gang Sha

ATRIA BOOKS
New York   London   Toronto   Sydney
Heaven's Library
Toronto

ATRIA
BOOKS

Heaven's Library

A Division of Simon & Schuster, Inc.   Toronto, ON
1230 Avenue of the Americas
New York, NY 10020

First Atria Books trade paperback edition June 2008

ATRIA BOOKS and colophon are trademarks of Simon & Schuster, Inc.
Heaven's Library and Soul Power Series are trademarks of
Heaven's Library Publication Corp.

For information about special discounts for bulk purchases,
please contact Simon & Schuster Special Sales at
1-800-456-6798 or business@simonandschuster.com.

Designed by Jaime Putorti

Manufactured in the United States of America

3   5   7   9   10   8   6   4   2

Library of Congress Cataloging-in-Publication Data

Sha, Zhi Gang.
Soul wisdom : practical soul treasures to tranform your life /
Zhi Gang Sha. — 1st Atria Books trade pbk. ed.
p.   cm.
1. Spiritual life.   2. Spiritual healing.   I. Title.
BL624.S4756 2008
204'.4 — dc22   2008017216

ISBN-13: 978-1-4165-8893-1
ISBN-10:   1-4165-8893-0

A previous version of this work was published by
Heaven's Library Publication Corp. in 2007.

Contents

PART 1

SOUL LANGUAGE
Universal Communication

PART 2

SOUL SONG
The Song of the Heart and Soul

Contents

Soul Power Series

The purpose of life is to serve. I have committed my life to this purpose. Service is my life mission.

My total life mission is to transform the consciousness of humanity and souls in the universe, in order to join all souls as one to create love, peace, and harmony for humanity, Mother Earth, and the universe. This mission includes three empowerments.

My first empowerment is to teach *universal service,* to empower people to be unconditional universal servants. The message of universal service is:

> *I serve humanity and the universe unconditionally.*
> *You serve humanity and the universe unconditionally.*
> *Together, we serve humanity and all souls in the universe unconditionally.*

My second empowerment is to teach *healing,* to empower people to heal themselves and heal others. The message of healing is:

> *I have the power to heal myself.*
> *You have the power to heal yourself.*
> *Together, we have the power to heal the world.*

My third empowerment is to teach soul secrets and wisdom and to transmit *Divine Soul Power,* to empower people to use Soul Power to transform every aspect of their lives and enlighten their souls, hearts, minds, and bodies.

The message of Soul Power is:

> *I have the Soul Power to transform every aspect of my life and enlighten my soul, heart, mind, and body.*
> *You have the Soul Power to transform every aspect of your life and enlighten your soul, heart, mind, and body.*
> *Together, we have the Soul Power to transform every aspect of the world and enlighten humanity and all souls.*

Soul Power is my most important empowerment. It is the key for my total life mission. It is the key for transforming my physical life and spiritual life. Soul Power is the key for transforming your physical life and spiritual life. It is the key for transforming every soul in the universe.

The beginning of the twenty-first century is humanity's, Mother Earth's, and the universe's transition period into a new era, which is named the Soul Light Era. The Soul Light Era began on August 8, 2003. It will last fifteen thousand years. Natural disasters—tsunamis, hurricanes, earthquakes, floods, fires, drought, extreme temperatures, famine, disease—and terrorism and political, religious, and ethnic wars and other such upheavals are part of this transition. Millions of people are also suffering from depression, anxiety, fear, anger, and worry. They suffer from pain, chronic conditions, and life-threatening illnesses. Humanity needs help. The consciousness of humanity needs to be transformed. The suffering of humanity needs to be removed.

The books of the Soul Power Series are brought to you by Heaven's Library and Atria Books. They reveal soul secrets and teach soul wisdom, soul knowledge and soul practices for your daily life. Soul Power can heal, prevent illness, rejuvenate, prolong life, and transform every aspect of life, including relationships and finances. Soul Power is vital to assist humanity and Mother Earth through this transition period. Soul Power will awaken and transform the consciousness of humanity and all souls.

In the twentieth century and for centuries before, *mind over matter* was emphasized. In the Soul Light Era, *soul over matter* — Soul Power — will transform all life.

There are countless souls on Mother Earth — souls of human beings, souls of animals, souls of other living things, and souls of inanimate things. *Everyone and everything has a soul.*

Every soul has its own frequency and power. Jesus had miraculous healing power. We have heard many heart-touching stories of lives saved by Guan Yin's[1] compassion. Mother Mary's love has created many heart-moving stories. All of these great souls were given Divine Soul Power to serve humanity. In all of the world's great religions and spiritual traditions, including Buddhism, Taoism, Christianity, Judaism, Hinduism, Islamism, and more, there are similar accounts of great spiritual healing and blessing power.

I honor every religion and every spiritual tradition. However, I am not teaching religion. I am teaching Soul Power, which includes soul secrets, soul wisdom, soul knowledge, and soul practices. Your soul has Soul Power to heal, rejuvenate, and transform life. An animal's soul has the power to heal and rejuvenate. The souls of the sun, the moon, an ocean, a tree, and a mountain have the power to heal and rejuvenate. The souls of healing angels, ascended masters, holy saints, Taoist saints, buddhas, and other high-level spiritual beings have great Soul Power to heal, rejuvenate, and transform life.

Every soul has its own standing. This spiritual standing, or soul standing, has countless layers. Soul Power also has layers. Not every soul can perform miracles like Jesus, Guan Yin, and Mother Mary. Soul Power depends on the soul's spiritual standing in Heaven.

The higher a soul stands in Heaven, the more Soul Power that

---

1. Guan Yin is known as the Bodhisattva of Compassion and, in the West, as the Goddess of Mercy.

soul is given. Jesus, Guan Yin, and Mother Mary all have a very high spiritual standing.

Who determines a soul's spiritual standing? Who gives the appropriate Soul Power to a soul? Who decides the direction for humanity, Mother Earth, and the universes? The top leader of the spiritual world is the decision maker. This top leader is the Divine. The Divine is the creator and manifester of all universes.

In the Soul Light Era, all souls will join as one and align their consciousness with divine consciousness. At this historical time, the Divine has decided to transmit his soul treasures to humanity and all souls to help humanity and all souls go through Mother Earth's transition.

Let me share two personal stories with you to explain how I reached this understanding.

First, in April 2003, I was teaching a soul workshop to about one hundred people at the Land of Medicine Buddha in Soquel, California. During my teaching, the Divine appeared. I told the students, "The Divine is here. Could you give me a moment?" I knelt to the floor to honor the Divine. (At age six, I was taught to bow down to my tai chi masters. At age ten, I bowed down to my qi gong masters. At age twelve, I bowed down to my kung fu masters. Being Chinese, I learned this courtesy throughout my childhood.) I explained to the students, "Please understand that this is the way I honor the Divine, my spiritual fathers, and my spiritual masters. Now I will have a conversation with the Divine." I began by saying silently, "Dear Divine, I'm very honored you are here."

The Divine, who was in front of me above my head, replied, "Zhi Gang, I come today to pass a spiritual law to you."

I said, "I am honored to receive this spiritual law."

The Divine continued, "This spiritual law is named the Universal Law of Universal Service. It is one of the highest spiritual laws in the universe. It applies to the spiritual world and the physical world." (The Divine pointed to himself.) "I am a universal servant." (The Divine pointed to me.) "You are a universal servant." (The Divine swept his hand in front of himself.) "Everyone and everything is a universal servant. A universal servant offers universal service unconditionally. Universal service includes universal love, forgiveness, peace, healing, blessing, harmony, and enlightenment. If one offers little service, one receives little blessing from the universe and from me. If one offers more service, one receives more blessing. If one offers unconditional service, one receives unlimited blessing."

The Divine paused for a moment before continuing. "There is another kind of service, which is unpleasant service. Unpleasant service includes killing, harming, taking advantage of others, cheating, stealing, complaining, and more. If one offers a little unpleasant service, one learns little lessons from the universe and from me. If one offers more unpleasant service, one learns more lessons. If one offers huge unpleasant service, one learns huge lessons."

I asked, "What kinds of lessons could one learn?"

The Divine replied, "The lessons include sickness, accidents, injuries, financial challenges, broken relationships, emotional imbalance, mental confusion, and disorder." The Divine emphasized, "This is how the universe operates. This is one of my most important spiritual laws for all souls in the universe to follow."

After the Divine delivered this universal law, I immediately made a silent vow to the Divine: "Dear Divine, I am extremely honored to receive your Law of Universal Service. I make a vow to you, to all humanity, and to all souls in the universe that I will be an unconditional universal servant. I will give my total GOLD [gratitude, obedience, loyalty, devotion] to you and to serving you. I am honored to be your servant and a servant of all humanity and all souls." Hearing this, the Divine smiled and left.

My second story took place three months later, in July 2003, while I was holding a soul retreat near Toronto. The Divine came again. I again explained to my students that the Divine had appeared, and asked them to wait a moment while I bowed down 108 times and listened. On this occasion, the Divine told me, "Zhi Gang, I come today to choose you as my direct servant, vehicle, and channel."

I was deeply moved and said to the Divine, "I am honored. What does it mean to be your direct servant, vehicle, and channel?"

The Divine replied, "When you offer healing and blessing to others, call me and I will come instantly to offer my healing and blessing to them."

I was deeply touched and replied, "Thank you so much for choosing me as your direct servant."

The Divine continued, "Very often, I offer my healing and blessing by transmitting my permanent healing and blessing treasures."

I asked, "How do you do this?"

The Divine answered, "Select a person and I will give you a demonstration."

I asked for a volunteer with serious health challenges. A man named Walter raised his hand. He stood up and explained that he had liver cancer, with a two-by-three-centimeter malignant tumor that had just been diagnosed from a biopsy.

I then asked the Divine, "Please bless Walter. Please show me how you transmit your permanent treasures." I saw the Divine send a beam of light from the Divine's heart to Walter's liver. The beam shot into his liver, where it turned into a golden light ball that instantly started spinning. Walter's entire liver shone with beautiful golden light.

The Divine asked me, "Do you understand what software is?"

I was surprised by this question but replied, "I do not understand much about computers. I just know that software is a computer program. I have heard about accounting software, office software, and graphic design software."

"Yes," the Divine said. "Software is a program. Because you asked me, I have just transmitted or downloaded my Soul Software for Liver to Walter. It is one of my permanent healing and blessing treasures. You asked me. I did the job. This is what it means for you to be my chosen direct servant and channel."

I was astonished. Excited, inspired, and humbled, I said to the

Divine, "I am so honored to be your direct servant. How blessed I am to be chosen." Almost speechless, I asked the Divine, "Why did you choose me?"

"I chose you," said the Divine, "because you have served humanity for more than one thousand lifetimes. You have been very committed to serving my mission through all your lifetimes. I am choosing you in this life to be my direct servant. You will transmit countless permanent healing and blessing treasures from me to humanity and all souls. This is the honor I give to you now."

I was moved to tears. I immediately bowed down 108 times again and made a silent vow: "Dear Divine, I cannot bow down to you enough for the honor you have given to me. No words can express my greatest gratitude. How blessed I am to be your direct servant to download your permanent healing and blessing treasures to humanity and all souls! Humanity and all souls will receive your huge blessings through my service as your direct servant. I give my total life to you and to humanity. I will accomplish your tasks. I will be a pure servant to humanity and all souls." I bowed again.

Then I asked the Divine, "How should Walter use his Soul Software?"

"Walter must spend time practicing with my Soul Software," said the Divine. "Tell him that simply to receive my Soul Software does not mean he will recover. He must practice every day to restore his health, step by step."

I asked, "How should he practice?"

The Divine gave me this guidance: "Tell Walter to chant repeatedly: *Divine Liver Soul Software heals me. Divine Liver Soul Software heals me. Divine Liver Soul Software heals me. Divine Liver Soul Software heals me.* He can also repeatedly chant his Soul Language."

I asked, "For how long should Walter chant?"

The Divine answered, "At least two hours per day. The longer he practices, the better. If he does this, he could recover in three to six months."

I shared this information with Walter, who was excited and deeply moved. Walter said, "I will practice two hours or more each day."

Finally, I asked the Divine, "How does the Soul Software work?"

The Divine replied, "My Soul Software is a golden healing ball that rotates and clears energy and spiritual blockages in Walter's liver."

I again bowed to the Divine 108 times. Then, I stood up and offered three Soul Softwares to every participant in the workshop as divine gifts. Upon seeing this, the Divine smiled and left.

Walter immediately began to practice as directed for at least two hours every day. Two and a half months later, a CT scan and MRI showed that his liver cancer had completely disappeared. At the end of 2006, I met Walter again at a signing in Toronto for my book, *Soul Mind Body Medicine*. Walter told me that there was still no sign of cancer in his liver after three years. His Divine Download and his Soul Language healed his liver cancer. He was very grateful to the Divine and his Soul Language.

This major event happened in July 2003. As I mentioned, a new era for Mother Earth and the universe, the Soul Light Era, began on August 8, 2003. The timing may look like a coincidence, but I believe there could be an underlying spiritual reason. Since July 2003, I have offered divine transmissions to humanity almost every day. I have offered several divine transmissions to all souls in the universe.

I share this story with you to introduce the power of divine transmissions or Divine Downloads. Now, let me share a commitment.

From now on, I will offer Divine Downloads in every book I write.

Divine Downloads are permanent divine healing and blessing treasures for transforming your life. There is an ancient saying: *If you want to know if a pear is sweet, taste it.* If you want to know the power of Divine Downloads, experience it.

Divine Downloads carry divine frequency with divine love, forgiveness, compassion, and light. Divine frequency can transform the frequency of all life. Divine love melts all blockages, including energy and spiritual blockages, and transforms all lives. Divine forgiveness brings inner peace and inner joy. Divine compassion boosts energy, stamina, vitality, and immunity. Divine light heals, prevents sickness, rejuvenates, and prolongs life.

A Divine Download is a new soul created by the heart of the Divine. The Divine Download transmitted to Walter was a Soul Software. Since then, I have transmitted several other types of Divine Downloads, including Divine Soul Transplants.

A Soul Transplant is a new divine soul of an organ, a part of the body, a bodily system, cells, DNA, or RNA. When it is transmitted, it replaces the recipient's original soul of that organ, part of the body, system, cells, DNA, or RNA. A new divine soul can also replace the soul of a home or a business. A new divine soul can be transmitted to a pet, a mountain, a city, or a country to replace their original souls. A new divine soul can even replace the soul of Mother Earth.

Everyone and everything has a soul. The Divine can download any soul you can conceive of. These divine soul downloads are permanent divine healing, blessing, and life-transforming treasures. They can transform the lives of anyone and anything. Because the Divine created these soul treasures, they carry Divine Soul Power, which is the highest power among all souls. All souls in the highest layers of Heaven will support and assist Divine Downloads. Divine Downloads are the crown jewel of Soul Power.

Divine Downloads are divine presence. The more downloads you receive, the faster your soul, heart, mind, and body will be transformed. The more downloads your home or business receives, the more downloads a city or country receives, the faster their souls, hearts, minds, and bodies will be transformed.

In the Soul Light Era, the evolution of humanity will be created by Soul Power. Soul Power will transform humanity. Soul Power will transform animals. Soul Power will transform nature and the environment. Soul Power will assume the leading role in every field of human endeavor. Humanity will deeply understand that *the soul is the boss.*

Soul Power, including soul secrets, soul healing, soul wisdom, soul knowledge, and soul practices, will transform every aspect of human life. Soul Power will transform every aspect of organizations and societies. Soul Power will transform cities, countries, Mother Earth, all planets, stars, galaxies, and all universes. Divine Soul Power, in the form of Divine Downloads, will lead this transformation.

I am honored to have been chosen as a divine servant to offer Divine Downloads to humanity, to relationships, to homes, to businesses, to pets, to cities, to countries, and more. Over the last few years, I have transmitted countless divine souls to humanity and to all universes. I repeat to you now: **I will offer Divine Downloads within each and every book of the Soul Power Series.** Clear instructions will be provided in the next section, "How to Receive the Divine Downloads Offered in This Book," as well as on the appropriate pages of each book.

I am a servant of humanity. I am a servant of the universe. I am a servant of the Divine. I am extremely honored to be a servant of all souls. I commit my total life and being as an unconditional universal servant.

I will continue to offer Divine Downloads for my entire life. I will offer more and more Divine Downloads to every soul. I will offer Divine Downloads to every aspect of life for every soul.

I am honored to be a servant of Divine Downloads.

Human beings, organizations, cities, and countries will receive more and more Divine Downloads to apply Divine Soul Power to transform and enlighten themselves. The Soul Light Era will shine Soul Power. The books in the Soul Power Series will spread Divine Downloads, together with Soul Power—soul secrets, soul wisdom, soul knowledge, and soul practices to serve humanity, Mother Earth, and the universe. The Soul Power Series is a pure servant for humanity and all souls. The Soul Power Series is honored to be a total GOLD[2] servant for the Divine, humanity, and all souls.

The final goal of the Soul Light Era is to join every soul as one. This means that the consciousness of every soul will be totally aligned with divine consciousness. There will be difficulties and challenges on this path. Together, we will overcome them. We call all souls of humanity and all souls of all universes to offer universal service, including universal love, forgiveness, peace, healing, blessing, harmony, and enlightenment.

The Divine gives his heart to us. The Divine gives his love to us. The Divine gives his downloads to us. Our heart melds with his heart. Our soul melds with his soul. Our consciousness aligns with his consciousness. We will join hearts and souls together to create love, peace, and harmony for humanity, Mother Earth, and all universes.

I love my heart and soul.
I love all humanity.
Join hearts and souls together.
Love, peace and harmony.
Love, peace and harmony.

Love all humanity. Love all souls. Thanks to all humanity. Thanks to all souls.

Thank you. Thank you. Thank you.

Zhi Gang Sha

---

2. Total GOLD means total gratitude, total obedience, total loyalty, and total devotion to the Divine.

How to Receive the Divine Downloads Offered in the Books of the Soul Power Series

The books of the Soul Power Series are unique. For the first time in history, the Divine will download his soul treasures to readers as they read these books. Every book in the Soul Power Series will include Divine Downloads that have been preprogrammed. When you read the appropriate paragraphs and pause for a minute, divine gifts will be transmitted to your soul.

Allow me to explain. The Divine has placed a permanent blessing within certain paragraphs in these books. These blessings allow you to receive Divine Downloads as permanent gifts to your soul. Because these divine treasures reside with your soul, you can access them twenty-four hours a day, as often as you like, wherever you are.

It is very easy to receive the Divine Downloads in these books. As you read some of the special paragraphs where they are preprogrammed, close your eyes. Receive the special download. It is also easy to apply these divine treasures for healing and life transformation. After you receive a download, I will show you immediately how to apply it for healing, blessing, and life transformation.

You have free will. If you are not ready to receive a Divine Download, simply say *I'm not ready to receive this gift.* You can then continue to read the special download paragraphs, but you will not receive the gifts they contain. The Divine does not offer Divine Downloads to those who are not ready or not willing to receive his treasures. However, the moment you are ready, you can simply go back to the relevant paragraph and tell the Divine, *I am ready.* You will then receive the stored special download when you reread the paragraph.

The Divine has agreed to offer specific Divine Downloads in these books to all readers who are willing to receive them. The Divine has unlimited treasures. However, you can receive only the ones designated in these pages. Please do not ask for different or additional gifts. It will not work.

After receiving and practicing with the Divine Downloads in these books, you could experience remarkable healing results in your physical, emotional, mental, and spiritual bodies. You could receive incredible blessings for your love relationships and relationships with others. You could receive financial blessings and all kinds of other blessings.

Divine Downloads are unlimited. There can be a Divine Download for anything that exists in the physical world. The reason for this is very simple. Everything has a soul. If you are wearing a ring, that ring has a soul. If the Divine downloads a new divine soul to your ring, you can ask that soul to offer divine healing and blessing. A house has a soul. The Divine can download a soul to your house that can transform its energy. The Divine can download a soul to your business that can transform your business.

The Divine has preprogrammed Divine Downloads to these books. When you read them, you can receive those divine souls, which can then bless and transform your life.

I am honored to have been chosen as a servant of humanity and the Divine to offer Divine Downloads. For the rest of my life, I will continue to offer Divine Downloads. I will offer more and more of them. I will offer Divine Downloads for every aspect of every life.

I am honored to be a servant of Divine Downloads.

What to Expect After You Receive Divine Downloads

A permanent Divine Download is a new soul created from the heart of the Divine. This soul is transmitted to your own soul. Your own soul will meld with this new divine soul. When this happens, some people will feel a strong vibration. For example, they could feel warm or excited. Their bodies could shake a little. Some people will not feel anything because they are not sensitive. Advanced spiritual beings with an open Third Eye will actually see a huge golden, rainbow, or purple light soul enter and join with them.

This divine soul is your *yin* companion for life. It will stay with your soul forever. Even after your physical life ends, this divine treasure will continue to accompany your soul into your next life and for all your future lives. In these books, I will teach you how to invoke this divine soul anytime, anywhere to give you divine healing or blessing in this life. You also can invoke this soul to leave your body to offer divine healing or blessing to others. This divine soul has extraordinary abilities to heal, bless, and transform. In your next life, if you develop advanced spiritual abilities, you will discover that you have this divine soul. Then you will be able to invoke this divine soul in the same way in your next life or in your many lifetimes to come.

It is a great honor to have a divine soul downloaded to your own soul. The divine soul is a pure soul without bad karma. The divine soul carries divine healing and blessing abilities. The download does not have any side effects. You are given more love and light. You are given greater abilities to serve yourself and others. Therefore, humanity is extremely honored that the Divine is offering this service. I am extremely honored to be a servant of the Divine, of you, and of all humanity and all souls to serve you in this special way. I cannot thank the Divine enough. I cannot thank humanity enough for the opportunity to serve you. I cannot thank all souls enough for the opportunity to serve them.

Thank you. Thank you. Thank you.

Foreword

I have admired Dr. Zhi Gang Sha's work for some years now. In fact, I clearly remember the first time I heard him describe his soul healing system, Soul Mind Body Medicine. I knew immediately that I wanted to support this gifted healer and his mission, so I introduced him to my spiritual community. Ever since, it has been my joy to witness how those who apply his teachings and techniques experience increased energy, joy, harmony, and peace in their lives.

Dr. Sha's techniques awaken the healing power already present in all of us, empowering us to put our overall well-being in our own hands. His explanation of energy and message, and how they link consciousness, mind, body, and spirit, forms a dynamic information network in language that is easy to understand and, more important, to apply.

Dr. Sha's time-tested results have proven to thousands of students and readers that healing energies and messages exist within specific sounds, movements, and affirmative perceptions. Weaving in his own personal experiences, Dr. Sha's theories and practices of working directly with the life-force energy and spirit are practical, holistic, and profound. His recognition that Soul Power is most important for every aspect of life is vital to meeting the challenges of twenty-first-century living.

The worldwide representative of his renowned teacher, Dr. Zhi Chen Guo, one of the greatest qi gong masters and healers in the world, Dr. Sha is himself a master of ancient disciplines such as tai chi, qi gong, kung fu, I Ching and feng shui. He has blended the soul of his culture's natural healing methods with his training as a Western physician, and generously offers his wisdom to us through his Soul Power book series. His contribution to those in the healing community is undeniable, and the way in which he empowers his readers to understand themselves, their feelings and the connection between their bodies, minds, and spirits is his gift to the world.

Through his Soul Power book series, Dr. Sha guides the reader into a consciousness of healing not only of body, mind, and spirit, but also of the heart. I consider his healing path to be a universal spiritual practice, a journey into genuine transformation. His professional integrity and compassionate heart are at the root of his being a servant of humankind, and my heartfelt wish for his readers is that they accept his invitation to awaken the power of the soul and realize the natural beauty of their existence.

Dr. Michael Bernard Beckwith
Founder, Agape International Spiritual Center

Preface

oul Wisdom: Practical Soul Treasures to Transform Your Life is a unique book. In it, I will teach you Soul Language, Soul Song, Soul Movement, Soul Tapping, and Soul Dance. I begin by teaching you what Soul Language is, why Soul Language is important, and how to translate it. I will offer you practical techniques to bring out and speak your Soul Language as quickly as possible. Then I will show you how to apply Soul Language to heal and prevent illness; rejuvenate your soul, mind, and body; and bless your relationships and finances.

This book is also unique because it is the first to offer Divine Downloads. There are divine blessings stored in these pages that will accelerate your ability to bring out and apply your Soul Language. After receiving these permanent divine blessings, you can access them anytime, anywhere, as many times as you wish. They can instantly uplift your Soul Power for healing, rejuvenation, and life transformation.

As you read this book, my soul will always be with you. In fact, you can call on me anytime, anywhere, and my soul will be with you to be your servant. Even after my physical life ends, my soul will still be your servant. I will be your servant forever. That is my commitment to humanity. That is my commitment to all souls, in order to fulfill my mission. My total mission is to transform the consciousness of humanity and all souls in the universe to create love, peace, and harmony for humanity, Mother Earth, and all souls.

Soul Language is the language of your soul. It carries your Soul Power. It can bring out the soul potential you have accumulated over hundreds of lifetimes. Soul Language stores the wisdom you have not yet realized. It is a communication treasure. You can use Soul Language to directly communicate with the Divine, with souls of high spiritual standing, and with the entire universe. You can use Soul Language to heal and prevent sickness, and to rejuvenate and transform all life, including your relationships and finances.

As you speak your own Soul Language, I will download Divine Soul Language to you. Divine Soul Language carries divine wisdom, divine power, divine knowledge, and divine secrets. You can use Divine Soul Language to transform and enlighten your life. You will become a divine servant by using Divine Soul Language to serve others.

The second part of this book is about Soul Song. Soul Song is the song of Soul Language. It carries incredible love and light. I have sung Soul Song since 2005, and it has touched thousands and thousands of people. People love my Soul Song because it expresses my love, care, and compassion. With it, I offer my service to humanity and all souls. I am delighted to give you a Soul Song for Healing and Rejuvenation of Brain and Spinal Column that you can download from my website: www.drsha.com. I will tell you how to gain maximum benefits from it in the section on "A Special Gift" at the end of this book.

Let me reveal a soul secret. As a universal servant, I call a soul conference every day to offer soul service. I call every soul of every human being and every soul in all the universes to gather together. I offer them my love, light, compassion, and kindness.

When you read this book, and when you listen to my Soul Song, you may think "This sounds familiar," because your soul has heard my Soul Song before. I have sung it to you many times already. The beauty of Soul Song will bring you joy. You will feel relaxed and comfortable when you hear it. Soul Song is a new form of song in Mother Earth. It will shine its light more and more. It will be a great service. Billions of people in the future will sing a Soul Song.

The third part of this book is about Soul Movement. Soul Movement is based on ancient practices such as tai chi and qi gong but, as in all of my teaching, it adds Soul Power.

Soul Movement is soul-guided movement. It is very simple and practical. You will learn how a few minutes of practice, a few times a day, can give you incredible benefits for boosting energy, healing, rejuvenation, and even enlightenment.

The fourth part of this book is about Soul Tapping. Soul Tapping is the most advanced soul healing technique that is available to everyone. However, advanced does not mean difficult or complicated. In my book *Soul Mind Body Medicine*,[3] I introduced one-minute soul healing techniques. Soul Tapping is even simpler! This practical soul treasure can be used for healing, preventing illness, rejuvenating, prolonging life, and transforming every aspect of life. It is my great honor to reveal this and all of the Soul Power secrets contained in this book.

The fifth and final part of this book is about Soul Dance. Soul Dance is soul-guided dance. Which parts of your body need to be stretched? Your soul knows. Where is the main energy blockage in your body? To remove the blockage, your soul will guide you on how best to stretch your body, where to move your arms, and how to turn your neck.

When you start to do a Soul Dance or sing a Soul Song, you will not want to stop. They bring inner joy and happiness. They bring inner and outer beauty. They remove energy and spiritual blockages. They transform and enlighten all life. I am honored to reveal these soul secrets to humanity.

Soul Wisdom is the first book in the Soul Power Series. Subsequent books will come one after another. Every one will have divine

---

3. New World Library, 2006.

permanent blessings stored within. Every one will be a divine practical treasure you can use to transform and enlighten your life.

Let this book be your pure servant. Let all books in the Soul Power Series be your pure servants. Let me be your pure servant. Let us join hearts and souls together to create love, peace, and harmony for humanity, Mother Earth, and the universe.

Thank you. Thank you. Thank you.

PART 1

Soul Language

Universal Communication

Introduction

We have just entered a period known as the Soul Light Era. During this era, whose dawn coincides with the change of the millennium, the soul will be central. The major transition into this era occurred on August 8, 2003, when there were great shifts in those who are on duty in the Soul World.

Some of you will shake your head and say, "Ah, I knew that date was important." You may be able to recall various events that happened on or near that date which let you know that this particular day was one of great significance. In many ways, it would be accurate to say that August 8, 2003, was actually the New Year's Day for this year, this century, and this era.

Changes are still occurring among those on duty in the Soul World. These changes will continue to occur for several more years. I share this background information to give you an idea of what has been happening in the Soul Light Era. Since we are living in the first part of that era, I would call this the Soul Light Century. This is information and teaching that I have received from my most revered teacher, Master and Dr. Zhi Chen Guo, as well as directly from the Soul World and from the Divine.

There are several aspects of this new era that are quite different from the previous era. Many of you may know from your own spiritual journey, from your teachers, or from other sources that the times in which we live today are very different from the times just a few short years ago. To some of you, this might be an obvious understatement.

I am not speaking of the physical surroundings in which we live, although they are also different and that is also an understatement. My main focus is to present and develop teachings regarding the Soul World. Specifically, how do we interact with the Soul World and how do we explain and understand that a great shift has taken place? What is the significance of that shift? We are leaving an era that was dominated by the mind, by the rational, by that which is tangible. We have actually left that behind.

Some people are very confused and conflicted. Some are caught in great struggles because they were greatly invested in the old rational approach — sometimes financially, sometimes professionally, sometimes with attitudes, beliefs, and behaviors. The investment was in the primacy of the mind and in that which is called "tangible."

This is not to say that we should ignore the mind and its great power and benefits. In this century, the mind is still important. We must respect it. However, it is the *soul* that now has priority. There is a growing realization and understanding that it is the soul that is the most significant entity in determining one's life direction and choices. Those who acknowledge this reality are able to live in a calm and peaceful way even while facing major challenges in their lives.

What is the soul? Soul is spirit or message. Soul is the essence of life. Everyone and everything has a soul. For anything in the universe, the soul is the essence of that thing. Your soul is an independent entity that resides in your body. The soul of anything is also an independent entity that resides in that thing. It can be seen by those with the advanced spiritual capability of an open Third Eye. Your soul resembles you, but it has its own consciousness, thoughts, likes, dislikes, and will. It has emotions, feelings, and creativity. Your soul carries great wisdom that it has acquired from its hundreds of lifetimes. Your soul can communicate with you and with any soul in the universe. Your soul has great power to heal, bless, and transform your life.

Living the reality of the Soul Light Era simply means that life choices, activities, and direction—all that is important—are in harmony with the soul's directions. Your soul loves you. Your soul cares about you deeply. Your soul always has your best interests at heart. To live in harmony with your soul is to live your true purpose. Your soul's journey is your true journey. Your soul's destiny is your true destiny.

Acknowledging the primacy of the soul is a very simple statement. To some of you, its importance might be obvious. However, even though it seems very simple, it is not an easy statement by which to live.

We came from an era dominated by the mind. The mind does not give up its dominance easily. It has developed many strategies and tactics to maintain its position of power, prestige, and admiration. The mind has done wonderful things, given great service and helped humanity in countless ways. We can point to many changes in recent years, decades, and centuries that are identified as progress. Almost all of these changes resulted from the analytic and creative abilities of the mind.

Even though all of this has been and, to a large extent, still is very true, in this new era the mind must live the reality that, in fact, it is the *soul* that sets the direction. It is the soul that makes the true choices. The mind must be willing to accept those choices. This is a great shift in consciousness. This century and era will be led by the spirit. This will be a time when the spiritual is acknowledged, appreciated, and allowed to be the aspect, the approach, the *one* that will be considered decisive whenever important choices need to be made.

A comparison might be helpful here. Think about the importance of the conductor to an orchestra. In this century and era, the soul is the conductor. When an individual pays attention to the soul's directions, everything is harmonious and beautiful. When an individual resists following the soul, it would be similar to an orchestra playing without a conductor.

It would be as though every member of the orchestra were playing his own melody, with its own tempo and rhythm, and with total disregard not only of the conductor but also of the other members of the orchestra. You can just imagine what the result would be. Few would describe it as harmonious and peaceful.

In the Soul Light Era, when we follow the direction of the soul, our individual lives will be harmonious and peaceful. Our interactions with others will also be harmonious. When large numbers of people come to the realization that following the direction of the soul is a priority, the entire social picture will change for the better.

This era is a particular gift. We will all learn that we are honored, privileged, and blessed to be living at this time. Each of us has a special role to fulfill. Each of us has a special responsibility to carry out. It is an honor and a blessing to do that. In this century and this era, Soul Language—and Soul Song and Soul Dance as well—will be a most special and significant treasure. Soul Language is not new to this era. It has existed in some form for centuries. It has been used by some groups for centuries. But in this century and era, Soul Language will become very common. The ability to translate it will also become very common. This will be a time when we will easily and truly be able to speak to one another soul to soul and be able to translate those messages.

This book will give more details, more explanation, and more teaching regarding Soul Language, including how to develop it and how to use it. As you read these pages, you will receive the blessings to be able to do what you are reading about. The level of success will vary from reader to reader, but there is a very strong possibility that you will be able to use Soul Language by the time you have finished reading this book. Many of you will be able to use Soul Language much sooner.

You will learn that one very important aspect of Soul Language (and of Soul Song, Soul Movement, Soul Tapping, and Soul Dance) is healing, including both self-healing and the healing of others. Soul Language, Soul Song, Soul Movement, Soul Tapping, and Soul Dance are all aspects of soul healing, which, as I have explained in other books including *Soul Mind Body Medicine,* is the most essential and most powerful form of healing.

For those of you who already speak and use Soul Language, it is possible that you will be able to translate Soul Language by the time you have finished reading this book. This will enable you to use Soul Language much more powerfully and to gain much greater benefits from it. Speaking is one aspect of Soul Language. Translation is the other aspect. Like the yin and the yang, neither is complete without the other.

Now that I have presented these introductory ideas to you, we are ready to begin Chapter 1. You have a brief but sufficient background as to the significance of the times in which we live and the fact that the book you are reading is much more than simply a book. This book will give you much more than just information. In fact, this book is also a healing and blessing tool, so the information you will receive is accompanied by many blessings. I am honored to serve you in this way.

Thank you. Thank you. Thank you.

1

What Is Soul Language?

There are nearly seven thousand known languages used on Mother Earth today. Many thousands more have been lost to history. Language is the communication tool for life. If you watch a movie but do not understand the language being spoken, you may feel very lost. If you visit a country where you do not speak the language, the simplest activities may be very difficult for you.

Language expresses your feelings and thoughts. Language can make you happy or miserable. Language enables you to learn wisdom and knowledge. Language is written in e-mails, books, magazines, newspapers, and advertisements. It is spoken over the telephone, on television, in movies, theaters, and on the Internet. Language is the daily communication tool between family members, work colleagues, and countries. It is very hard to imagine life without language.

I have something very important to share with you: there is only one Soul Language. Every soul can speak it. Every soul can understand it. Every soul can communicate with it.

Soul Language is the soul communication tool in all universes. Many people think there is only one universe. I believe there are countless universes. Every universe is divided into two parts: a yang world and a yin world. The yang world is the physical world, such as the one we know, which includes Mother Earth, our solar system, and countless stars and galaxies. The yin world is the spiritual world or Soul World. All souls form the Soul World, which includes healing angels, ascended masters, buddhas, and holy saints, as well as demons, monsters, and ghosts. Soul Language can be understood by every soul in the Soul World, which is every soul in all universes.

Yin/yang philosophy, theory, and practice are a major universal law. Yin and yang are opposites, such as night and day. But they are interrelated. We cannot explain night without explaining day, and vice versa. Yin and yang also can transform into each other. Think about night transforming into day and vice versa.

There is one important concept of yin and yang of which people may not be aware. This is that yin is always within yang and yang is always within yin. Think about the yin/yang symbol (☯), which consists of a white fish and a black fish. The black fish has a white eye, while the white fish has a black eye. The white fish represents the physical world. The black fish represents the spiritual world. The black eye of the white fish represents yin within yang. The physical world connects with the spiritual world through this black eye. The white eye of the black fish represents yang within yin. The spiritual world connects with the physical world through this white eye.

As a human being, you have a physical body, which belongs to yang. You also have a soul, which belongs to yin. Your soul resides inside your body. This is yin within yang.

In the spiritual world, there are countless angels. An angel is a soul. Soul belongs to yin. You may not realize that a soul consists of "tiny," or subtle, matter. Matter belongs to yang. This is yang within yin.

This wisdom about yang within yin and yin within yang explains that yin/yang is one body. Souls are in the spiritual world. They are also in the physical world. There are countless souls in the universe. A human being has a soul. An animal has a soul. All living things have souls. All inanimate things—for example, mountains—also have souls. When you speak Soul Language, all souls understand it. The entire yin world communicates through Soul Language.

Do you realize that an organ has a soul? Five thousand years ago,

The Yellow Emperor's Classic of Internal Medicine, the authoritative text of traditional Chinese medicine, revealed this wisdom. It named the souls of five major organs: liver *hun,* the soul of the liver; heart *shen,* the soul of the heart; spleen *yi,* the soul of the spleen; lung *po,* the soul of the lungs; and kidney *zhi,* the soul of the kidneys. When you speak Soul Language, the souls of these organs understand it and respond to it.

In my book *Soul Mind Body Medicine,* I further explained this wisdom. Every organ has a soul. Every cell has a soul. The nucleus of every cell has a soul. Every cell unit has a soul. Every molecule of DNA and RNA has a soul. When you speak Soul Language, all of these souls understand it and respond to it.

In physical life, we experience every day that language can make us happy, peaceful, or excited. Language can inspire and motivate us. Language can bring inner joy. There has been a great deal of research that explains these phenomena. Nobody doubts that language has great power to influence our lives.

Soul Language can influence our lives even more than physical language. There may be nearly seven thousand languages used on Mother Earth at this time, but there is only one Soul Language in all universes. Each physical language is powerful. Imagine the power of seven thousand languages serving every human being on Mother Earth, nearly seven billion souls in all. Soul Language, however, serves every soul of the universe, and there are countless souls — many more than seven billion. Because the scope of its service is so vast, the power of Soul Language is beyond that of any physical language. It is beyond comprehension.

The Universal Law of Universal Service, which I shared in my introduction to this book, states that *the more you serve, the more blessings you receive.* Soul Language serves the greatest possible number of souls in the universe. Consequently, it carries power that is unlimited and incomprehensible.

You will deeply experience the power of Soul Language in this book. Prepare yourself at the soul, mind, and body level for excitement and joy when you speak Soul Language, and for even more excitement and joy when you apply Soul Language for healing and transformation of your life.

Everybody's Soul Language sounds different. Still, Soul Language is the universal language. English is the most important language in the world today, but its reach is still limited. Soul Language is the language for all souls of humanity. Soul Language is the language for all souls in all universes. When you speak Soul Language, every soul of the universe understands it and responds to it.

I started to teach Soul Language in 1996. In early 2008, the number of people who speak Soul Language and apply it for healing, rejuvenation, and blessings is in the thousands. This is still a very limited number.

At this transition time for Mother Earth, people are searching for wisdom and guidance. They need practical tools to help them deal with the challenges of life. Soul Language is an incredible soul treasure to heal and transform your life. More and more, people are ready to learn and benefit from Soul Language. You are reading this book because you are one of these people.

In the future, Soul Language will become a true universal language. Peoples of every nation will speak Soul Language. They will understand each other. They will communicate with each other through Soul Language. Imagine the transformation this will create!

I dream of holding a Soul Language workshop in the not-too-distant future in which I will speak only Soul Language from beginning to end. Participants must consciously understand Soul Language, which means they must be able to translate Soul Language. People who do not understand Soul Language could attend the conference also, but translators would be needed to offer translations of the Soul Language into physical world languages. Although it may take years to spread Soul Language teachings worldwide, and it may take more years for humanity to truly understand and appreciate the power and ability of Soul Language, I know my dream will become a reality.

Soul Language directly connects with the Divine and high spiritual teachers in the spiritual world. As your spiritual journey progresses, your Soul Language brings deeper wisdom and knowledge from the spiritual world and the Divine.

Soul enlightenment is the goal of every soul. Soul enlightenment is the goal of every spiritual being. To have an enlightened soul is to be aligned with divine consciousness and to have great commitment to serve humanity and all souls. There are layers of soul enlightenment. The higher the layer of enlightenment you reach, the greater the divine abilities you are given by the Divine.

Higher enlightenment means a higher spiritual standing in Heaven. The higher your spiritual standing, the greater the Soul Power you are given and the deeper the wisdom you bring from the Divine and Heaven. Your Soul Language abilities will be totally different. Soul Language is an incredible soul healing treasure. It is also a powerful, life-transforming treasure. The power of Soul Language is immeasurable and unlimited.

×

You have learned that Soul Language is the unique form of communication that will be used universally during the Soul Light Century and Soul Light Era. The highest realms of the Soul World communicate with one another through Soul Language. Humans can communicate with and receive communication from the highest saints through Soul Language. Some of the most powerful healing and blessing mantras in history are in Soul Language. Soul Language itself can be considered to be a most powerful mantra. It is a very pure form of communication that comes directly from the heart and directly from the Message Center (also known as the "heart chakra"), which is located in the center of your chest. Soul Language is very pure because its origin and expression are from the very pure and clear part of your being and essence.

Specifically, Soul Language gives expression to what is pure and clear in the Message Center, as this most important energy center and spiritual center is named in my teachings. The messages held within the Message Center often are so profound and have been part of one's soul journey for so long that it can be difficult to articulate them in conventional speech and language.

Soul Language makes it possible to connect with the deepest, most profound, and most ancient teachings and wisdom held within your soul. It also makes it possible to connect with the deepest, most profound, and most ancient teachings and wisdom held within the universe, within Mother Earth, within those around you, and in fact within all of the Soul World. Soul Language is the vehicle that makes it possible to connect with *every* soul in a way that is not filtered—a way that is authentic and faithful to the message of each soul.

There are some major differences between conventional language and Soul Language. One of the most important is that conventional language needs to be processed in and assisted by the left brain. For Soul Language, the processing and expression are in the right brain. This is quite a significant difference. Those of you who know a little about anatomy and physiology will be aware of how different the processing is in the two hemispheres of the brain. Conventional speech requires a certain amount of logic, and so the facilities and functions of the brain that are connected with logic need to be involved.

With Soul Language there is a very different set of connections. The connections are "uncluttered" by what has been learned, by the mind-sets, attitudes, and beliefs that you developed during the course of your life. All of this is quite important in understanding and appreciating the answer to the question "What is Soul Language?" Just as that is a very simply stated question, the answer could also be a very simple statement. However, as is true for so many aspects of the soul journey, what can be stated in a simple way does not necessarily mean that all the layers of wisdom and teachings present within that simple statement are obvious.

For the question "What is Soul Language?" we could respond very simply that *Soul Language is the language of the Soul World*. That would include every aspect of the Soul World. It includes the saints, the buddhas, the Divine—all of those who dwell in light in the highest layers of the Soul World. It also includes the countless souls on the opposite end of the spectrum of the Soul World. It includes all souls who dwell on Mother Earth. Pay attention to that last statement because it includes much, much more than the souls of other human beings. The souls of all those throughout the universes are also included. All that exists is included because *everything* has a soul. The souls of those before time, in future times and beyond time, as well as those in what we call the present time, are all included.

So Soul Language embraces a countless number of possibilities—a countless number of souls who are able to communicate using this particular method. It is quite extraordinary and exciting to think about the limitless possibilities. It is useless to refer to numbers or even to try to use quantitative words or concepts to express the possibilities of those with whom you can communicate through Soul Language. It is even more exciting to realize that these souls really desire to communicate in this way, that Soul Language is in fact their preferred method of communication.

An example may help you understand what this means. Those who were born and raised in the United States speak its official language, English. English is the language of those who live in the United States, which means it is the preferred form of communication for every aspect of daily life. English is also the accepted language of communication for everything that takes place in the institutions of the United States. The language of the government in the United States is English. It is not difficult to understand why a common language is important and helpful. We can say that the official preferred language in the United States is English. In the same way, we can say that the official preferred language in the Soul World is Soul Language. This little comparison may help you understand and appreciate more fully the brief answer given above to the question "What is Soul Language?"

Soul Language is also a mantra. A mantra is a special sound. It is a special message. To say that it is a special message means that it is much more than information. The word *message* can be interchanged with *spirit* and with *soul*. So Soul Language is a special soul. In other words, this means of communication is a soul in and of itself. This special soul connects all souls who use Soul Language. This is a very important aspect of Soul Language to keep in your awareness.

This role of Soul Language, its capacity and ability to connect the souls of all those who are communicating with one another through it, is very special. It is a unique quality and characteristic of Soul Language. Knowing this about Soul Language will help you appreciate even more the extraordinary power and ability of this method of communication. It is not only that the sounds of Soul Language connect, but also that the sounds connect because they are an expression of the soul. This soul, spirit, or message brings about a unity and harmony among the souls who are using this form of communication, a unity and harmony that are very pure and very true.

Soul Language promotes this unity and harmony in part because, in its expression, the ordinary encumbrances of conventional language are not present. There is a freedom from the mind-sets, attitudes, and beliefs associated with particular words, expressions, and forms of speech in conventional language. All of these limiting mind-sets, attitudes, and beliefs are avoided when Soul Language is used. This is another very special and important characteristic of Soul Language to keep in mind. You will encounter this idea in several places throughout this book, related to other aspects of Soul Language. Each time you do, your understanding of its significance will increase. It will be brought to another level, another frequency, another vibration. This is actually an important benefit of reading this book, and I will give a fuller description of this and other benefits later in this chapter.

It may be very helpful for you to reread this section of the book about the fact that Soul Language is a mantra and that this mantra is more than a special sound. It is also a special message. In fact, you may benefit by coming back to it and rereading it several times as you continue going through the pages of this book. For many of you, it will be a new idea, a new understanding that the mantra itself is also a very special soul. This mantra has a particular ability that is connected to the fact that it is a special soul. This ability is over and above the ability that the vibrations of the sounds themselves have. Knowing that Soul Language is also a special mantra will help add to your appreciation of how important and powerful this gift is and how it is a most appropriate and significant expression and manifestation of the Soul Light Era. As you continue to read, you will actually begin to experience what I have explained.

Uses of Soul Language

Soul Language is a truly universal language. It goes beyond national boundaries and other barriers. Pause for a moment to consider the many implications of this very simple statement. Through Soul Language, people who live in different countries could converse with one another, exchange ideas, and share wisdom and teachings in a way not possible before. The complete range and very rich depths of information, wisdom, and teachings that exist would become available to everyone. This is an amazing gift that opens many opportunities. Soul Language can eliminate any existing barrier that prevents access to exclusive information and teachings.

Let me elaborate by offering examples of using Soul Language with others who are not physically present with you. For example, how could you communicate with those who live in other parts of the world? You could communicate using Soul Language by simply arranging a time when this communication would take place. This could be done with those whom you want to respond directly to your Soul Language or whom you want to translate your Soul Language. You could also communicate with events and situations in other parts of the world. I will develop this concept later in this book, but it is important to mention it here.

Soul Language could also be used to facilitate a group of people who speak different languages. Imagine a large group of people gathered together who speak twenty different native languages. They could all communicate consciously on a soul level through Soul Language and translation. The translation could be in the language of the speaker. The translation could be in the languages of the listeners, as is done at the United Nations. However, the most exciting possibility would be for the translation to be in a language common to the entire group, namely Soul Language! Envision how this would remove one of the biggest barriers separating the people in the group.

Normal language is a common barrier in contemporary society, especially in major urban centers in our most "advanced" societies. Many people living in the same geographic region, city, or even neighborhood cannot communicate with one another because their native tongues are different. Conversely, each country has its own language and most people raised there are limited to knowledge of their native language. With Soul Language, these limitations and barriers will no longer be significant. With Soul Language, any soul can communicate with any another soul. There is no such thing as Soul Language that is specific or unique to a particular country or region.

When you learn Soul Language and translation, economics is not a factor. The most important factors are your spiritual standing and virtue. With a high spiritual standing and a large amount of virtue (usually, these go hand in hand), you can connect with very high levels of the Soul World. You also can connect with others who are on a level similar to yours. Those with limited funds would have the same access as those with comfortable incomes. This would bring about many changes and much transition in our society as we know it now. Authentic unity in society will become possible. The value of one's information and other contributions to discourses would be based not on personal wealth or external power or position, but on spiritual standing and virtue. All aspects of life today would change dramatically as we move beyond all barriers.

Let us consider more implications of these changes. With Soul Language and translation capabilities, the wealth of information, treasures, and secrets of ancient teachings—wonderful discoveries known to very few—would become widely available. All of this teaching and wisdom could be communicated through Soul Language. Those of you who have experienced Soul Language realize that very brief amounts of Soul Language, spoken for perhaps not even a full minute, can be translated into many, many paragraphs or even several pages. This Soul Language "compression technology" has existed throughout the ages.

Those of you who can speak Soul Language or translate the Soul Language of others will appreciate fully what I mean when I say this technology has existed for a very long time. Soul Language is a very condensed teaching, wisdom, and message. All it contains can be present in a few phrases, sentences, or perhaps one minute of speaking. It is a tremendous gift and blessing to be able to say very briefly what would normally take a long time to express. Furthermore, when anything is expressed through Soul Language, no editing is necessary. This is an exquisite treasure. Soul Language makes it possible to almost instantaneously communicate the essence of any teaching and any wisdom. The ability to do this almost instantaneously, without regard to geographic distance, makes Soul Language a very important and very significant tool for humanity at this time.

Another great advantage of Soul Language for those who are currently separated by differing native tongues is that people from various countries, even if they are unfriendly or hostile toward one another, could actually communicate freely and openly—heart to heart and soul to soul—with one another.

When those who realize we are on the same soul journey truly share a commitment to unconditional universal love, forgiveness, peace, healing, blessing, harmony, and light—and communicate this to one another—the results will be truly amazing. There are many people who live in troubled areas of the world whose heart's desire is to do whatever they can to resolve differences and conflict. These people can now offer, through Soul Language, unconditional love and forgiveness to the conflict, to those who are perpetuating it, to those who are assisting in the continuation of it, and even to those who may be profiting from it. The only way to achieve lasting peace is by offering unconditional love and forgiveness. Soul Language is a means of doing this.

When these individuals communicate with one another through Soul Language, amazing transformation is possible. Bridges of light will go over, around, and through any barriers. The energy of love and the energy of forgiveness can actually begin to dissolve these barriers. These energies can melt walls that seemed impossible to tear down, much less melt. Unconditional universal love can transform anything. *Love melts all blockages.* In fact, only love can remove barriers and melt obstacles. Those who realize this can bring love and forgiveness to the situation through the use of Soul Language, even if they find themselves on different sides of the barriers and in the midst of conflict.

This capability of Soul Language is an extraordinary and magnificent gift that can be used anytime and anywhere. It can be used on an individual basis or with others. Wonderful things can manifest through this most precious gift of Soul Language and translation.

We could stop and reflect at length on the many implications of what is possible when people of different attitudes and ideas can communicate with one another through Soul Language. People with very different perspectives could come together and use Soul Language to obtain guidance to resolve the assumptions, questions, and beliefs that separate them.

At this particular time, given the nature and history of societies on Mother Earth, this may not happen on an official level. However, it can most certainly happen on the level of "ordinary folks" who perform the jobs that keep society moving. "Ordinary folks" have many different perspectives on any one single question. Unfortunately, conversations between people who have differing perspectives often do not come to useful conclusions. Frequently, the opposite is true. Those who have differing perspectives can become even more determined to stay bound to their particular approach or perspective. Often, the result is that such discussions do not result in more openness, flexibility, compromise, or resolution. Instead, many of the participants become more rigid and closed.

When guidance and answers are sought and received through

Soul Language, the only real possibility is to become more and more open. Participants who agree to even take such an approach already have a degree of openness and a willingness to connect to a part of the Soul World that is not available to most people on a daily basis. People with differing ideas and approaches to particular questions can come together and ask for guidance through Soul Language. The responses and answers received will truly lead to forgiveness on the part of each one—both forgiveness that is given and forgiveness that is asked. When this happens, peace can exist, spread, and flourish, even though it may not happen immediately on an "official" level.

The very fact that ordinary people could begin to meet with one another and have conversations in this way creates an entirely different kind of energy around the situation being addressed. Instead of having energy blocked or locked into a particular pattern, a flow of flexibility can begin. This new flow of energy can break the old patterns and help to establish a new way of approaching the situation. It may seem like a very small thing when a few individuals come together to do this; however, the ripples from this small beginning extend far beyond the direct participants. The light that is released by this process touches not only all aspects of the situation, but also all aspects throughout Mother Earth and beyond.

It is very difficult, perhaps impossible, to get a really accurate and valid understanding and appreciation for the great significance and importance of initiating this process with even a small group of people. It will really make a tremendous difference. Think in terms of your physical body, which you know so very well. When you have a headache, it affects your whole body. It affects you completely. And the more intense the headache, the more you are affected. However, you probably remember what a difference it made to your entire body and your outlook on life when your headache went away.

This is analogous to having just a small group of people using Soul Language address a particular issue. When the headache goes away, it makes a difference to the entire body. In the same way, when a small group of those with very differing ideas and attitudes becomes less closed, more flexible and have a flow of light and energy among them, it can make a difference to the entire problem or situation, even an ongoing one of long standing.

Do not underestimate the significance of being the one who brings light and transformation to any situation. It is also important to know that every effect that is named will be blessed and multiplied many times by the entire Soul World. This is just another example of what can happen through the use of Soul Language. It is both significant and beneficial because, in fact, the significance of doing this flows into many benefits. Those benefits will be discussed later in this chapter.

There are other possibilities connected with the idea that people from different parts of the globe can come together and communicate with one another in a form that is universally available. Perhaps the most familiar image of people coming together from different continents and countries is the Olympic Games. Another image that many people will recognize is the events following Pope John Paul II's death, when his successor was elected. There was an international response; people from all around the world attended and participated in those ceremonies. However, they could not understand one another without the services of a translator. If the participants had Soul Language capabilities, a translation service would not have been required. They could simply translate each other's Soul Language. Those communicating with one another could translate for each other. This would be an incredible service for any number of different situations. Imagine the Olympics or other large events led and taught by someone using Soul Language. This would truly be revolutionary.

You may be familiar with the Christian scriptures and the story of Pentecost. On Pentecost Sunday in the Christian era, people came to the Holy City of Jerusalem to celebrate the special holy days of the Jewish people. These pilgrims traveled from many different areas and countries and spoke many languages and dialects. Part of the significance of Pentecost Sunday for Christians is the transformation that took place in the disciples of Jesus and all those who had gathered to wait and pray for the coming of the Holy Spirit. Jesus had directed them to do this before he ascended into Heaven. The disciples and others waited and prayed in an upper room that was locked and shuttered. When Jesus sent his spirit to them, it was obvious because light appeared above each one's head and the sound of an enormous wind could be heard. This sound was so powerful that it was heard throughout the city and pilgrims gathered at the site to find out what had taken place.

Peter began speaking to them and each person in the gathered crowd understood him as if he was speaking in their own language. The pilgrims marveled at this and commented that although they were from different countries, they all could understand this person from Galilee. Peter was speaking in Soul Language. The pilgrims were spontaneously able to translate.

The Pentecost event of Soul Language and translation was experienced by at least three thousand people. They were so moved by what they heard that they became followers of The Way, a term that identified those who accepted the message and teachings of Jesus and lived them in their daily lives. As more people learn Soul Language and translation, Pentecost-like events may take place many times and in many places on Mother Earth.

Even though this Pentecost story was quite dramatic and significant, the number of language groups represented was small compared to an event like the Olympics. There would be no need for simultaneous translation by a third party and everyone would receive the same teachings at the same time. The only differences in what each person receives would be in accordance with their standing in the Soul World and their virtue. It would be an extraordinary experience for people to come together and learn in this way. A conference like this would not have to take a week, several days, or even hours because much can be said through Soul Language in a brief amount of time.

Soul Language condenses the message into just a very short few phrases that can contain many, many paragraphs of teaching. With an otherwise traditional teaching approach, just this one feature alone would make Soul Language teaching extraordinary. The advantages are numerous. What might normally take several days in a normal conference could now be collapsed into a day or two or just hours! And all of the discussion and sharing done afterward could also be accomplished in a much shorter amount of time through the use of Soul Language. In fact, in this kind of international gathering, it is very important to *avoid* having "normal" discussions in the same native language. The whole point is to have those with different native languages interacting with one another and, in this way, bring about greater harmony and greater peace on our planet.

Further reflection upon these ideas can lead to an almost endless string of possibilities. There could be an international conference where the participants would be able to stay in their own homes. This, too, would be revolutionary. It would not need to rely on technology or other conventional facilitators. Although there would be a need for coordination and organization, the entire conference could unfold in a way that is completely new, a way that has never before existed for humanity.

You can probably think of many ways that such a conference could be held even at this present time. Holding conferences using Soul Language and translation is something truly transforming. All of the problems that currently exist when people from different areas, with different ideas, attitudes, political views, and all of the other things that people identify as "differences," could be completely avoided. Through Soul Language and translation, all of these so-called blocks, obstacles, and barriers to communication would be overcome. Through Soul Language and translation, we could unlock ancient sources of wisdom and access deep healing for very ancient wounds. This type of wisdom and healing can be brought directly into the present through Soul Language and translation. This would be an incredible service and treasure.

This wisdom and healing could be revealed when any two or more people gather together. People from different areas who are very different from each other and even openly hostile could experience rich healing and deep wisdom teachings. Soul Language and translation would greatly magnify these healing experiences and wisdom teachings. To have "different" people come together and use Soul Language to reveal the Soul World's perspective on their situation—to learn the real truth—will be truly amazing. To say this will be revolutionary is not enough. To say this will be healing is only a tiny hint of what can happen. Words really fail to express adequately the possibilities of this type of soul conference. There are literally as many possibilities for these kinds of gatherings as there are people on earth.

At this particular time, the only way this type of communication can take place is through Soul Language. Since the participants would translate for one another, the authenticity and the truth of the message would be revealed, appreciated, and understood by all present. Situations like these again demonstrate how the significance and benefits of Soul Language blend together, although I will discuss further benefits later in this chapter.

Many groups are easy to identify by their different mind-sets, attitudes, and beliefs concerning one another. Just look throughout the world at the many places where people are fighting with one another. To bring mutual understanding of the truth of the situation would be an astounding and amazing gift, not only to those involved in the conflicts, but also to all of Mother Earth. Remember, when there is conflict between two groups, it is never limited just to the area of the conflict. It affects the entire global community, just as a headache affects the entire physical body.

These are some of the most significant aspects of the uses of Soul Language. There are many other things that are significant about the use of Soul Language and translation. What has been said should be sufficient to give you a beginning appreciation for what a very powerful, beautiful tool and blessing treasure Soul Language is; how it is perfectly suited to the era in which we live; and why it is so important that there be more and more people who can speak and translate Soul Language. Soul Language is indeed a treasured and precious gift to humanity at this time in the history of Mother Earth.

Significance of Soul Language

We have already referred to one of the most important reasons Soul Language is significant: it is the purest voice. The significance of this is magnified at this time of transition from the prior era to the Soul Light Era. So many things are in transformation that it can be very confusing to many. "What is the truth of what is happening? What is the truth of the information that we are given? What is the truth of the various teachings that are presented to us? What is the truth of the various institutions that have for so very long claimed to be the guardians and the protectors of our journey?" It is difficult to sort this out. It is difficult to hear the truth in these different situations and experiences. And the questions about "what is the truth" could go on for several pages. The examples I have presented are more than enough to give you an idea of the type of confusion that many people have at this time.

On the other hand, there are also many people who *are* able to see clearly and understand in great depth what the truth is. They can sort through the confusion and, even if they cannot state clearly what their awareness is, they have a very deep understanding and conviction that much of what is being presented is, in fact, completely authentic. Frequently the voices that are heard are not in the purest form. This is not to criticize or to complain about those voices. To criticize or complain adds to the confusion and the unrest surrounding us. Instead of this type of negative approach, it is much better to offer love and gratitude, to offer appreciation for all that is occurring, even for the confusion and conflict that is part of the present situation, or that is part of your own personal journey.

In the midst of all this confusion and conflict, there is the possibility that you can receive answers that will come with the purest voice in the purest form. The way that those answers can be received is through Soul Language. The questions can be asked and the responses will always be given in the purest voice. It is important to point out that if a group of three or five or even larger, perhaps hundreds, asks a question and each person speaks and translates Soul Language in order to receive the answer to that question, what is received by each person will be a little bit different. The reason for this is that each person has a different frequency, vibration, and spiritual standing. For this reason, the Soul Language expressed by each person is also different. I will say more about this in Chapter 2 when I explain fully how to develop Soul Language.

At this point, I will just say that each person's Soul Language will be different from the Soul Language of others. That does not make one right and another wrong. It simply means that the frequency, vibration, and standing are unique to each person. Therefore, the Soul Language will be unique to each person and the information received will also be unique to each person. Again, more will be said about this later in this book, when I discuss how to translate Soul Language.

When Soul Language is used, the Divine is present. This is most certainly true in other situations also. However, it is particularly true for Soul Language. Its purity and the fact that it is the mode of communication throughout the Soul World will help you understand why Soul Language is a form of communication that brings the presence of the Divine in a unique way. In some ways it is possible to say it is the preferred form of communication for the Divine in this era. It is a way for the Divine to be present with us and among us at any time and in any place. This is a very special gift that will help to shape this beginning part of the Soul Light Era.

There are many situations where the presence of the Divine is needed in a strong and dramatic way. The conventional ways of introducing the presence of the Divine are not always acceptable in these situations. To use Soul Language and to have wherever you are and whatever you are doing transformed by the presence of the Divine is a very special blessing. It is such a treasure and the most extraordinary gift from the Divine. It is amazing and quite overwhelming and breathtaking to realize that the Divine desires to be with us and assist us so much that we have a tool for making this happen, anytime and anywhere.

I want to mention that Soul Language can be spoken silently. This is important because you may be thinking of situations or experiences where it would be very difficult and may, in fact, even intensify the difficulty of the situation to use Soul Language out loud. Some of you may have read the last several paragraphs thinking, "Right. If I tried using Soul Language in these situations, it would not work." So, understand that Soul Language can be silent. With this knowledge, there is absolutely no place or time when Soul Language cannot be used to bring in the presence of the Divine, even in settings that seem very unwelcoming.

An example may be helpful. Think of a time when you attended a meeting and the meeting accelerated in intensity and the clashing of ideas. These situations happen in almost everyone's life, if not in a meeting then perhaps in a family setting. It is probably safe to say that everyone reading this book has been in some situation in which the conversation accelerated in intensity and moved toward a real conflict of ideas.

In this setting, silently chanting Soul Language is an absolute treasure and a most wonderful blessing and gift. The benefits and blessings for each person who is involved in the conversation will be significant. Most especially, the benefits for the one who uses the Soul Language will be amazing. To use this wonderful gift in a situation of escalating conflict can actually help transform it into a situation that has the possibility of being healing, of being the presence of harmony and blessing. It can also remind the one who is using Soul Language of the importance of always offering unconditional love and forgiveness. Only by offering unconditional love and forgiveness can the possibility of authentic peace come into being. All of this potential for total transformation is connected with the reality that Soul Language is a unique form of divine presence and so carries with it all of these blessings. This one aspect of Soul Language alone is very powerful and allows you to appreciate the extraordinary significance of Soul Language.

Another significant aspect of Soul Language is that it is a means of unity that cannot be stopped by any barrier. It is a way of being together with others regardless of location and time. This is a wonderful characteristic and quality to really appreciate about Soul Language. It is not necessary to actually be physically present in the same place where the Soul Language is being used. People can be in communication with one another through silent chanting of Soul Language. This can happen over great distances. It can also happen with those who are removed from us and who have made their transition to the Soul World.

Benefits of Soul Language

The benefits of Soul Language are numerous. Many have already been described. One major benefit is to have direct access to the Divine and to the highest realms of Heaven. Communicating in this very pure form with the Divine and the Soul World allows you to have access to wisdom that is not available to you in other ways. This wisdom can be applied to all aspects of your life.

You can use this wisdom to have greater clarity about your role. Having clarity about what the Divine and the Soul World want you to do during this lifetime is a very special treasure. With this clarity, much confusion and uncertainty is eliminated from your life. This clarity will also bring a feeling of great calm and peace. It will give you tremendous benefits on the emotional and mental levels.

> *Transform the soul first; then transformation of the mind and body will follow.*

Everything that happens for you on the level of your soul also benefits you on every other level. This is especially true when you have greater clarity about what you are meant to do. You can avoid the constant back and forth that many people experience between "Should I do this?" and "Should I do that?" Some people have even greater vagueness. They have a sense that they are meant to be doing something but it is simply not clear. They struggle and search for what they are being called to do. It is almost like trying to walk or drive through a very thick fog. By using Soul Language, that fog can lift.

The comparison to having the fog lift is a very good one because when the fog lifts, it is possible to see clearly and proceed in a way that is full of energy. Not only can you see your own path clearly, you can also see all that surrounds your path and how your path is influenced by other events, situations, and people. You can also appreciate how your path will bring great service to all those who surround you, and to everything that surrounds you. Keep this comparison to having the fog lift in your awareness. This comparison will help you to appreciate not only the contents of this book but also the events of your life.

Another benefit of Soul Language is that it brings you in direct connection with divine consciousness. This is such an extraordinary gift. It has been referred to earlier but I would like to develop this teaching further. To say that you are connected with divine consciousness means that everything that is part of divine consciousness is available to you on your level. The possibilities are infinite and extraordinary. It is very difficult to grasp or believe that you have this available to you through this wonderful tool of Soul Language. It is not possible to describe all aspects of divine consciousness in this book, but stop to think for just a few moments about what that phrase means. It is a most precious treasure.

Divine consciousness means that you have the possibility of entering into and communicating with that aspect of the Divine which allows you to have divine awareness of everything. This one aspect alone of entering into divine consciousness will bring many changes to your life. Having awareness from the perspective of the Divine will change the way you view all of life. It will change your responses to all of life. Many of the things that had been problems for you will begin to melt. As you connect with divine consciousness, you will become aware that what is considered a problem on the human level is often just not an issue for the Divine. Those blockages and obstacles that had seemed at times almost insurmountable will take on a smaller and smaller proportion. The events and situations in your life that were triggers for anxiety, anger, grief, fear—whatever—will be viewed differently. Instead of draining and creating blocks in your energy, you will begin to receive them as blessings and gifts.

Divine consciousness views humanity and all of creation, all events and situations very differently than we do when we approach from the perspective of logical thinking, or even when we approach from our own specific spiritual tradition. The biggest difference is that when we connect with divine consciousness, there are no limits. Everything has infinite possibility. Connecting with divine consciousness through Soul Language puts a range of possibilities in front of us that is not available in other ways. This is a truly extraordinary benefit of Soul Language.

As you read these ideas and teachings, I am certain that they spark within you a degree of hope and enthusiasm. Knowing that you have a readily available tool that can bring infinite potential into your life is a very exciting idea indeed. This is another example of the extraordinary generosity of the Divine and the entire Soul World. In the same way you connect with divine consciousness, you would also connect with your guides, special saints, special holy people, angels—with whoever in the Soul World has helped you in your journey so far. Doing this makes your soul journey much clearer to you. It eliminates many obstacles. Things become much simpler. Even though simpler does not always mean easier, having simplicity enter your life to a greater and greater degree is another benefit of using Soul Language. This simplicity is also very closely linked to the clarity I have described.

These benefits will affect not only your life but the lives of all those with whom you interact. You can imagine easily enough how wonderful it will be for you to have clarity. You can imagine what a delight it will be for those who are near and dear to you to live with and know someone who has this clarity. The benefits will go out beyond even those you know; they will be released to all on Mother

Earth and beyond. What a wonderful milestone on your soul journey to realize that you can appreciate such a blessing in your life as service as well. This may be a new idea for you, to realize that the gifts that come to your life can also become service to others. This is another benefit of using Soul Language.

All that has been described definitely is a benefit directly for you. When you benefit and reach another level in your soul's journey, when your soul's standing increases, everything you do moves to that new level. All that you now do becomes a higher quality of service. The blessings you give, the chanting you do, the interactions you have with others all move to a new level. This is another example of divine generosity. It makes it very clear that all souls, all of us, are working together. This brings a new depth of understanding to what universal service means.

I have mentioned so far several of the blessings and benefits of Soul Language that will become a daily part of your life. The more often you use Soul Language, the more you will experience these blessings and benefits.

Another great benefit of using Soul Language is that it brings understanding from the soul. This benefit is yet another exquisite treasure. Many people habitually resort to using logical thinking and that is indeed a very good approach in some situations. However, in the Soul Light Era, logical thinking will not do an adequate job for us. Many people have already experienced this in their lives. They use logical thinking and end up running around in a circle. They feel as though the ideas are just spinning in their heads and only become more and more anxious about the situation or question they would like to resolve.

This type of approach is no longer necessary. Soul Language will allow you to connect directly with your soul to receive information from your soul and from the soul of the event, situation, or question you would like to resolve. This will make life much more tranquil. This benefit alone will be a treasure for many people. This continual circling around something that is troubling you is a very common experience and the stress and anxiety that result are also very common.

Using Soul Language is a marvelous and efficient way to resolve questions. It makes it possible to reach solutions within minutes. In today's "instant" world, this will be very appealing to many. It will no longer be necessary to sit and reflect and mull over questions day after day. Simply speak and translate Soul Language and the solutions will come immediately. What a wonderful, precious tool! What a generous gift from the Divine! To have solutions come directly to you from the Soul World will end your circling. It also brings all the blessings and benefits that the Soul World continually gives.

So, not only will you have the solution to your question, you will also have many other blessings from the Soul World. You may become aware of some of these other blessings immediately. You may become aware of other blessings more gradually. It really is not important *when* you become aware of these blessings. You have received the blessings and they are part of your soul's journey. When you need to be aware of them, the awareness will come to you. In fact, you could use Soul Language to find out when the proper time will be for you to receive the awareness of the many blessings that accompany every solution and every response that you receive.

When you use Soul Language the way I have described, it is possible to say that you are a divine messenger. After all, what happens when you connect with the Divine and the Soul World through Soul Language? You receive their messages and, in some situations, you convey those messages directly to others. Clearly, this makes you a divine messenger. To be a divine messenger is a great privilege and honor.

In other situations, you will become a divine messenger because the teachings, wisdom, and guidance you receive will become part of you. They will become part of your soul's journey. They will also become part of your conscious awareness. You will live the information, the guidance, and the wisdom that you have received. As you do this, you become the presence of that guidance, wisdom, and teaching. You become their messengers. You become a divine messenger. You become this divine messenger in every aspect of daily life. Everything is influenced and touched by it. Sometimes you will be very conscious that this is what is happening. Sometimes in your conversations with others you will hear words coming out of your mouth and you will wonder to yourself, "Who is talking?" At these moments, you will have the realization that you are expressing what you have received through Soul Language and that what is coming out of your mouth is from the Divine. It is from the Soul World. And this experience will be one that will help you to appreciate what it means to be a divine messenger.

The more frequently you use Soul Language, the more messages, teachings, guidance, and wisdom you will receive. This makes it possible for you to become a divine messenger of an ever higher frequency, vibration, and quality. It also makes it possible for you to share more profound messages with those around you.

This explanation will help elucidate what I said earlier about giving service through the use of Soul Language. This is a somewhat obvious example of giving service. There are numerous other examples. This particular possibility is a special treasure because, as you have the awareness that the source of what you are sharing is definitely from the Soul World, your appreciation for this wonderful tool will increase. Your connection on a conscious level will move to a higher standing. Having this awareness on a conscious level is very important. Not only will you be able to observe in your conversations that the information, wisdom, and teachings are from another source, you will also appreciate this in your daily responses. All of these things are blessings received from the Soul World and the Divine.

Soul Language is also a treasure for meditation. You can make whatever request you like of your Soul Language. You may want to open your Message Center, strengthen your Lower Dan Tian, or enter the condition of universal unconditional love. You may want to enter the condition of emptiness. Whatever it is, request it and then begin to use Soul Language. As you use Soul Language, you will connect with your request on the level of the soul, on the level of the Divine, and on the level of the entire Soul World. As you continue to chant Soul Language, your request will become part of your meditation.

When you use Soul Language, it is like turning on a water faucet. Do not have expectations. As soon as expectations enter, it is like turning the water faucet off. This comparison makes it perfectly clear why expectations cannot enter into your meditations or anything else for that matter. Using Soul Language for meditation gives you the possibility of entering into your request on the level of the soul of your request. This is an extraordinary and boundless possibility. Allow yourself to receive what is given to you and receive it with complete gratitude. Whatever happens for you during your time of meditation is exactly what the Soul World desires to give to you at that moment.

Continue to use Soul Language and focus on your request. As you use Soul Language, you may become aware of a shift in your consciousness. You may become aware of messages connected to your request. When this happens, you can stop the Soul Language and connect with the awareness and with the messages, because these are gifts that you are being given at that moment.

There is an enormous difference between receiving messages that come from the use of Soul Language and the distractions that many people experience during their time of meditation. The difference is very clear. The distractions fall into the category of logical thinking. When you are distracted, it is as if your mind is jumping around like a flea. When this happens, you are not experiencing messages from the Divine and the Soul World. Divine Soul World messages are accompanied by deep, profound, and transforming peace.

If you experience distractions, treat them as gifts and teachers. Do not become upset. Do not try to push them away. Respond to them with gratitude and continue with your Soul Language. When you do this often enough during your time of meditation, you will begin to experience a change in the quality of your meditation. You will begin to enter into the condition of your request.

Once again, it is very important to avoid having expectations. Expectations will stop the process faster than almost anything else. From the example of turning off the water faucet, it is clear what happens when expectations enter the picture. A way to avoid expectations is to use this precious tool of Soul Language. You can even respond to your expectations the way that you do to your distractions. Thank them. Receive them as a gift and a teacher, for they truly are teachers. They have great wisdom to share with you. When you respond in this way, your expectations and distractions actually become guides and helpers in your meditation process. Using Soul Language to gain wisdom from your expectations and distractions is a wonderful way to accelerate the process of having them become your guides and helpers.

I have identified many benefits of using Soul Language. There are more; however, the ones I have mentioned and explained are those that will make great differences in your soul's journey. They are ones that are clear and easily understood and appreciated. As you begin to experience the benefits that I have described, you will also become aware of other benefits in your own personal soul journey. These are precious and priceless gifts from the Divine, and the wonderful thing about these gifts is that the more they are used, the more they increase. This is another example of divine generosity. Use Soul Language often and you will experience the reality of all these benefits in your life.

Gratitude

You have probably noticed the many times that I have mentioned gratitude in these pages. The importance of gratitude cannot be stressed strongly enough. When you approach your life from the perspective of gratitude, everything looks different. Your experiences begin to feel different. In fact, all of your life will be a most profound experience of transformation.

It is somewhat similar to a kaleidoscope. Think of all the colored pieces that are in the kaleidoscope. If you simply put those pieces on a table in front of you, that's all there is to look at: a collection of beautiful pieces of colored glass. They are simply scattered colored pieces of glass.

When you put those same pieces in a kaleidoscope, they become an exquisite, ever-changing pattern. They then become a source of delight and enjoyment. Similarly, when you look at all of your experiences through the lens of gratitude, instead of seeing separate, fragmented events, you see beautiful patterns that are a source of great delight and enjoyment. This is a very good comparison to keep in mind: gratitude can act as a kaleidoscope for your life.

When you respond to the events of your life with gratitude, you will see seemingly negative events in a completely different way. You will begin to perceive these events as gifts and as very special wisdom figures. This is especially true when the events are particularly difficult or painful. This is part of the process of the soul's journey. When something particularly difficult has been ongoing in your life, it reveals to you an aspect of yourself that needs to be transformed into light. That aspect may have been part of your present life for many, many years. It may have been part of your soul's journey and your soul memories for many lifetimes.

When this is the case, transformation will often be difficult. It will require very conscious and consistent effort on your part. When these events or situations come to your awareness, and you look at them from the perspective of gratitude, there is a very deep and profound realization that you have been given a gift. This is a very special wisdom teacher in your life. What other response can there be to an exquisite gift and the presence of a profound wisdom teacher? When you begin to consider "troublesome" events in this way, the only appropriate response is gratitude. Let me give you an example to help clarify what I mean.

When you are resisting a teaching or when you have a strong negative response to a certain individual, this indicates that this is a gift and teacher. When these events are received with gratitude, you

become conscious of an underlying pattern in your life that you have
had for many years. Very frequently these patterns are identified as
virtues. For example, the quality of honesty is held in great regard by
many people. People who value this quality highly are often individuals who want to be identified with this special virtue. They connect
their personality with this quality. Now I want to be very clear that
honesty is, in fact, extremely important. In no way am I suggesting
that you can treat honesty lightly. It is an important quality that needs
to be part of everyone's life in a very concrete and practical way.

What I am talking about is the type of response to honesty that
carries what I call an emotional "charge"—the kind of honesty that
gets people angry or agitated. When you create this kind of response,
you have left the virtue and moved into the connection between this
very important quality and your personality. This is the clearest signal that you are now dealing with an ego issue. It is not really connected to the quality of honesty at all. Honesty has been your way of
protecting an aspect of your personality that truly needs healing. This
realization will make your soul journey and your healing journey
much simpler. The realization that you have actually used honesty as
a way of protecting and defending your ego is a precious gift. It truly
is an exquisite wisdom teacher.

When you come to this realization, it is next necessary to release
your ego attachment. This can be done by chanting Soul Language. It
can be done by being grateful for the gift received. All of these approaches
are profoundly effective. It can also be done by going into the condition
of divine gratitude and, in this condition, offering gratitude to the awareness you have just received. This is a very powerful practice.

Let's do this practice together now:

> *Dear soul, mind, and body of my mind, I love you.*
> *Dear soul, mind, and body of my ego, I love you.*
> *Dear soul, mind, and body of my Soul Language, I love you.*
> *I realize that my ego has created some blockages for my*
> *journey.*

I am very grateful for this realization.
I ask my ego to release its attachments — to being defensive, to
being protective, to having its say, to being "right."
I ask my Soul Language to bless and help my ego and my mind
to release their attachments.
I am very grateful.
Thank you.

Now, totally relax. If you have opened and "brought out" your Soul Language, chant your Soul Language for a few minutes. If you cannot speak Soul Language, I will lead you to bring out your Soul Language in the next chapter. For now, chant 3396815 repeatedly in Chinese, *San San Jiu Liu Ba Yao Wu,* pronounced "sahn sahn joe lew bah yow woo." I will explain the significance of this number sequence, which is a special mantra and a secret code, in the next chapter.

Go into the condition of gratitude, of total gratitude, of *divine* gratitude for the realizations and insights you have received, for your commitment to remove your own ego and mind blockages, and for the blessings of your Soul Language and 3396815.

After a few minutes, close the practice by saying:

Hao! Hao! Hao!
Thank you. Thank you. Thank you.

Hao, pronounced "how," means "good, perfect, healthy, strong." All positive wishes are included in that one word. We finish by expressing gratitude.

This simple practice will be of great help in transforming what has been an ego attachment to the presence of more profound light in your life. This is an example of how gratitude can touch those areas of your life that need healing.

When you have the awareness that a particular quality has actually become a defense or a protection mechanism, you can offer that area of your life healing blessings. You can go into the condition of unconditional universal love or unconditional universal forgiveness and offer these to whatever your ego has become attached to. Very frequently, those things that are part of your life pattern that are connected to your ego are a manifestation of things that need forgiveness and love. More than likely, when you offer your ego or personality forgiveness and love, you will become conscious of individuals or events in your life that trigger great pain and sorrow. When you offer them unconditional universal love or unconditional universal forgiveness, your healing will be so profound that you will be amazed.

You will likely experience a very deep releasing and be moved to tears. These tears may literally cleanse the wound that has been part of your life for so very long. Allow yourself to truly release these hurts, to truly allow the tears to heal whatever it is that needs healing. These are precious gifts. These are wisdom teachers that are not available in any other way. To have these gifts and these wisdom teachers enter your life is indeed a reason for the most profound and sincere gratitude. When you begin to realize that these difficult events introduce you to deep healing and wisdom teachers, you will find it more and more possible to respond with sincere gratitude.

This example will help you appreciate what I have said earlier: when things come into your life that seem negative, difficult, or painful, they are actually gifts. They represent your "readiness" to receive healing and the wisdom teachers. If you were to receive the healing or the wisdom teacher directly without this readiness, it could be overwhelming. In the Divine's goodness and tender mercy toward us, we receive only after we have been prepared through the necessary readiness.

What I have said is equally true for things that we resist changing. Resistance to change is most often connected with a mind-set, an attitude, or a belief that may be connected to soul memories. It is difficult to heal soul memories directly but it can be done. Once again, resistance to change is the readiness. It is your introduction to a mind-set, attitude, or belief that needs to be healed and released.

These may appear in your life in a variety of ways. Frequently, they assume the guise of "efficiency." If you are a professional person, they may show up as one of the hallmarks of your profession that you have worked to develop over the years, perhaps as what is known as "common knowledge." They may appear as a statement that begins, "It is very clear that the best practices are . . ." and the conclusion of the statement will vary according to your own life pattern. When you begin to notice that you say things like this on a regular basis, it is your indicator that readiness is taking place and that you are being introduced to an exquisite wisdom teacher and a profound healing experience.

Another common statement that signals readiness begins, "People need to talk about these things . . ." What makes things tricky is that there is some truth in each of these statements. However, when you begin to have an emotional charge connected with your statement, that is a clue that you have left the arena of truth for the arena of a mind-set, attitude, or belief that needs healing. When you have some degree of rigidity about whatever you are expressing, that is another very good clue that you are now receiving the readiness for precious, exquisite healing and profound wisdom teachings.

My previous teaching on healing the hurts in your life applies here also. You can use the same approaches to receive the precious treasures of this gift and teachings. The wonderful result will be the healing of soul memories. When this happens, not only is your soul journey transformed to a most exquisite light and to a higher frequency and vibration, but all of those who were part of those soul memories also have more light become part of their soul journeys. Their soul journeys are literally transformed. This is a very high level of service. It will affect your soul's standing and the soul standing of many others in a profound way.

By now I hope it is easy for you to understand and appreciate why gratitude is very important in your life. I want you to look at gratitude from the perspective of your own personal story during this lifetime and your soul journey through many lifetimes. When you also appreciate gratitude as an essential manifestation of the Divine, your appreciation will be even greater. By "essential manifestation," I mean that gratitude is of the very essence, the very core of the heart, soul, and mind of the Divine. It is of the purest aspect of divine light. To connect with this is deeply transforming. The more frequently you connect with gratitude and the more you *become* this divine presence, the more you are able to manifest these essential and core aspects of the Divine. This is an incredible privilege and honor.

Becoming aware of this additional role of gratitude in your life will generate even greater gratitude. Expressing gratitude is somewhat like rolling a snowball down a hill. Once you set it in motion, it will grow and accelerate by itself. The momentum of your gratitude will extend and expand the gratitude. This is a wonderful gift from the Divine. As soon as you begin to connect with this quality in your life, as soon as you are able to have it as your first response, you have started the snowball on its way down the hill. Every snowball hits some bumps along the way. It is my hope and my blessing to you that you will respond to those bumps with gratitude—a gratitude that is heartfelt, a gratitude that comes from the depths of your soul, mind, and body. When this happens, you will live and express gratitude as a natural part of who you are and as a natural part of the rhythm of your day.

To enter into the gratitude I have described, the most important key is to be relaxed. When you notice you are resisting something, when there is a degree of rigidity in your responses to events or people, or when something is painful or hurtful to you, it is very important that you allow yourself to become relaxed around that particular awareness. Most often, when you become aware of one of these situations, your immediate response is to become tense, stressed, irritated, angry, or fearful.

As soon as you become aware of one of these reactions, say to yourself, "What I need to do now is to relax." Of course, just saying "I am going to relax, I am going to relax" to yourself might not work. You can in addition speak to the soul of relaxation and ask for its blessing. You can use Soul Language to find out how to relax. You can go into the condition of divine relaxation. Whatever approach you use, as soon as you become aware of your response, use that awareness as your reminder that what is needed at the moment is to become relaxed. Relaxation is the key for opening the door to gratitude. And gratitude is the key for opening the door to transformation.

These are very simple qualities to incorporate into your life, but they will bring about changes on every level of your being. As you practice gratitude, you will become aware that you have more gentleness, increased flexibility, and more humor and joy in your life. These are all wonderful gifts. They will make an enormous difference in the quality of your daily life. They will also make an enormous difference in the quality, frequency, and vibration of your soul journey and your soul standing. The changes in daily life and in your soul journey are connected and interact. Changes in one facilitate changes in the other. You will become aware of this in your daily life as well. This awareness will help you put into practice the gratitude that I have described in these pages.

Now let me discuss "complaining," which can block gratitude. Complaining can come in very easily identifiable ways. Complaining can also come very subtly into your life. For those who are serious about their soul journey and who are really sincere in their efforts to transform on every level, complaining is one of the first things to eliminate from your life. It is easy to identify those areas where complaining is obvious. It is more difficult to identify the more subtle forms of complaining, although I have referred to several of them in the section above.

When you make statements such as "Everyone knows . . ." or "People need to talk about . . ." or similar statements, however you complete the sentence, you are actually complaining. These are actually socially acceptable ways of criticizing and complaining, because they camouflage your complaint. We can rephrase the statement "Everyone knows that . . ." into one that is obviously a complaint. Turn that statement around and say "Whatever is happening here is all wrong and anyone with an ounce of sense would be able to recognize this." When you transform the statement in this way, it is very easy to recognize it as a complaint or criticism. Avoid making these kinds of statements.

This may be a huge challenge for some. One of the mantras you may have developed in your life is "honesty is a core value to me; my personal integrity is the most important thing in my life." If these happen to be your mantras, you will have a particularly difficult time releasing these forms of complaining. When honesty and integrity are not respected in public life, people are shocked. This is just not acceptable in today's society. For this reason, it may be difficult to release this form of complaining. For many people, these messages from their cultural setting are very strong and enter easily into their life pattern. However, I suggest that we need to look closely at what is really going on and reflect on what I have already mentioned—that using these phrases is actually a subtle form of complaining.

Another subtle form of complaining is comparing yourself to someone else. Many people do this frequently throughout the day. Most adults will not admit to doing this because society has taught us that this is not an appropriate response to another person's accomplishments. But whether or not the comparison is voiced out loud does not matter. Whenever you compare yourself to someone else, you are actually registering a complaint or a criticism.

You can understand this by turning the statement around. Some of my students say, "My Third Eye ability is not as good as Joyce's. My Third Eye ability is not even close to the ability of Artemas." As soon as you make such a comparison and have a feeling of dissatisfaction, sometimes even sadness, you have strong cues that you have entered into a very subtle form of complaining or criticizing.

Let me turn those statements around for you. The "statement behind the statement" could be something like this: "Dear Divine, you have given Joyce such wonderful Third Eye ability but what you've given to me isn't so good and I am not at all happy with it." Restating the comparison in this way may be a little shocking. I don't think there is one person reading this book who would actually say such a thing to the Divine. (If you ever do say something like this to the Divine, very quickly follow it with, "I am so sorry. Please forgive me.") So, you can understand why these comparisons truly are complaints and criticisms. They are an indirect way of telling the Divine that the Divine has not really done a very good job in giving you whatever gifts or abilities you have. You are telling the Soul World, your guides, and special protectors that they have not done a very good job.

There are some things you truly cannot do. If you have not studied French and it is not your native language, you cannot speak French. That is an accurate statement. If you have not studied higher mathematics and you do not have this as an intuitive gift, you cannot do calculus or probability theory. That is an accurate statement. Some statements are accurate. Other statements fall into the category of very subtle complaining or criticizing.

Let me give you another example. Say you have been given a task to perform in your job that falls outside your area of competency. Your tendency might be to say, "I cannot do that. I do not have the gifts or abilities to do that." As soon as you make this statement, you are offering those limitations to the Divine. The Divine will receive them and return them to you. This concept is worth reviewing because it is very common. Consider this yet another gift you can receive as readiness for a wonderful healing experience and the introduction to profound wisdom teachers. Everything I have described is part of life. It is part of our human journey. What is very important is to avoid feeling sad, guilty, or frustrated. Replace those emotions with gratitude.

At this point it should be very clear that making these types of statements to the Divine and to the Soul World is not the best way to make progress in your soul journey or to experience improvement and healing at the physical, mental, and emotional levels of your being. I hope these examples of rephrasing the problematic statements will help you avoid this type of complaining and criticizing. I hope they will help you become aware of the many times throughout the day that you may be making these types of comparisons.

By now I have offered you the teaching on gratitude several times. Each time I have presented it, you have also received very powerful blessings that will make it possible for you to put these teachings into practice in your daily life. As you put these teachings into practice, you will experience magnificent changes — transformations that you could not imagine. All of these changes and transformations will happen more quickly than you have ever experienced.

Some of my students have had the experience of instant transformation. Almost all of them have said that the changes that have become part of their lives, whether they took place over a few years or, for some, within just a few months, are absolutely unimaginable. They thought that such changes would take many years or perhaps even lifetimes to occur. Following the teachings in these pages will accelerate your soul's journey also. Receiving the blessings in these pages will make a profound difference in every aspect of your life.

2

Bring Out Your Soul Language

Y ou have just read about the significance and benefits of Soul Language. You could be very inspired. I hope you are eager to bring out your own Soul Language. When people first speak Soul Language, they can be very excited and emotional. Some people cry. Others laugh uncontrollably. Some feel their heart beating very rapidly. If you experience any similar reactions when you first speak Soul Language, know that they are all normal.

Everyone can speak Soul Language but few are aware of it. Soul Language generally remains hidden. When you suddenly open your Soul Language channel and your Soul Language flows out, it can be very exciting. I remember a chiropractor who ran around the room for several minutes when he began to speak Soul Language. He just couldn't stop speaking and moving. That was quite dramatic.

I am telling you this to explain that it does not matter what your particular reaction may be or how excited you become. Opening your Soul Language channel is very safe. Do not be concerned about any reaction you may have. You will receive great benefits for healing, rejuvenation, and life transformation when you bring out your Soul Language. Prepare!

Secret Soul Code to Bring Out Your Soul Language

Some of you may already be able to speak Soul Language. You may think this chapter is not necessary for you and skip right over it. Let me tell you that this would be a mistake. Remember that every word, every letter, every space in this book is a blessing tool. If you skip this chapter, you will skip over thousands of blessings. This chapter also contains the first two Divine Downloads ever given within a book.

I have taught thousands of people around the world to bring out their Soul Language using a secret code that was received by my spiritual father in China, Master Zhi Chen Guo, in the 1970s. One morning as he was meditating, he received this code from Heaven. It carries incredible Soul Power for healing, blessing, and opening spiritual channels. This code is the number sequence 3396815, *San San Jiu Liu Ba Yao Wu* in Chinese, pronounced "sahn sahn joe lew bah yow woo."

This secret code and special mantra has been used by hundreds of thousands of people in both China and the West. One of the special gifts of this mantra is its ability to connect your soul with the soul of the Divine. It is a very special mantra for opening your soul communication channels. Many other benefits and capabilities are connected with this mantra. Numerous gifts come from using this mantra. They will be the subject of another book. For our purposes, let's just say that this mantra opens soul communication. Since Soul Language is a form of soul communication, there is only one secret to bringing out your Soul Language. Chant this secret code repeatedly:

> *San San Jiu Liu Ba Yao Wu*
> *San San Jiu Liu Ba Yao Wu*
> *San San Jiu Liu Ba Yao Wu*
> *San San Jiu Liu Ba Yao Wu . . .*

Chant faster and faster. Chant as fast as you can. Suddenly, you will begin to utter strange sounds in a special voice. You have probably never heard this voice before. This special voice is your soul voice. The strange sounds are your Soul Language!

If you want to be sure that you are speaking Soul Language, stop your special voice and return to chanting 3396185, *San San Jiu Liu Ba Yao Wu, San San Jiu Liu Ba Yao Wu, San San Jiu Liu Ba Yao Wu, San San Jiu Liu Ba Yao Wu.* Suddenly, the special voice will come out again. It may sound exactly like it did the first time. It may sound different. When you hear this special voice again, you can be sure it is your true Soul Language.

As I mentioned at the beginning of this chapter, when your Soul Language flows out, you could become emotional. You could feel somewhat excited, even very excited. Your body could shake. If you get overexcited, do not be scared. Give a command to your mind to *stop* or *slow down* your Soul Language and everything will become calm.

Receive Soul Blessings and Practice to Bring Out Your Soul Language

Now, prepare yourself. I am going to lead you in a practice to bring out your Soul Language. At the same time, I am going to offer a Divine Download to help bring out your Soul Language. When you read this section, it is just like being at one of my workshops. You will chant with me exactly as you would in one of my Soul Retreats.

This book is the first book of my Soul Power series. The Divine guided me to write it in a special way to give you the opportunity to experience Divine Downloads. Many of you will bring out your Soul Language in the next few minutes if you follow my instructions and do the practice with me.

With just a few minutes of practice, many of you can bring out your Soul Language immediately. If you spend eight minutes practicing seriously, most of you will bring it out. Some of you may need to do the practice a few more times. If this is the case for you, just keep practicing and your Soul Language will come.

RECEIVE A DIVINE DOWNLOAD
TO BRING OUT YOUR SOUL LANGUAGE

I am now going to offer you a Divine Download.

I started to offer Divine Downloads in July 2003. Usually, people receive a download remotely by registering on my website and gathering in my weekly *Sunday Divine Blessings* teleconferences.

I am honored that the Divine has agreed to give certain downloads to every reader of this book. This is the first time in history that Divine Downloads are being offered in this way. From now on, I will offer this Divine Download service in every book in the Soul Power Series.

The first Divine Download I am going to transmit is called *Divine Soul Transplant of Divine Golden Light Ball and Golden Liquid Spring of Divine Soul Language.* This Divine Download is a gift that the Divine will transmit to your soul.

This gift has two parts. The Divine Golden *Light Ball* is a divine yang treasure. The Divine Golden *Liquid Spring* is a divine yin treasure. This download is a divine soul of Divine Soul Language. The Divine has given me the honor of offering this treasure to every reader.

Prepare. If you wish to receive this Divine Download, it will be offered to you in just a few moments. If you do not wish to receive this Divine Download, simply say, *Thank you. I am not ready to receive this gift.* You will not receive the download but you can still continue to read these paragraphs.

When you are ready in the future, please come back to this page. Tell the Divine, *I am honored to receive this gift.* Then open your heart and soul. Read the following four paragraphs one more time. You will then receive the download of your own free will.

TOTALLY RELAX. To receive the divine blessing stored
in this book, open your heart and soul. Sit up straight.
Keep your feet flat on the floor. Put the tip of your

tongue as close as you can to the roof of your mouth without touching.

DIVINE DOWNLOAD: *Divine Soul Transplant of Divine Golden Light Ball and Golden Liquid Spring of Divine Soul Language from the Divine's heart and soul to your soul. Silent download!*

Now, close your eyes for one minute to receive and welcome this divine soul treasure to your soul.

Congratulations! You have received the first divine permanent healing and blessing treasure offered in this book. Every time you reread the download paragraph, you will receive a boost. This is the Divine's plan for this download. If you ask for additional downloads or other gifts, it will not work. The Divine Downloads for you and other readers of this book are specific.

PRACTICE TO BRING OUT YOUR SOUL LANGUAGE

First, I offer my soul service to you and to every reader of this book. Before you do this exercise, call on my soul. My soul is your servant. It is available to serve you twenty-four hours a day, anytime, anywhere.

Once again, sit up straight and totally relax. You are going to practice with me to bring out your Soul Language. Call my soul first by saying: *Dear soul of Master Sha, please come now to give me a blessing to bring out my Soul Language when I practice. Thank you.*

Remember another important secret: when you chant, be natural. Do not be too serious. Relax when you chant.

Start to practice by chanting:

San San Jiu Liu Ba Yao Wu
San San Jiu Liu Ba Yao Wu
San San Jiu Liu Ba Yao Wu

San San Jiu Liu Ba Yao Wu
San San Jiu Liu Ba Yao Wu
San San Jiu Liu Ba Yao Wu
San San Jiu Liu Ba Yao Wu . . .

Chant faster!

San San Jiu Liu Ba Yao Wu
San San Jiu Liu Ba Yao Wu
San San Jiu Liu Ba Yao Wu
San San Jiu Liu Ba Yao Wu
San San Jiu Liu Ba Yao Wu
San San Jiu Liu Ba Yao Wu
San San Jiu Liu Ba Yao Wu . . .

Chant even faster!

San San Jiu Liu Ba Yao Wu
San San Jiu Liu Ba Yao Wu
San San Jiu Liu Ba Yao Wu
San San Jiu Liu Ba Yao Wu
San San Jiu Liu Ba Yao Wu
San San Jiu Liu Ba Yao Wu
San San Jiu Liu Ba Yao Wu . . .

Chant faster and faaaasssssstttteeeerrrr!

San San Jiu Liu Ba Yao Wu
San San Jiu Liu Ba Yao Wu
San San Jiu Liu Ba Yao Wu
San San Jiu Liu Ba Yao Wu
San San Jiu Liu Ba Yao Wu
San San Jiu Liu Ba Yao Wu
San San Jiu Liu Ba Yao Wu . . .

Chant as faaast as you can!

> *San San Jiu Liu Ba Yao Wu*
> *San San Jiu Liu Ba Yao Wu*
> *San San Jiu Liu Ba Yao Wu*
> *San San Jiu Liu Ba Yao Wu*
> *San San Jiu Liu Ba Yao Wu*
> *San San Jiu Liu Ba Yao Wu*
> *San San Jiu Liu Ba Yao Wu . . .*

Continue to chant for five to eight minutes. As you do this, you will discover that continuing to pronounce each word becomes more and more difficult. In fact, it will become impossible. That is *exactly* what you want to happen. You want to say the words so quickly that they lose their distinct individual pronunciations and instead become a blur of sound. You may emit a variety of different sounds. When this happens, you have opened your Soul Language.

Suddenly, a special voice that you have never heard before will flow out of your mouth. Continue to let that special voice and its special sounds flow out. That is your Soul Language.

To confirm that it truly is your Soul Language, follow this guidance. Stop the special voice and return to chanting *San San Jiu Liu Ba Yao Wu* as fast as you can. If the special voice comes out again, then it is truly your Soul Language.

At the end of each practice session, always remember to say:

> *Dear soul of Master Sha, thank you. Please return now to Master Sha.*

It is spiritual courtesy to do this.

If your Soul Language flows out right away, congratulations! If your Soul Language flows out within eight minutes, congratulations! If your Soul Language does not come out within the first eight minutes, do not feel disappointed. Practice for eight minutes again later today or tomorrow. Do a few eight-minute practice sessions per day.

Every time you practice, invoke your new Divine Download to bless you. Here is the simple Say Hello formula:

> *Dear Divine Golden Light Ball and Golden Liquid Spring of Divine Soul Language, I love you, honor you, and appreciate you. Please bring out my Soul Language. Thank you.*

Start to practice again by chanting:

> *San San Jiu Liu Ba Yao Wu*
> *San San Jiu Liu Ba Yao Wu*
> *San San Jiu Liu Ba Yao Wu*
> *San San Jiu Liu Ba Yao Wu*
> *San San Jiu Liu Ba Yao Wu*
> *San San Jiu Liu Ba Yao Wu*
> *San San Jiu Liu Ba Yao Wu . . .*

Chant faster!

> *San San Jiu Liu Ba Yao Wu*
> *San San Jiu Liu Ba Yao Wu*
> *San San Jiu Liu Ba Yao Wu*
> *San San Jiu Liu Ba Yao Wu*
> *San San Jiu Liu Ba Yao Wu*
> *San San Jiu Liu Ba Yao Wu*
> *San San Jiu Liu Ba Yao Wu . . .*

Chant even faster!

> *San San Jiu Liu Ba Yao Wu*
> *San San Jiu Liu Ba Yao Wu*
> *San San Jiu Liu Ba Yao Wu*
> *San San Jiu Liu Ba Yao Wu*
> *San San Jiu Liu Ba Yao Wu*

San San Jiu Liu Ba Yao Wu
San San Jiu Liu Ba Yao Wu . . .

Chant faster and faaaassssssttttteeeerrrr!

San San Jiu Liu Ba Yao Wu
San San Jiu Liu Ba Yao Wu
San San Jiu Liu Ba Yao Wu
San San Jiu Liu Ba Yao Wu
San San Jiu Liu Ba Yao Wu
San San Jiu Liu Ba Yao Wu
San San Jiu Liu Ba Yao Wu . . .

Chant faaaast as you can!

San San Jiu Liu Ba Yao Wu
San San Jiu Liu Ba Yao Wu
San San Jiu Liu Ba Yao Wu
San San Jiu Liu Ba Yao Wu
San San Jiu Liu Ba Yao Wu
San San Jiu Liu Ba Yao Wu
San San Jiu Liu Ba Yao Wu . . .

Continue to chant for five to eight minutes.

Be confident! Your Soul Language will come out!

When your Soul Language comes out, continue to flow your Soul Language for a few minutes. Let the voice of your soul and the special sound of your Soul Language flow fluently.

Apply Soul Language to Heal Yourself and Others

Now, let us practice using Soul Language to offer a healing to yourself and others. Sit up straight. You may do the following practices aloud or silently.

HEALING YOURSELF

Let's start with the Say Hello invocation:

> *Dear my Soul Language, I love you, honor you, and appreciate you. Please give me a healing for my . . .*

Complete your request by naming an organ, system, or cells in some part of your body—knees, back, neck . . . —or name an illness or emotional imbalance that needs healing.

> *Thank you.*

You could also use the permanent divine healing and blessing treasure that you received a few pages back:

> *Dear Divine Golden Light Ball and Golden Liquid Spring of Divine Soul Language, I love you, honor you, and appreciate you. Please heal my . . . Thank you.*

Or, invoke both your Soul Language and your Divine Download:

> *Dear Divine Golden Light Ball and Golden Liquid Spring of Divine Soul Language and dear my Soul Language, I love you, honor you, and appreciate you. Please heal my . . . Thank you.*

Then start to chant *San San Jiu Liu Ba Yao Wu* faster and faster until your Soul Language comes out. Continue to speak Soul Language for three to five minutes, either silently or out loud.

Close your eyes and focus on the area for which you requested a healing. You may feel warmth, coolness, or vibration there. If your Third Eye is open, you may see a dark area there turning to light. This shows that energetic and spiritual blockages are being removed. If you have advanced Third Eye abilities, you may see all kinds of images. You could see angels or other high spiritual beings coming to your assistance. You could see healing images of your parents, grandparents, or other loved ones who care for you. You could see healing images from nature. You could see parts of your own body radiating light and health.

After three to five minutes of chanting your Soul Language, say:

> *Hao. Hao. Hao.*
> *Thank you. Thank you. Thank you.*

Hao means "perfect" or "get well" in Chinese. To say *thank you* is to show gratitude to your Soul Language, your own soul, and the Divine.

I recommend that you do this self-healing practice as many times as you can per day. You can also do this practice to boost your energy; simply make that request! Spend three to five minutes each time. For chronic, serious, or life-threatening conditions, close your eyes and practice ten to fifteen minutes per session, as many times a day as you can.

There is no limit to how long you can practice self-healing with Soul Language per session. There is no limit to how many times you can practice each day. Even after you have self-healed yourself, continue the practice. Your Soul Language will automatically change from a healing tool to a rejuvenating tool!

IMPORTANT: If you speak Soul Language lying down, do not chant out loud. Chanting Soul Language or any mantra out loud while you are lying down can drain your energy. Chant silently instead. Chanting silently is a good practice for any body position, any time, anywhere. If you are not lying down, it is also a good practice to alternate chanting out loud with chanting silently. Chanting out loud vibrates the big cells and spaces of the body. Chanting silently vibrates the small cells and spaces of the body.

HEALING OTHERS

Now, I would like to lead you to experience healing others with your Soul Language. Choose a person nearby or someone close to your heart to whom you would like to give a healing. You could silently Say Hello as follows:

> *Dear my Soul Language. I love you, honor you, and appreciate you. Please give a healing to* . . . (name the person) *for* . . . (name the unhealthy condition, organ, system, emotional imbalance, etc.).

Start to chant Soul Language. Continue for three to five minutes. At the end of the healing session, say:

> *Hao. Hao. Hao.*
> *Thank you. Thank you. Thank you.*

Do not forget to also invoke your Divine Soul Language Download to offer healing to others. Here's how:

> *Dear Divine Golden Light Ball and Golden Liquid Spring of Divine Soul Language. I love you, honor you, and appreciate you. Please give a healing to* . . . (name the person) *for* . . . (name the unhealthy condition, organ, system, emotional imbalance, etc.).

Start to chant Soul Language. Continue for three to five minutes. Close:

> *Hao. Hao. Hao.*
> *Thank you. Thank you. Thank you.*

To receive a Divine Download is to be empowered to offer divine healing and blessing to yourself and others. You can quickly experience the power of Divine Downloads for healing and blessing. Always remember to honor the Divine Download.

How does this Divine Download work? Divine Soul Language is a divine soul downloaded from the heart of the Divine to your soul. When you invoke this treasure, this Divine Soul Language soul will vibrate and radiate to offer divine healing to yourself or others.

At the end of your practice, do not forget to honor by saying *thank you* from the bottom of your heart. Gratitude is a vital spiritual practice and courtesy.

Do this healing practice as many times as you can per day, the more, the better.

Apply Soul Language to Boost Energy for Yourself and Others

Now, let me show you how to apply this Divine Download to boost your energy and vitality. Say silently or out loud:

> *Dear Divine Golden Light Ball and Golden Liquid Spring of Divine Soul Language, I love you, honor you, and appreciate you. Please boost my energy and vitality. Thank you.*

Then, chant *San San Jiu Liu Ba Yao Wu* to bring out your Soul Language for three to five minutes. Do it now. After three to five minutes, check your energy level. Compare how you feel now with how you felt three to five minutes ago. You may feel lighter, more relaxed or happier. Whatever you feel is perfect.

You can boost your energy in this way anytime, anywhere. At the end of three to five minutes of chanting, always say:

> *Hao. Hao. Hao.*
> *Thank you. Thank you. Thank you.*

You may experience benefits instantly. You may not experience results immediately, but this does not mean that Divine Downloads do not work. It could take more practice. Remember this very important point: to receive a Divine Download does not mean you will automatically recover. You *must* practice in order to receive optimum healing benefits. The more you practice, the better.

You also can invoke your own Soul Language to boost your energy and vitality.

You also can invoke your own Soul Language and your Divine Download at the same time. This principle can be applied to every practice.

To invoke a Divine Download and your own Soul Language together produces better results.

Apply Soul Language to Do Remote Healing

Now, let me lead you to apply your Divine Download to offer healing and energy boosting to whomever you choose, wherever they may be. Your Divine Download soul will go out to offer distant healing and energy boosting.

Choose a person you want to receive this remote healing service. You can pick up the phone and call him or her to offer this service, or you can offer the remote healing without connecting physically.

Let's do it!

> *Dear Divine Golden Light Ball and Golden Liquid Spring of Divine Soul Language and dear my Soul Language, I love you, honor you, and appreciate you. Please heal* . . . (say the name of the person you wish to heal) *for* . . . (request the kind of healing you want to give). *Thank you.*

Then chant *San San Jiu Liu Ba Yao Wu* for three to five minutes to bring out your Soul Language. Do it now. After chanting for three to five minutes or longer, always say, *Hao. Hao. Hao. Thank you. Thank you. Thank you.*

You have now received the first Divine Download in this book and applied it to do self-healing and to boost your energy and vitality. You have also experienced using your divine gift to offer healing to others and to offer remote healing. The download you have received is a permanent divine soul. This soul will stay with you forever. You can invoke both it and the soul of your Soul Language anytime, anywhere, to offer healing and energy boosting at your request.

Remember, if you receive instant results by applying Divine Downloads, say "thank you" from the bottom of your heart. If you do not receive instant results, please also say "thank you" from the bottom of your heart. It could take a little more time and practice to receive healing results.

A divine soul can offer healing results beyond your imagination and comprehension. I wish for you to receive more and more healing results by applying Divine Downloads.

There is another Divine Download to be given in this book. These permanent divine souls could bring you remarkable life transformation.

Apply them. Benefit from them.

Let It Flow

Each person's Soul Language sounds different. Soul Language can sound like the babbling sounds of baby talk. It can sound like a foreign language you've never heard before. Others may experience a clicking sound. Some Soul Language actually sounds like a song, with a clear melody. The possibilities go on and on. They are without limit. Whatever your Soul Language sounds like is completely appropriate for you and your soul journey at this moment. Avoid any form of censorship.

What I mean by that is to receive and accept whatever comes out of your mouth as Soul Language. Avoid saying, "This cannot possibly be Soul Language; it sounds so strange." Change that to, "This is Soul Language even if it does sound strange." Or, "It does sound very strange so it must be Soul Language! I could never produce this by myself." If you want to check whether or not what is coming out of your mouth truly is Soul Language, try to go back to a very clear pronunciation of *San San Jiu Liu Ba Yao Wu*. If, after trying to articulate it clearly several times, you slide back into the strange sounds, you will know that you have truly opened your Soul Language. If you are able to clearly pronounce *San San Jiu Liu Ba Yao Wu* and if you can continue to pronounce each sound distinctly even when you accelerate your speed, then you simply need more practice to bring out your Soul Language.

Some of you may try to produce the strange sounds by thinking about it, by logically going about making strange sounds. This simply will not work. It will actually block your ability to bring out your Soul Language. Avoid logical thinking. Focus all of your attention on developing your Soul Language naturally. Focusing on the Soul Language itself will be the key for some of you. You may say, "I feel so absolutely ridiculous doing this. This is embarrassing. I feel so foolish." You may feel uncomfortable and self-conscious. In such a situation, you need to shift your focus from how you *feel* to a focus on Soul Language.

When you focus on how you feel, you are slipping into a focus on your ego. Your ego is sending out all sorts of messages that are going to be barriers and blockages to bringing out your Soul Language. Practice losing your focus on your ego and bringing out your Soul Language will become easier.

Blessings

As you read these pages, you are receiving enormous blessings. You may think that in order to receive blessings, you must have a physical connection with the one who is blessing you, that you need to either see or hear him or her. This is not accurate.

I am very honored and privileged to extend blessings through this book. You could say this book is a physical extension of my presence. In addition to the permanent Divine Downloads, you will receive numerous blessings each time you read this book. You will receive the particular blessings that you need for any aspect of bringing out or developing your Soul Language by reading the section on that aspect. This is a great advantage of this book. You could say that I am giving you your own invisibly guided tutorial.

This book will give you your own individualized set of blessings. The only thing you need to do is go to the section of the book that teaches about your particular need or interest. When you read that section over and over, you are receiving specific blessings that will help you with that aspect. This is a very special gift associated with this book and other books that I have published. The more blessings you receive, the more accelerated the improvements in your Soul Language will be. Your ability to bring out your Soul Language — and to develop and improve your Soul Language — is also related to the blessings you have received.

This may discourage those of you who think your opportunities to receive blessings are limited because you live at a distance or because your finances are limited. Once again, I remind you that this book is a healing and blessing tool. Anytime you feel the need for more blessings in order to continue with your soul journey, just read parts of this book again. Or, when you have completed the book, begin reading it again from the beginning.

You have already experienced how powerful and transforming the blessings that you receive by reading this book can be. In fact, this book is a constant source of blessings for you. Take full advantage of this marvelously generous gift from the Divine. Take every opportunity to benefit fully from this continual and constant stream of blessings. This is a unique opportunity that is offered to each of you. It is a possibility that is now available to everyone in the Soul Light Era.

As a blessing tool, this book has greater power in the Soul Light Era than it would have had in a previous time. This is another unique characteristic of the era in which we live. Use this gift in every possible way that comes to your awareness. It has been given to you so that you may have every advantage in progressing in your soul journey. I am delighted to be able to serve you in this way. Some of you may be thinking, "I don't want to be greedy." That is an incorrect idea, so let go of it right now. Instead of thinking you are being greedy by following my suggestions often, transform your thinking and begin to think of the book in terms of a candle.

When you read this book, you are lighting your first candle. The more often you read the book, the more candles you are lighting. So instead of being greedy by using this book to increase the blessings you receive, you are actually adding divine light to your own light and to the light that is present on Mother Earth. This is a great service. Think of reading the book in this way and you will have an accurate picture of what is really happening. Do not hesitate to follow the suggestions I have made. Following these suggestions will give you other benefits that you will become aware of as you read this book.

Practice

Blessings are vital but not enough to transform your opening and development of Soul Language. Your own personal practice is also needed. This is true because your own practice is actually a manifestation of your willingness to follow the teachings on complete gratitude. There is no need to explain this more fully. When you practice by yourself, you have the opportunity to express your gratitude for the teachings and the gift of Soul Language. Besides gratitude, it is also important in the soul journey to be devoted and to be willing to follow the teachings. Your practice is also an opportunity to manifest this devotion and willingness. This is extremely important for your soul journey and the uplifting of your spiritual standing.

Be active in your participation and progress. Putting in your own effort shows your goodwill. It also shows your willingness to offer this kind of service. When you do this, you will be delighted by the improvement that will take place. Your own practice will bring a special quality of joy, delight, and healing to your life. All the benefits of

Soul Language I have described will become part of your life each time you practice. This is an extraordinary possibility and opportunity for you.

A comparison may be helpful. Think about learning to play a musical instrument. You take lessons. At home, you practice what you have learned. Reading this book and receiving its teachings is similar to taking music lessons. Then, what you do during your own time of practice will help you understand and increase your ability and proficiency in what you learned. This is why practice is very important.

The blessings are effective, powerful, and necessary, just as taking a music lesson would be effective and necessary. The lesson makes it possible for you to improve and advance to the next level of proficiency. However, if you do not practice between lessons, the benefits you experience would be limited. Similarly, when you practice as I have described in this book, you are accelerating your ability to open Soul Language and you are greatly accelerating your ability to use and benefit from Soul Language. It is also a great service for you to use Soul Language.

The idea of being able to give service by using Soul Language may be surprising to you because your first focus is opening your own Soul Language and developing your own abilities. In fact, your practice time *is* also great service. Every time you connect with the Soul World and with the Divine through your practice, you are entering the most magnificent presence of the most powerful light and energy. The Divine and the entire Soul World respond with complete generosity, so that you and every soul around you receive blessings. Even the place where you are practicing receives blessings. All of your light becomes more intense and of a higher quality, vibration, and frequency. Amazingly, your practice can be of great benefit to others even if you have not specifically set that intention. It is another example of divine generosity that many souls can benefit every time you use, or even try to bring out, your Soul Language. These are some important aspects and benefits of your practice time.

Other benefits include the improvement in your soul's intelligence and creativity. These are wonderful gifts to receive. They will facilitate transformation in your soul journey. All of the significance and benefits of Soul Language become part of your life to a greater degree with every practice session. This improvement is easily available to you. All that you need to do is set a time to do this practice and keep your appointment.

When your Soul Language has opened, you can even practice as you are driving your car, sweeping the floor, or in between activities. Those interactivity transition times are especially good for practicing Soul Language. Often those transition times are stressful or frustrating. They may be times when you have to add something new to your plate. Practicing Soul Language will bring all of its benefits to those transition times. Practicing Soul Language at those times will also bring profound blessing to all the things that you will be doing next. Practicing throughout your day will make Soul Language a constant source of divine light.

Most of you have numerous times during the day when you change from one activity to another. For those of you who multitask, there are numerous times when you change from several activities to several others. Practicing Soul Language at these transition moments will bring about a transformation that will be an absolute delight. Instead of feeling frazzled, you will feel much more peaceful. The more you remember to practice Soul Language during those moments, the deeper your experience of peace, love, and light will become.

The benefits to you will be extensive. The benefits to all those who will be touched by your activities will also be extensive and will reach far beyond the activities that you are immediately aware of. For example, if your next activity is to make a phone call or to send an e-mail to many people, the recipients will benefit when you practice Soul Language first. In turn, all the people who interact with those people will also benefit. It, for example, the person who receives your phone call is working in an office, the entire office setting will benefit. The blessings, love, and light radiate to the entire setting. This is quite extraordinary and is another example of the service offered by using and practicing Soul Language.

    Let's practice together now!

> *Dear Divine Golden Light Ball and Golden Liquid Spring of*
> *Divine Soul Language and dear my Soul Language, I love*
> *you, honor you, and appreciate you.*
> *Please bless my* . . . (name your next activity or task).
> *Please bless me and all others involved* (you may name them).
> *Please bless the activity so that it may be completed with love,*
> *peace, and harmony.*
> *I am very grateful.*
> *Thank you.*

Chant your Soul Language for a few minutes, and then close the practice. If you don't have a few minutes, even doing this practice for twenty or thirty seconds will bring great blessings, love, and light. It is great service to the activity and to all involved in or affected by it.

    The more service you offer, the more your soul standing is uplifted. The virtue you receive is very powerful. All of this virtue will make it more possible for you to fully open and develop your Soul Language. It is a spiral of ever-increasing benefits. When you practice, you are sending out blessings, love, and light. Actually, it is more correct to say you are radiating out the blessings, love, and light. And the more you radiate out, the more it reflects and returns to you. The more it returns to you, the more you radiate out. These are some of the most significant reasons why practice is very important.

Using Soul Language

When you follow my suggestions and use the Divine Download offered earlier in this chapter, your Soul Language will open and develop. Now that you have Soul Language, it is necessary to use it. As you use Soul Language, the benefits described will become a greater and greater part of your life and your soul journey. Your use of Soul Language will improve simply by using it. Think again of the comparison to playing the piano. Every time you play a particular song for the pleasure of the experience, you are also improving your skill and increasing your gift. When you practice Soul Language, not only do you improve your skill and the quality of your gift, the improved quality radiates out far beyond you.

As described, you offer great service simply by practicing Soul Language. The benefits for your meditation will be greatly increased. The quality of your meditation will change significantly. Soul Language is a powerful tool that is very easy to use.

It can be every bit as powerful to use Soul Language silently as aloud. You often may not be able to use Soul Language aloud because of your work setting or family situation. Using Soul Language silently is every bit as powerful. Sometimes silent Soul Language brings benefits that audible Soul Language cannot. Silent Soul Language radiates and vibrates the tiniest cells and clears the tiniest spaces. It can bring about transformation at an extraordinarily deep level. Sometimes people are disappointed that they cannot use Soul Language aloud, because they feel that they are not offering the service that others can. That is not true. The possibilities associated with silent Soul Language are extraordinary.

Avoid the inclination to compare silent and audible Soul Language. Remember all that I said before about comparisons. Those teachings apply in this situation also. Simply be grateful for whatever opportunity you have and rejoice that you have the possibility of using Soul Language throughout your day. As you use it, you will be amazed at the benefits. Listing and describing all the benefits is not possible. They will vary from person to person. Know simply that your own soul journey will be touched in a very deep and profound way. Each person's soul journey is different. The details and the settings are different. Because of this, it is impossible to be very specific about how you will benefit by using Soul Language. You must have the experience.

When you are conversing with someone, you may become aware of healing that is needed in your life, in the lives of others, or in a particular situation. When you use Soul Language, that healing will take place immediately. There will be transformations on every level. This is an example of the unlimited benefits that you will experience as you use Soul Language. Your intention might be simply to use it for meditation or for the delight and joy of being able to connect with the Divine, the highest saints, and other souls. Frequently, as you do this, you will receive an inspiration or a new awareness. In fact, as you use Soul Language a great deal is happening within you, much of which cannot be anticipated or even perceived. This is what I mean when I say that the benefits are so extensive and so profound that it is impossible to completely describe them.

These benefits will be different for each one of you. In every situation, however, the benefits will radiate out beyond you and beyond the healing you may be receiving or offering. They will radiate out to Mother Earth in a most extraordinary and generous way. Every time you practice Soul Language, your vibration and frequency increase. The quality of light present within you increases. Your presence as a being of light also increases. All that was described as the significance and benefits of Soul Language becomes present within you. It is an extraordinary privilege and honor to be able to use Soul Language and to serve in this way.

3

Soul Language and Healing

One of the most powerful benefits of Soul Language is the impact it has on healing. When you think about it, this makes perfect sense. Soul Language is the purest form of connection with the Soul World and with the Divine. All of the healing potential of the Soul World and the Divine is available to you when you make this connection. With this potential, the possibilities for healing are without limit. The immediacy of healing is also without limit. Realizing the power of Soul Language for healing is very important. However, it is also important to balance this realization by releasing expectations. When Soul Language is used for healing, it must be done in a way that will allow the free flow of divine light, love, and healing blessings. It must be done with unconditional love, compassion, and forgiveness. It must be offered as unconditional universal service.

Offering a healing in this unconditional way will automatically make the healing free of expectations. This balance is needed for the healing blessings to truly flow. As I said earlier, bringing expectations to any situation is like turning off a faucet. When giving a healing blessing, it would be counterproductive to have an expectation about the results—almost like giving the blessing and taking it back at the same time.

Using Soul Language for healing blessings connects you to the soul of whatever it is that needs healing. This connection is powerful and transforming, because it brings all the possibilities of the Divine and the entire Soul World. Of course, with divine wisdom, whatever is being healed will receive the blessings that are appropriate at the moment. The situation, the illness, and the person will receive precisely the healing that they are ready to receive. It is necessary to keep this awareness in your conscious mind as you use Soul Language for healing. If the results are less than you hoped for, there are many possible reasons for this. One of those reasons is that the person or situation is not ready to receive greater healing.

If this is the case, it is great kindness and mercy on the part of the Soul World to minimize or limit the benefits. This aspect of "readiness" on the part of the receiver of the healing blessings through Soul Language is very important and should always be kept in mind. This awareness will help you avoid expectations. It will also help you avoid the tendency to complain because the results are less than hoped for. The more you use Soul Language for healing, the more you will experience results that are actually significant and dramatic.

When you use Soul Language for healing in this way, you are entering into the purest healing energy of the Divine and the Soul World. In fact, Soul Language gives you the ability to enter that energy by allowing you to put aside your logical thinking and your ego involvement. You become connected to this purity. With this connection, not only is the person who receives the healing blessed by this very clear energy, you are also blessed. Your own purification process is accelerated. Every time you use Soul Language and are able to enter into this very pure flow of divine light, you are purifying at every level of your being.

As you become a more and more pure messenger, you pass along higher and higher frequencies and vibrations to those you serve. This is a wonderful honor and privilege. The more pure you become, it would be accurate to say, the more divine you become. You are in greater harmony with very powerful frequencies. You are in greater unity with the Divine and with the Soul World. You become a clearer instrument. You will experience clarity and purity on the physical, mental, and emotional levels of your life and in your soul journey. This clarity will allow you to be the presence of divine light in an extraordinary way. Your Soul Language will become more and more powerful. The benefits others will receive will become more and more powerful. The service you perform will radiate out with greater and greater intensity. You will be blessed on every level of your life.

You may have a concern that some of the people you serve are fragile and may not be able to withstand intense energy. There is no need for concern. Soul Language is self-adjusting; it modifies the intensity with which it is received by the recipients of your healing blessings. Although you yourself may experience great intensity, if the person to whom you are giving the healing blessing is not able to absorb or withstand that intensity, they will receive what they are ready to receive. They will receive what is appropriate to them.

When my students offer healing blessings, many of them silently make a request of the Soul World, the Divine, and of their healing gifts to give healing blessings that are appropriate for the recipient. All of the characteristics associated with the use of Soul Language make it a very safe way to give healing blessings. There is no need to be concerned about causing problems for the ones you serve. There is no need to be concerned about negative side effects or an intensification of the existing difficulty. Using Soul Language avoids all of these concerns. I will say more about this later in this chapter in the section on healing others.

You Have the Power to Heal Yourself

In this section I will discuss teachings connected to a fundamental part of my mission. This aspect of the mission that I have been given by the Divine can be expressed in the statement: *You have the power to heal yourself.* This statement cannot be overemphasized. I hope many of you have experienced the truth of this statement. Some of you may be saying with your logical thinking, "Yes, that's true. That's obvious." However, your grasp of this statement will stop on the level of your logical thinking. What I wish to happen is for you to have the truth of this statement resonate and radiate in your heart and soul.

The statement "You have the power to heal yourself" is essential in your healing journey. It is essential in your journey as a healer. Radiate and vibrate this statement in your heart and soul and you will be able to approach healing others with confidence, conviction, and the experience that they, too, can heal themselves.

This statement is an essential part of the foundation of your healing journey. When you appreciate and realize from experience how true this statement is, everything in your life will begin to transform rapidly. There are many reasons for this. One of the most powerful reasons is that this statement, which you can consider to be a mantra, is the top aspect of my second empowerment. It connects very closely with what the Divine wants to happen on Mother Earth. This close connection carries a set of healing abilities and blessings.

The blessings that go to those who really practice the teaching "You have the power to heal yourself" are multiplied many times. This is true because you are the "early birds," the pioneers. You do not have the advantage of seeing many other people who have benefited from using this teaching. You are the ones who are creating the experiences that others will use as a reference. This may not seem very important, but its significance is vast.

You have a unique connection to my healing channel and to that of the Divine. It is strong and very powerful. Because you have been willing to accept and practice this teaching, you are rewarded and blessed in abundance far beyond what you can imagine. Your soul journey accelerates at an amazing rate. The trust that you demonstrate by accepting and practicing this teaching is also blessed at an extraordinary rate. Some of you may be surprised by that last statement. You may not feel a high degree of trust. There may be some areas where your confidence is very limited. Let me assure you that your willingness to be one of the first to accept and then to manifest the truth of this statement is truly significant.

The blessings you receive are continual and, in fact, you are demonstrating amazing trust. The realization that trust is an important aspect of your soul journey will become more and more obvious to you. As it becomes more obvious, your self-confidence will increase in a way that you can easily recognize. All of these are very special blessings. They are all connected with your living the teaching, "You have the power to heal yourself." The more you live this teaching, the more you become its physical presence. People who have known you in the past will not need you to tell them "You have the power to heal yourself." They will see that something dramatic has happened in your life. Many of them will even ask you, "What has happened for you?" At that time you can tell them very simply that you are practicing this teaching. Your life itself will be the explanation. The transformation that they observe in you will complete the teaching.

The benefits and blessings that you will receive as this happens are also amazing. Simply living your life as a person who is healing is service. All who meet you will be touched by the teaching that you live and manifest. This may be surprising to some of you, but it is only yet another example of divine generosity. Absolutely everything that you do which is a heartfelt response to the Divine is blessed, multiplied, and returned to you. When you accept and live the teaching "You have the power to heal yourself," that is accepted, blessed, multiplied, and returned to you. You will experience blessings on every level of your life.

This teaching is not new. What is new is the approach for the Soul Light Era. Connecting with the soul greatly accelerates the healing process, because true healing power is *soul healing* power. With the power of the soul, the healing process becomes integrated and complete in a way that is not otherwise possible. Specifically, connecting to the soul through Soul Language accelerates and multiplies the healing process in a way that can be immediate. If your response is not immediate, you simply need more time for the blockages to be removed. Do not be frustrated, discouraged, or compare yourself to others.

I have taught all of this earlier in this book. If you are feeling a little frustrated or discouraged at this moment, go back to those sections and read them again. When you do this, you will receive the blessings contained in those sections again. You need to go through these feelings and transform them to light. Your ability to do this is another example of the blessings received when you accept and live the teaching "You have the power to heal yourself." When you manifest healing in your own life, you have taken a very positive action. As the old adage says, "Actions speak louder than words." Even without words, your healing process is a very powerful teacher that will catch the attention of many. You will be one of the ones to lay the foundation for this teaching to be spread to many others.

When you use Soul Language to integrate this teaching with your very being, the message will radiate to the entire Soul World. Reflect on this extraordinary statement. Hold it in your heart and soul. Your healing process will become a teaching not only to those who knew you and are amazed at the transformation in your health, it will become a teaching for the entire Soul World. The benefits you can receive by offering this kind of service are unimaginable.

The major observable benefit will be the transformation of your health on a *physical* level. Physical changes are easy to observe and describe. Medical records and test results provide a measurable way of making your transformation tangible.

With all the different complementary and alternative healing approaches available, many people are confused or suspicious. This is understandable. Many of the healing approaches offered are questionable. Often, the most questionable approaches receive the greatest amount of media coverage. This makes it difficult for many people to accept new teachings about healing, especially a teaching that is unique. Most complementary and alternative medicines use concrete tools such as herbs, magnets, or oils. Each of these approaches does bring benefits. These approaches have been very helpful in the past.

What is different now is that we are in the Soul Light Era. That means it is vital to connect with the *soul* of your health condition. When you make this connection, your improvement can be amazing. When you make this connection, you also participate in my healing channel in a very profound way. The teaching "You have the power to heal yourself" will release amazing amounts of energy within you. This phrase also opens the possibilities for gratitude.

I strongly recommend that you reread the section on gratitude that concludes Chapter 1. You will receive the blessings contained in those pages again. Those blessings are specifically connected to your ability to heal yourself. This connection will intensify and multiply the benefits to your healing process.

"You have the power to heal yourself" can be used as a mantra. This mantra has power on many levels. When you use this mantra and allow it to go into Soul Language, the healing blessings on every level of your being will be very powerful. Using this teaching as a mantra maintains it as a constant flow of energy for you throughout your day. It quite literally transforms your day into a healing process. As you go through your day and become aware of the need for healing, use this teaching. Say "You have the power to heal yourself" to yourself many times. Say it with the realization that this is a special and privileged connection to my healing channel. You will receive very powerful transformations. For health issues that are recent, you may even experience a complete reversal and a return to health. Your blockage may be completely removed and transformed to the presence of healing energy and light. These are all extraordinary benefits and blessings.

When you accept and live this teaching, you have a connection to the Divine that will bring about profound changes on every level of who you are. These changes are not limited to your physical health. The first and most powerful change will actually be on the level of soul. As your soul is healed, as it is purified and becomes more and more pure light, it will give stronger and more powerful messages to your mind. This is a very special gift in this era in which the soul is in charge. The soul directs every other aspect of who you are. When the soul gives more powerful directions to your mind, you release limiting mind-sets, attitudes, and beliefs. You release patterns associated with limitations on your physical level. When the soul becomes more and more the presence of divine light, this divine presence has greater influence on all aspects of who you are.

In this Soul Light Era, the transformation of the soul will be easier than it was in previous eras. *Heal the soul first; then healing of the mind and body will follow.* Although I have discussed healing on the physical level first, healing actually begins with the soul. When you accept and manifest the teaching "You have the power to heal yourself," you connect to the Divine on the soul level. As more and more individuals manifest the dramatic results of this teaching, more members of the public will accept the truth of this teaching. This is the message the Divine wants us to experience on Mother Earth at this time. You are a messenger for the Divine. This is an extraordinary honor and privilege.

Your willingness to be such a messenger is blessed in abundance. Your soul journey and soul standing increase more rapidly than you can imagine. All that was said about healing on the physical level is also true about healing on the level of the soul. Those who have known you will also be aware of changes that take place on the level of the soul. They may not be able to identify specifically what they are observing, but most of them will have a sense that something is different about you. Some of them will even express it. When they do, you have a wonderful opportunity to introduce them to the teaching "You have the power to heal yourself."

Some of your friends and acquaintances will be grateful to hear this teaching. Some of them have a great yearning within their souls for this teaching and its blessings. Their souls have been waiting for this teaching for a very long time, in this lifetime and in previous lifetimes. The joy and gratitude they experience on the soul level will be very moving for them. You bring the presence of healing energy to them simply by being present. Your very self becomes the teaching.

When you give an explanation, this teaching becomes stronger and the souls receiving the teaching respond very powerfully. You may even be able to use Soul Language to give some of your friends and acquaintances a healing blessing. This will release incredible joy, delight, and gratitude within their souls and begin a powerful process of transformation for their soul journey.

As your friends and acquaintances change, some will begin to connect with the mission of empowerment for healing. This will be a very great blessing for them and for you. Whatever their response, the fact that you are the messenger of this teaching and that their souls have an opportunity to respond is very important. The results of the interaction are not most important. The results actually have very little to do with you. *The effort is yours, but the results belong to the Divine.* This realization is another way to release attachments to outcomes. Because the outcomes do not belong to you, you can be relaxed about introducing these ideas to others. You can present them as gifts. Whether or not the gift is accepted is not up to you.

The simple act of presenting the gift is important service. The more often you are the presence of the teaching "You have the power to heal yourself," the more often this teaching is a gift. As more and more people present this gift to others, the light and healing associated with this teaching will multiply. There will be a day when it will not be unusual for people to manifest the truth of this teaching.

All I have said about the healing of your soul is also true for the healing of your mind. Your mind-sets, attitudes, and beliefs will begin to transform. You will release limitations and patterns that have been part of your present physical lifetime. This release will have benefits on every level of your being. Your experience of light and liberation will be amazing. When those who have known you experience the new flexibility that you have, it will be a very powerful teaching for them. It is once again a very powerful service on your part. The virtue you accumulate will be extensive.

Note that doing something in order to accumulate virtue is counterproductive. If this is your motive, you will create barriers and blockages because you are not being unconditional. When you offer service unconditionally, that service will be rewarded with huge amounts of virtue.

You may find it difficult to differentiate between having an awareness that virtue is given and having virtue as your intention or motive. If so, it is because you are using logical thinking. You will not be able to sort things out with this approach. What you need to do is connect with the soul of your confusion. Let's do that now!

> *Dear soul of my confusion, I love you.*
> *Dear soul of my mind, I love you.*
> *You have the power to heal yourselves.*
> *Dear Divine Golden Light Ball and Golden Liquid Spring of*
>   *Divine Soul Language and dear my Soul Language, I love*
>   *you.*
> *Please bless my mind to release the mind-sets, attitudes, and*
>   *beliefs that are not beneficial to me, my healing journey, or*
>   *my soul's journey.*
> *I am very grateful.*
> *Thank you.*

Now, speak Soul Language (or 3396815) for several minutes. When you finish, you will probably experience peace and tranquillity. Your confusion will be transformed. It will not be completely gone, however, because your confusion is a signal that you need to release certain mind-sets, attitudes, and beliefs.

The great gift of your confusion is the awareness it brings of your need to do this kind of releasing. Furthermore, you have such a simple and practical tool to facilitate the releasing. Soul Language can bring about this shift very rapidly, even "easily" or "painlessly." These are wonderfully descriptive words that let you know yet again how abundantly blessed you are by the Divine when you enter into and use the teaching "You have the power to heal yourself." This may sound self-centered. However, the secret of this teaching, as you may have already discovered, is that it is *soul-centered*.

"You have the power to heal yourself" is a clear expression of a significant aspect of my mission. My mission is one that leads all souls who are willing to respond to access the highest levels in their soul journey. When you accept and live this teaching, you have entered into the realm of the soul and soul healing. Your soul has begun to direct your life in a way that is more powerful than you can imagine. This soul connection transforms every aspect of your life.

You will be able to say to others who are hesitant, "I know it can be done because I have done it." There is probably nothing more powerful than personal experience. You can probably think of many examples in your life where you have been willing to attempt something or accept something because of someone else's example. When others say to you "This seems unbelievable" or "This might work for someone else but I don't think it will work for me," and you can respond "I can relate to what you are saying," it is a wonderful gift. Relating to the hesitance that others feel as they begin this healing journey will be healing in and of itself. Saying this to others will release in them the possibility of accepting this teaching. It brings light to their doubts. As you do this for others, the changes that you experience will be significant and the gratitude that you experience will be transforming.

Gratitude will become an even stronger presence in your life. By now, you probably have a greater appreciation of what I said before about rolling a snowball downhill. That comparison will be dramatically evident to you. The more you accept and live the teaching "You have the power to heal yourself," the more rapidly the snowball rolls down the hill. The delight of this hill is that it has no bottom! The snowball can continue to get bigger and bigger. There is no end point for the improvements you can experience on the levels of the soul, mind, and body.

This is equally true on the level of emotions. You will be delighted and surprised at how quickly your emotional levels become more balanced. The reason is quite simple. The major emotions are associated with various organs.

- Anger connects with the liver and gallbladder.
- Depression and anxiety connect with the heart and small intestine.
- Worry connects with the spleen and stomach.
- Grief and sorrow connect with the lungs and large intestine.
- Fear connects with the kidneys and urinary bladder.

As each organ becomes stronger and more the presence of light, all the associated emotions will also be transformed. Anger will transform to peace and tranquillity. Depression and anxiety will transform to joy and contentment. Worry will transform to calm. Grief and sorrow will transform to a new quality of happiness. Fear will transform to confidence and authentic courage.

The benefits of these emotions transforming to light and becoming sources of energy and strength, rather than limitations and drains on your energy, are evident. The transformation of your emotions will in turn result in better health for your organs. If you are receiving counseling or other forms of assistance for your emotional life, I strongly recommend that you continue. When you reach the point when it is no longer necessary, you will be very aware of it. Your counselor will also be very aware of it. And so you will be able to conclude your relationship mutually when it is the appropriate time. It is in fact very important that this be done mutually.

As you experience further healing on the levels of soul, mind, and body, becoming the presence of more complete health on these levels, you can offer healing blessings to others. You will become a more and more pure and clear messenger. You will assist others in very powerful ways. You will help them become confident that they, too, have the power to heal themselves. To help even one person develop this confidence is an extraordinary treasure and blessing. It is like giving life to another, almost like a rebirth. For you to be part of that process is an extraordinary privilege and honor. This form of service is direct participation in the service of the Divine.

These are some important benefits of living the teaching, "You have the power to heal yourself." Now that you have an appreciation of this teaching, you are ready to appreciate your ability to use Soul Language to heal others.

Healing Others

Your ability to heal others is greatly increased when you use Soul Language. Your presence as divine healing energy will assist the healing process for your client. (For convenience, I will refer to the person you are healing as the "client," although it may be a relative or a friend.)

Using Soul Language to help your clients carries all the benefits that I have described for Soul Language. It also carries all the benefits described for healing yourself. Soul Language makes it possible for you to be the physical presence and sound of divine healing energy. As you use Soul Language for your clients, you may become aware that your Soul Language is different for each client. The reason is that the healing energy needed differs from person to person. Each person's soul journey is different. As you become aware of the differences in your Soul Language for each client, pay attention to how you experience that difference. This will help you assist each client better.

You are aware on the soul level of what your client needs. You will be grateful that your Soul Language can adjust to the needs of your client for you. Not only will you notice a difference from client to client, you will also notice a difference each time a particular client comes to you. This makes sense. Changes occur from moment to moment. Shifts in energy are taking place continually. This means that each person goes through transformation and healing continually.

This is also true for each organ. For example, if you are giving healing blessings to a client who is depressed, the organ involved is the heart. Your Soul Language may sound different when you give a healing blessing for someone experiencing anger, which is associated with the liver. What is true for each organ is also true for different illnesses. The changes in the way your Soul Language sounds directly address whatever organ or illness is receiving the healing blessing.

In Chapter 5, I will discuss translation of Soul Language. I only want to mention now that when you do a translation, the messages will be directed specifically to the healing blessing you are giving. They will offer teachings connected with the organ or illness involved. Occasionally it will be helpful to your client to have a translation of your Soul Language. Some clients will benefit by having in their conscious awareness all the teachings related to their particular health issue. In any case, these variations in your Soul Language can provide you with wonderful wisdom and healing suggestions for your clients.

For example, if your client is angry, it affects his liver and gallbladder. To understand why he carries that anger is very useful. It empowers your client to release the memories connected with that anger. It makes it possible for him to take his healing to the next level by entering the condition of unconditional universal forgiveness. When clients become aware of the situation that is the root of their anger (or depression, or worry—whatever), they will need to offer unconditional universal forgiveness in almost every case.

Some clients will be very grateful to have this opportunity. They will be ready to accept the connection between the issues that need forgiveness and their physical manifestation as illness. Other clients will not be ready for this. Respect the readiness of each client. Bring those who are not ready step by step toward readiness. You can do this by helping them appreciate the changes taking place on the physical level. When they have an adequate appreciation of these changes, you can present to them the connection between their physical symptoms and the emotions connected with particular organs.

You might be saying, "My clients do not have problems that are connected with an organ. Many of them come with pain in their back or their neck. Some have knee problems. Others have problems connected with their tendons." All of these are manifestations of blockages in different organs. If the pain is connected with the muscles, then the spleen and stomach are involved. If it is connected with the knees, again the spleen and stomach are involved. If it is connected with the tendons and ligaments, the liver is involved. The five major organs (liver, heart, spleen, lungs, kidneys) are connected with all the main systems in the physical body. For a more complete explanation of this connection, see my book *Zhi Neng Medicine*.

You can even use Soul Language to connect with your client's needs before your client arrives. This takes only a brief amount of time. You may already do this as part of your practice. For those of you who have not thought of doing this, using Soul Language before your client arrives makes your healing session much more powerful and effective, because it helps bring harmony to each soul participating in the healing. Before your client even arrives, the entire Soul World is present, with all of its healing energy. Your client will enter this extraordinary field of healing energy.

As soon as clients enter your healing space, healing will begin as their souls receive these blessings. You may notice an amazing rate of improvement when you begin using Soul Language regularly. Your clients will also be aware of a great difference as soon as they arrive for their healing blessings. Many of your clients will talk to others and the number of people coming to see you will increase by this word of mouth. The use of Soul Language in the healing of others is without limit. Allow your imagination to discover other possibilities. Use Soul Language to release these possibilities for assisting others in their healing journey. Every time you do this, you are serving others as an unconditional universal servant.

This practice will help you and all those you serve. Soul Language is not only a tool, a blessing, and a profound connection with the entire Soul World and the Divine; Soul Language is also a universal servant. When you think of Soul Language in this way, your ability to assist others in their healing journey will increase significantly. This will be a blessing for you and for all those who come to you for healing blessings. It will be a very special honor and privilege to work with Soul Language in this way.

Remote Healing

All that I have said about healing others is also true for remote healing. The greatest difference is simply that the client is not directly in front of you. The preparations that you make are the same. Your responses to your clients' requests will be done in the same way. You may choose to do remote healing over the telephone so that your connection with your client is more direct. You may choose a time when your client will sit quietly to receive your healing blessing without a direct connection.

Although these approaches can be helpful, they are not always necessary. If your client feels there is greater benefit with a direct connection, then by all means use one when offering your healing blessing. If your client does not have this need, there are countless ways in which you can do remote healing. Perhaps the easiest is to set aside a time in your day to offer remote healings. In some situations, you will want to give a remote healing to a person who is totally unaware of the healing. If you are working with a family member, relative, or close friend, in most cases it will be perfectly fine to do that.

If you have any question about the appropriateness of sending a healing blessing, you can ask the soul of the individual if it is all right to proceed. Many of you will immediately hear within your own soul "yes" or "no." If you do not receive this kind of response, you can add the phrase "if it is appropriate" to your healing blessings. Here's an example:

Dear soul, mind, and body of Nancy, I love you.
You have the power to heal yourself. Do a good job.

Dear soul, mind, and body of Nancy's sore back, I love you.
You have the power to heal yourself. Do a good job.
I would like to send you a healing blessing, if it is appropriate.
Dear Divine Golden Light Ball and Golden Liquid Spring of
  Divine Soul Language and dear my Soul Language, I love
  you, honor you, and appreciate you.
Please offer Nancy a healing blessing.
If it is appropriate for Nancy to receive this healing blessing,
  please let her benefit. If it is not appropriate, please send the
  healing blessing to those who need it and who are ready to re-
  ceive it.
Thank you so much.

Then, speak Soul Language for a few minutes. End the healing blessing by saying:

Dear Divine Golden Light Ball and Golden Liquid Spring of
  Divine Soul Language, please return to my soul.
Hao. Hao. Hao.
Thank you. Thank you. Thank you.

It is possible to send remote healings to several people simultaneously.
To do this, simply state their names and ask your Divine Download
and your Soul Language to send healing blessings to all of them. If
you know what their particular issue is, you can identify it. If you do
not know, you can simply ask your Divine Download and your Soul
Language to give the healing blessing that is appropriate and most
needed at this time. If you have Third Eye abilities, you will see areas
that are blocked or areas that need more light and energy. This will
make it possible for you to direct your request to those areas. If you
cannot see this, simply ask, "Please direct the blessings to wherever
they are most needed, as appropriate." Even if you do have Third Eye
abilities, it is always good to ask your Divine Download and your
Soul Language to give the blessings they know are most needed.

There is another request that would benefit your clients tremendously: "Please give healing blessings on all levels: physical, emotional, mind, and soul." Adding this phrase after you have identified specific areas that need healing will make your healing blessings much more powerful and effective. You are also assisting your clients to progress on their soul journeys. Their transformations can be very profound and powerful. And all of this can be done at a distance!

If you have been practicing these techniques already, reading about them in this section increases your abilities. As I have said often throughout this book, as you are reading the teachings, you are receiving profound blessings. These blessings will enhance your healing abilities and your own soul's standing. They change the quality of your healing abilities. Your intuitive understanding of this will move to a new level every time you read this section. The quality of light, love, compassion, forgiveness, and other divine qualities that are connected with your soul journey and your healing abilities, all move to a greater vibration and a higher frequency. This is an extraordinary blessing for you and your clients.

4

Soul Language as Service

The idea of Soul Language as service may be new to you. When you use Soul Language you are in fact giving great service, as I have described throughout this book. I have also referred to Soul Language as an unconditional universal servant. I will explain this teaching in more detail in this chapter, because it is important. Keep this teaching in your awareness. The more you understand Soul Language as an unconditional universal servant, the more you and others will benefit. The benefits will multiply and radiate out to all of Mother Earth and beyond. They will bless the lives of many you do not even know.

Giving this type of service is especially blessed because it is yin virtue, which means that it is unseen and unacknowledged. Yin virtue benefits your soul journey in an extraordinarily generous way. When your activities are acknowledged publicly, even by a limited number of people, you have already received most of your reward. When they are not acknowledged, then you receive all of your reward in the form of an increase in virtue. The blessings for you will be amazing. Furthermore, as you receive more blessings, everyone and everything associated with you will also receive more blessings. This is in turn additional service and virtue. You probably have not considered this even as a possibility, but it is only yet another example of the extraordinary generosity of the Divine.

It is also an example of the harmony and unity that exists among all souls. What happens for one soul can influence many other souls. When your soul journey is the most important aspect of your life, you are actually giving more service, because everything that happens in your soul journey radiates out to many others. It radiates out not only to those closely associated with you, but also to those you do not even know and to those who actually lived in a different time. This is part of the true meaning of universal service.

When you are practicing Soul Language, when you use it for the sheer delight and enjoyment of it, you assist numerous souls in their transformation to light. Many of you who know my role as a divine universal healer, teacher, and servant have a good idea of just how extensive the service I offer is. It radiates out and includes Mother Earth, our universe, all universes, all the souls (including the highest saints) in Jiu Tian (the nine layers of Heaven that most people understand and connect with) and Tian Wai Tian (the Heaven beyond Jiu Tian). When you are connected and associated with my mission, the service you give also radiates out far beyond where it would if there were no connection with my teachings.

I hope this teaching will help you better understand the nature and scope of universal service. Whenever a new teaching becomes part of your conscious awareness, that teaching becomes a powerful part of what you do. Using Soul Language will help you bring more and more knowledge and wisdom into your conscious awareness. Soul Language will help unlock the doors to some of the most amazing wisdom held within the universe. It can connect you with very ancient, sacred wisdom that has not been revealed before. Attaining and living this wisdom is also service. This service will also radiate out far beyond yourself to assist others in their soul journeys and to increase their soul standing. The possibilities are limitless, because whenever you enter the realm of the highest saints and the Divine, you enter into the realm of the infinite.

It is quite amazing to realize that whatever you do for your own soul journey will also benefit many other souls. This "side effect" only has benefits. If you are still struggling with bringing out your Soul Language, I hope this teaching will inspire you to continue to practice. By this point in the book, you will be very close to experiencing success, no matter how you have struggled to open your Soul Language. In fact, almost all of you will have experienced success. If you have not, you may want to return to the sections that describe developing your Soul Language and receive the blessings there yet again. Opening your Soul Language will open the treasure chest of everything that I describe in this book.

Communicating with the Soul World

In this section, I will continue the teachings that I began in Chapter 1 on the significance and benefits of communicating with the Soul World. As is true for everything connected with the Soul World, it is impossible to give a complete explanation. Here, I will approach these teachings from a different perspective—that of service.

One aspect of using Soul Language and connecting with the Soul World from the perspective of service is using Soul Language for healing, as discussed in Chapter 3. Another aspect of using Soul Language for service is giving healing blessings to those who have passed from this life. Using Soul Language is a very powerful way to assist those who have made this transition. When you offer this type of service, it is vital to add the phrase, "if it is appropriate" or "for the souls who are ready."

There are some souls whose karma is so powerful that you may not have enough virtue to offer blessings with your Soul Language. In order to avoid draining yourself of your virtue, it is very important to add one of the qualifying phrases. It is also necessary to realize that some people must purify their own karma. It is not appropriate to interfere with the Divine's plan for some souls. The individuals who carried that karma when they left Mother Earth need to carry it for a certain amount of time. Understand that time has different meanings in the Soul World. This may seem very harsh, but you must realize that the burdens of karma that each soul carries are also an opportunity for them to learn important lessons. When an individual has a karmic debt to pay, these lessons may be ones the individual missed in their lifetime on Mother Earth.

Some individuals may have not only missed the lessons but chosen to ignore them. They need to learn those lessons so they can fully participate in their journey to light. It is actually not harsh on the part of the Divine at all. It is actually very generous for the Divine to keep giving those individuals opportunities to learn the lessons essential to their transformation to light and increased soul standing. It is inappropriate for you to offer these individuals blessings connected with the use of Soul Language.

Some of you may still feel uncomfortable with this teaching or have a whole range of other responses. This is a wonderful opportunity for you to look at those reactions. Again, do what I suggested earlier in this book. Speak Soul Language connected to your reaction. Pay very close attention to all that comes to you as you do this. You will get very helpful and useful information. Much of the information you receive is associated with having no attachment.

Those who have strong reactions are particularly blessed. Those who do not have a strong reaction have already passed through this type of attachment and you were blessed. Whatever group you belong to or wherever you fall between the two, remember what I said to you about making comparisons. If you are having strong reactions, I suggest again that you go back to the section on attachments so that they become a source of light to you.

Some of you are very annoyed at this time and are vigorously resisting my suggestion to go back and read that section again. Such a response is a perfect indication that going back to reread it is exactly what you are called to do by the Divine and the entire Soul World. Perhaps you would like to allow yourself a little space of time before you go back to that section. You could chant Soul Language so that you feel a degree of calm and peace before you go back to that section. When you read those sections again, they will become more and more part of you. After you receive the blessings associated with those teachings again, continue with this section.

To conclude my teachings about those who have very heavy karma, there are some masters and teachers on Mother Earth at this time whose virtue is so extensive and powerful that they have the authority from the Divine to offer blessings of light to those souls who have passed from this life carrying very heavy karma. The Divine does not abandon any soul. However, the beings who are able to offer this type of service must have very specific authority from the Divine. If you are wondering whether or not you have that authority, you can rest assured that the answer is *no*. When a person receives this authority, it is very clear and very direct. There will be no question about it. Having this clarity is very important. It is not enough to simply be inspired or to have one of your teachers tell you that you can do this. It is necessary to have a very clear and powerful message from the Divine. It is necessary to have great virtue and very high standing in the Soul World to offer this kind of service.

If you are saying to yourself, "But I have received this information in my meditation; my teacher, my master has told me to do this," you may want to check again. I cannot emphasize enough that you must be extraordinarily careful about doing this. If you have not received the authority and do not have the virtue to do this, the effect on your life can be very serious. You can become so drained that you actually end up in a life-threatening condition. Take this teaching with great seriousness.

Communicating with Mother Earth

It is possible to communicate with every aspect of creation through Soul Language. You can offer service through this form of communication with Mother Earth and beyond. In the rest of this chapter, I will describe ways of doing this. If you already practice these approaches, you will appreciate these teachings in a very special way.

As you read these pages, the blessings you receive will raise your service to a higher level. The insights that you will receive about your practices will also bring your service to a higher level.

These ideas may be new or unusual to you. You may not have thought of these possibilities before. But as you read these teachings, you may say to yourself, "of course." You may have a feeling of going home. You may have a sense of familiarity connected with these teachings. You may have a sense of joy and delight at the possibilities. Whatever your response, the blessings you receive will be very powerful and will bring greater transformation to your responses, to your practices, and to you.

You may not have considered how to use Soul Language to bless and serve Mother Earth before. To give and receive blessings from Mother Earth is very important at this time. This will assist Mother Earth in her transition and purification in very powerful ways. The healings our dear little planet will receive from those who use Soul Language will be amazing.

When you use Soul Language to communicate with Mother Earth, you connect with those parts of Mother Earth that need healing blessings. You can offer blessings for those areas suffering from political or religious conflict or a natural disaster. Offering healing blessings through Soul Language will benefit all those areas powerfully, because Soul Language connects Mother Earth and her needs with the very highest levels of the Soul World.

You can offer healing blessings to the many areas of Mother Earth damaged by human beings. For example, there are many areas where pollution is so extreme that the water is undrinkable without extensive purification processes. Offering healing blessings to the water would be a great act of service.

You can probably make a long list of the various forms of pollution on Mother Earth. Offering healing blessings to any of these areas of pollution will make a huge difference to our dear planet. The gratitude she will have for being sent these healing blessings will be profound. This gratitude will resonate throughout all of Mother Earth. Offering this kind of service is a special blessing and gift associated with Soul Language.

Let's offer such a blessing together now. Think of a polluted entity (lake, river, area of land, a business, etc.) near you.

> *Dear soul, mind, and body of* (name the polluted entity), *I love you.*
> *You have the power to heal yourself.*
> *Dear Divine Golden Light Ball and Golden Liquid Spring of Divine Soul Language and dear my Soul Language, I love you, honor you, and appreciate you.*
> *Please offer a healing blessing to* (the entity) *as appropriate at this time.*
> *I am very grateful.*

Chant your Soul Language for a few minutes and close in the usual way.

Another example of how humans have damaged Mother Earth is through the removal of her resources by mining. Even though much of this was done unconsciously, insufficient thought was given to the long-term results. Mining has left enormous scars and open wounds on Mother Earth. Tremendous healing is needed in these situations. Using Soul Language for this kind of healing is very powerful.

When you offer healing blessings to Mother Earth, I suggest you also include everyone who was part of creating the pollution or damage. At this moment, you may be angry at the thought of what has happened to Mother Earth. If this is the case, then please go into the condition of universal unconditional forgiveness. Do not practice Soul Language or try to offer healing blessings when you are angry. Stop first and enter into unconditional universal forgiveness. Only then should you continue to offer healing blessings. You and Mother Earth will both benefit greatly.

Other examples of Mother Earth's need for healing include the congestion that exists in many areas. This congestion can assume many forms. Many areas of Mother Earth have been paved over; farmland has been converted to "development." In some of these development projects, excessively large homes have been built. Some of these homes are so excessive that it is not really possible to describe them as family dwelling places. They are something else entirely. The weight that they place upon Mother Earth is enormous. As before, it would be very good to include all those who are part of these projects in your healing.

These are a few examples of communicating with Mother Earth to send healing blessings for areas and situations where healing is needed. The need for healing is very deep. This need has existed in some cases for hundreds, if not thousands, of years. With such a deep and long history, healing may take longer than days, weeks, or even months, but keep in mind that healing will be accelerated more than you can imagine with the use of Soul Language.

Besides giving healing blessings to Mother Earth, you can use Soul Language to communicate with the various aspects of Mother Earth that are a sheer delight to you. You can also ask to receive healing blessings. For example, if you want to be physically stronger, you can use Soul Language to communicate with the mountains. You can connect with the soul of the strength of the mountains to receive their blessings. If you want more joy in your life, you could use Soul Language to connect with the soul of those parts of Mother Earth that are particularly delightful to you. It may be the beauty of the sunrise or sunset. It may be the variety of the flowers that flourish on Mother Earth. It may be the beauty of the songbirds. The possibilities are almost limitless.

Choose the ones that bring the greatest delight to you. Connect with their beauty, joy, and delight. Communicate through Soul Language to become one with the soul of the sunset, the songbirds, or the magnificence of the blossoms. Doing this is a way of "going into the condition." Go into the condition of the joy and beauty of the sunset. *Become* that beauty. When you do this through Soul Language, you will be amazed at the transformation that takes place.

The beauty has many layers and levels because the beauty of the sunrise or sunset, the flowers and the songbirds is connected with all of the gratitude of those who have experienced this beauty, joy, and, for some, ecstasy. When you go into the condition of the beauty of the sunset, you receive the blessings of all of these souls. Not only will you benefit but the benefits will be returned to Mother Earth. This is a type of "recycling" that may be new to you. It carries blessings, light, and regeneration far beyond your ability to imagine.

You can also offer service to Mother Earth through Soul Language by simply using Soul Language for the pure delight and joy of it. When you use Soul Language in this way, you are simply connecting with Mother Earth in mutual harmony by connecting with her Soul Language. This connection is powerful and profound. You will receive profound and transforming teachings. You can connect with all of Mother Earth or with particular aspects such as the rivers, mountains, trees, and animals.

You may notice that your Soul Language changes. When you are in harmony with the mountains, you receive one kind of Soul Language. When you are in harmony with the streams or the waterfalls, you receive a different kind of Soul Language. With each form of Soul Language you receive different blessings and teachings. You also are giving the blessings that are needed by that aspect even if giving blessings was not your intention. Giving blessings is an automatic benefit of Soul Language.

Soul Language is a unique form of communication with Mother Earth. It is a unique way to offer blessings to Mother Earth. It is a way to connect Mother Earth with the highest levels of the Soul World and with all that exists beyond Mother Earth. These connections bring powerful and profound blessings. They help bring Mother Earth into a stronger vibration and frequency for healing, health, and wholeness. The connection of Soul Language with the entire Soul World is a particular kindness that you offer to our dear planet.

At this time, there is a great need for Mother Earth to receive this kindness. It is a very great kindness and a very high form of service to use Soul Language for Mother Earth. It is a particular kindness to return gifts to her when she has given you gifts in such abundance over the centuries. It is like showing respect and appreciation for your physical mother. Offering this type of service is connected with a very special quality of virtue. When this service is received by the Divine and the entire Soul World, it will be blessed, multiplied, and returned to you. This will most certainly make a difference in your soul's standing. It will also increase the power of the blessings you offer using Soul Language. The most marvelous thing about offering this type of service is that the benefits for Mother Earth will be truly amazing.

It is indeed a great honor and privilege to do this for Mother Earth.

Communicating Beyond Mother Earth

Through Soul Language, you can communicate with the planets, stars, and other universes. You can communicate with the space that surrounds Mother Earth. You can communicate with the space that exists between the planets and between the stars. You can communicate with the space that exists between all the universes and beyond.

To communicate through Soul Language with the planets, stars, and other universes will benefit and bless you in a way similar to what was described in the previous section for Mother Earth. The needs for healing of the planets, stars, and universes are also similar to the needs of our planet. The same is true for the blessings received.

In this section, I will teach you about space. For health, it is necessary for the spaces in the human body to be free of blockages, clear, and full of light. This is also true for the spaces around and beyond Mother Earth. It is true for all space. When the space is clear, it becomes the presence of light. This light can then circulate in a way that will promote health. It may seem strange to talk about the health of the space beyond Mother Earth, our solar system, and our universe, but it is very important. You will better appreciate the significance of this with some examples closer to home.

Think of the atmosphere around Mother Earth. At this point in the history of our dear planet, our atmosphere is quite polluted. Those who live in densely populated areas can frequently *see* the air. Sometimes it is possible to even smell or taste the air. This is absolutely not the way air is meant to be. When those who live in congested areas visit less populated areas, the difference in the air can be obvious and extraordinary. Your entire body responds favorably when breathing this pure air.

This example gives you a good idea of what it means to say "The space needs clearing." Quite literally, everything that pollutes the air needs to be transformed. The air needs to become clean once again. Everything in the environment that is a source or result of pollution is similar to excess energy stored in the body. Whatever blocks the space in our air needs to be transformed into freely flowing energy and light. As this process takes place, the air surrounding Earth will become clear. The space around Earth will become clear and clean.

When you communicate with our atmosphere, you can offer it healing blessings through Soul Language. This is one of the most significant activities you can do to benefit the environment. Using Soul Language for the healing of the atmosphere can be powerfully effective. It can transform the space into the presence of divine light and energy. The clearer the space is, the more easily divine light and energy will circulate in a balanced way around Mother Earth. When this happens, the health of Mother Earth will improve dramatically.

It would be wonderful if environmental groups could come to appreciate the significance and power of Soul Language. If their activities were joined to Soul Language, the results would be amazing. Their activities are expressions of the yang or physical world. Soul Language is an expression of the yin or Soul World. With both the yin and yang present, the impact of the environmental groups would be greatly magnified. The experiences of their members would also be transformed.

In the future, it is likely that various movements will include Soul Language as part of their programs. This will alter many current organizations and their activities significantly. Their members will use Soul Language organically across their activities. The benefits for their projects and the environment will be profound.

※

The usual sources and results of pollution are not the only things cluttering the air around Mother Earth. There are other things that create blockages. Many satellites and spacecraft that have been put into orbit around Mother Earth are also creating blockages. The process of transforming these enormous machines will require a level of virtue and light that few people have developed at this time. It will be possible to transform these objects; however, only those who have the requisite virtue can do it. Even if we are not able to completely transform this space debris, it is still important for us to send healing blessings to it by using Soul Language.

As I said before, the virtue of the entire Soul World comes to whatever is receiving the healing blessing that you offer when you use Soul Language. This is very powerful. You may wonder, "If the entire Soul World is assisting, why can't anyone bring about the transformation needed for these objects that have been left to orbit aimlessly in space?" The answer is quite simple. The Soul World responds to the request according to the standing of the requester. The higher your standing is in the Soul World, the more powerfully the Soul World responds to your request and to your Soul Language, and the more powerfully it participates in the blessings given through your Soul Language.

Whatever your soul's standing, it is an extraordinarily important service to send blessings to the space around Mother Earth and beyond by using your Soul Language. However, always remember: *The work is yours; the results belong to the Divine and the entire Soul World*. It is particularly important to keep this in mind in the days that are upon Mother Earth in her time of transition and purification. Offering service is in and of itself the most important thing. Always offer pure service as an unconditional universal servant.

With the examples of the pollution and clutter in the atmosphere around Mother Earth, you can appreciate the need to clear the spaces beyond this solar system—the spaces throughout this universe and in other universes. Because you have probably seen photographs of the pollution and of man-made objects in the atmosphere, it should not be too difficult to imagine the transformation process that can take place through Soul Language.

It might be more difficult to picture the transformation for the spaces far beyond Mother Earth. These spaces are so vast and seemingly remote that you may not have any idea what kinds of "pollution" they contain. Just transfer the picture that you have for all of Mother Earth and our solar system and apply it to the spaces beyond. The forms of pollution may be different and the forms of clutter may be different, but that is not important. The essence of this teaching is that all of these spaces need to be cleared, and that Soul Language is the most powerful way available to us to participate in offering the service of clearing. When those spaces are cleared, the health of every planet, star, and universe—of all that exists—will begin to improve. This is an extraordinary realization.

Very often we think only in terms of Mother Earth. It is important to think beyond those limits. When you begin to do this, you enter into another aspect of what it means to be an unconditional universal servant. Your service is not limited to where you live or to those you know. It is universal. It extends beyond—far beyond—Mother Earth. Offering this truly *universal* service also brings about the most amazing improvements in the physical, emotional, mental, and spiritual well-being of all creatures who live upon Mother Earth, as well as of all who live upon the planets, stars, and universes beyond Mother Earth. In offering service to clear the spaces, you offer a most powerful service that radiates out so far that it is not possible to imagine how extensive it is.

Helping to clear the spaces is a very special blessing. When the spaces are cleared, not only is there the presence of light, not only is the health of all who dwell on other planets, stars, and universes improved, but also the quality of emptiness becomes present. If you have some understanding or experience of the term *emptiness*, you can appreciate that this word does not mean what it normally does. *Emptiness* is the presence of the Divine. When spaces are cleared and transformed, they fill with divine light and energy. They become the presence of the Divine. They become *emptiness*.

As this happens around Mother Earth and beyond, throughout all universes, the soul journeys of all those in human form and other forms will be dramatically transformed. This form of service is highly blessed. When offering this type of service, it is important to also include the phrase that I have suggested previously: *if it is appropriate* or *for those spaces that are ready to receive this healing blessing.* Adding one of these phrases makes it possible to offer service that is appropriate for the amount of virtue you have. Clearing these spaces helps bring about the complete purification of Mother Earth and all that exists beyond Mother Earth.

When spaces between the planets, stars, and universes are cleared, the health of all that exists will improve. Once again, think in terms of a human body. The space within a cell, the spaces between cells, the spaces between organs, and the bigger spaces within the body—all need clearing. Each and every space, whether it is tiny or huge, influences the other spaces. The same is true when we speak of the spaces around Mother Earth, beyond Mother Earth, throughout the universe and all universes. What happens in one space influences and affects the other spaces.

If the concept of universes beyond this one is too difficult to accept at this moment, that is quite all right. Simply imagine this universe and say to yourself, "I know there are more." Do not force yourself to try to accept or appreciate this realization fully at this moment. The more you simply say "I know there are more," the more this realization will become part of your being, little by little in a gradual and natural way.

When you offer service beyond Mother Earth, you are doing all that has been described for Mother Earth and you are also clearing the space. These two approaches are very important. Besides offering service through healing blessings, you can use your Soul Language to enjoy the possibility of being in harmony with all that exists beyond Mother Earth. You can receive teachings and wisdom from beyond Mother Earth. Even receiving these teachings and wisdom is a form of service. The more teachings and wisdom you receive and begin to live, the more you will be transformed and the more your soul's standing will increase.

By now it is probably clear to you that *whatever* you do can be a form of service. Once you enter the condition of being an unconditional universal servant, every aspect of every part of your day carries the possibility of offering service. This is a wonderful understanding to have. It transforms everything you do. Your responses to everything in your life will also transform. You will appreciate what an honor and privilege it is to be an unconditional universal servant.

Translating Soul Language

Now that you have begun to speak Soul Language, I am sure you want to understand Soul Language. In this chapter, I am honored to teach you how to translate Soul Language. I will also offer you a Divine Download to improve your ability to translate Soul Language.

All that I have said about Soul Language and its limitless possibilities should make it easy to understand that the ability to translate Soul Language is extremely important. Connecting with the soul of the teachings and the soul of the wisdom in this book can be transforming. However, this transformation is limited. The ability to translate Soul Language will remove those limits.

The Importance of Translating Soul Language

Soul Language carries profound soul wisdom and knowledge. If you can translate it, many soul secrets will be released to you. You can use Soul Language to communicate with saints and other high-level spiritual fathers and mothers in Heaven. You can use Soul Language to communicate with the Divine.

LEARN WISDOM DIRECTLY FROM THE DIVINE
THROUGH SOUL LANGUAGE

Let me demonstrate how you can use Soul Language to learn sacred wisdom directly from the Divine.

First, I ask the question for which I wish to receive a divine teaching:

> *Dear Divine, I am honored to speak Soul Language to ask you a question.*
> *What is the importance of translating Soul Language?*

Then, I speak Soul Language for about one minute. When I am done, I ask the Divine:

> *Dear Divine, could you give me your answer through my Soul Language?*
> *Thank you.*

Then, I speak Soul Language again for one minute to receive the Divine's reply.

Here is my translation of the Divine's reply through my Soul Language:

> *Dear Zhi Gang, Soul Language translation is very important. You can understand my teaching directly through Soul Language and translation. You can receive my blessing through Soul Language and translation. You can understand directly the wisdom that I reveal to you.*
> *The Soul Language channel is a direct and pure channel. I can release my wisdom to anyone who asks me something using their Soul Language channel. But you must know how to translate Soul Language. Otherwise, you will not understand the wisdom at all.*

*Through Soul Language, I offer my direct guidance to human-
ity. If you have life challenges, ask me through Soul Language and I will explain the blockages in your life. Through
Soul Language, I will guide you with my wisdom to melt your
blockages and transform your life.*

*Through Soul Language, I can offer my healing to anyone.
Translating Soul Language can reveal the root blockage of a
person's health issues. Soul Language can also transmit my
healing blessing and remove this root blockage.*

*Soul Language and its translation can also offer rejuvenation.
Through Soul Language, you can learn how to rejuvenate
faster and better. Soul Language translation will provide an
explanation for whatever you ask.*

I deeply appreciate the Divine's reply through my Soul Language.

Thank you. Thank you. Thank you.

At the end of any conversation with the Divine using Soul Language,
always remember to say *thank you* three times to show your gratitude.

You can learn to use Soul Language in the way I just demonstrated. Ask the Divine a question using Soul Language and use Soul
Language to receive the Divine's reply.

You can use Soul Language to ask any question of any saint, any
buddha, any healing angel, and any ascended master. You can also
receive their replies through Soul Language. Soul Language is a
major spiritual communication tool for communicating with any soul
in the universe.

SOUL LANGUAGE TRANSLATION IS THE FOUNDATION FOR
OPENING OTHER MAJOR SPIRITUAL COMMUNICATION
CHANNELS

Soul Language is one of the four major spiritual channels. The others
are the Direct Soul Communication channel, the Third Eye channel,
and the Direct Knowing channel. With the Direct Soul Communication channel, you can have a direct conversation with the Divine and
any soul of the universe using your own physical language. With the
Third Eye Channel, you see spiritual images that allow you to understand the spiritual world's guidance. With the Direct Knowing channel, you simply *know* instantaneously the correct answer to your
questions.

Soul Language is the fundamental spiritual channel. If you wish
to open and develop your spiritual communication channels, open
your Soul Language channel first. After your Soul Language channel
opens and you gain the ability to translate your Soul Language, your
other spiritual channels will open quickly.

Soul Language Translation Has Layers

When you translate Soul Language, you can access the true secrets
of the spiritual world. You are given wisdom that you have never
had. The wisdom you receive through Soul Language translation can
be shared with and benefit humanity.

Even though this is true, it is also true that no translation of Soul
Language is complete. You receive what you and your soul's standing
are ready for at the moment. For example, if three people translate
the same Soul Language, the essence of the translations will be the
same. However, the specific details can be different. When you think
about it, that makes perfect sense. Each person's soul journey is different. Each person's soul standing is different. Because of these differences, each person's translations will include different details and
have different layers of meaning. Each translation is correct. Each

translation gives important information from the Soul World. What is the same in each one is the *essence*.

When you translate Soul Language, it is extremely important that you avoid any inclination to censor or edit. As soon as you censor or edit, you have left your soul's connection. You have left true translation and entered into logical thinking. Logical thinking completely closes the process of translating. As I said earlier about bringing out and developing Soul Language, completely accept what you are given with gratitude, even if your translation consists of a single word.

Also, avoid making comparisons between your translation and someone else's. Avoid making comparisons between other people's translations. Avoid saying, "Susan's translation is so much better than Nancy's." All that I said previously about making comparisons applies when you are doing or listening to a translation. When you do a translation, you are in yet another form of connection with the Soul World. You are receiving in your conscious mind the wisdom and teachings that the Soul World is presenting to you. Receiving in your conscious mind is essential to implementing those teachings and wisdom in your daily life.

When you do a translation, the guidance you receive is your own personal guide for your soul journey. It can be your personal guide for the healing blessings that you give. It is extraordinary to realize that the Soul Language translations are very special blessings to provide you with such wonderful information, wisdom, and teachings. They can bring about powerful transformation on every level of your being. Soul Language translations are special gifts from the Soul World.

When you translate your own Soul Language, you have access to all the wisdom of the universe, the Divine, and the entire Soul World. This is extraordinary. It is amazing to realize that the Divine and the Soul World are so generous. You could say that translation is the key to unlock the door of the library that holds universal wisdom and teachings. It is the key that unlocks our ability to participate in and learn from divine wisdom and teachings.

Soul Language translation is also service. What you receive when you translate Soul Language becomes part of your soul's journey on every level. That which becomes part of who you are can then, in turn, be used to serve others. What you receive becomes part of your wisdom. It can become part of what you teach through your words and your actions. It definitely becomes part of what you teach through your mind-sets, attitudes, beliefs, and behaviors. Soul Language translations are very powerful connections with the Divine, with the Soul World, and with the situation or issue for which you used the Soul Language. The ability to make these soul connections is a very powerful tool for transformation.

It is an amazing gift that this quality of transformation is available. The blessings for you and all universes will be profound. The quality of divine light, divine energy, divine love, divine forgiveness, and all the other divine qualities will increase significantly. Translations are also important for those who listen to Soul Language because not everyone will be able to translate. The translations allow others to benefit from the teachings and wisdom. Without the translations, the soul journeys of those who cannot translate would be slowed. Slowing the soul journey of another carries very heavy karma—yet another reason why translation is important.

There are other reasons why translation of Soul Language is important, but what I have mentioned gives you enough of an idea that translation is essential. Think about the yin/yang symbol (page 10). You could consider Soul Language as the yin and its translation as the yang. It is important to translate even if you are the only one to hear the translation. As I mentioned in Chapter 3 on healing, if you are able to tell your client what message the Soul World has for him, the client will often participate more fully in the healing process. These are some of the most significant reasons for translating Soul Language.

How to Translate Soul Language

How do you translate Soul Language? It is actually very simple. Some of you will be able to translate almost immediately. Others may need to read this section several times and practice before developing the ability to translate. The first and most important thing to do is to relax. I explained the importance of being relaxed in depth earlier. You can go back to that section and reread it, to receive its blessings again. When you read it again, mentally replace the words *Soul Language* with *translation*. Being relaxed allows you to connect with the Divine and the Soul World in a powerful way. When you are relaxed, your ego has stepped out of the picture, which is very important.

Some of you will find yourself monitoring, editing, or censoring the translation as it comes. Avoiding these processes is absolutely essential. The very moment that you shift to censorship or editing, you are entering logical thinking, which will stop the translation. Gratitude is also necessary as you prepare to translate. Being relaxed and grateful for the opportunity to receive information from the Divine, from the highest saints, from your client's illness, from nature, from Mother Earth and beyond, will greatly enhance your ability to translate. Your gratitude will be blessed, multiplied, and returned to you.

SECRET FORMULA FOR TRANSLATING SOUL LANGUAGE

The Soul Language channel starts from the Message Center, also known as the heart chakra, and flows up the center front of the body to the brain. Now, let me reveal to you the secret formula for translating Soul Language:

> *Dear soul, mind, and body of my Soul Language channel, I love you.*
> *When I speak Soul Language, could you send the message from my Message Center to my brain and mouth?*
> *Let me speak the exact meaning of my Soul Language.*
> *Thank you.*

This Say Hello greeting is a key to opening your ability to translate.

PRACTICE TRANSLATING SOUL LANGUAGE

Now, let me lead you to translate your Soul Language.

First, call my soul:

> *Dear soul of Master Sha, please come to give me a blessing and*
> *assist me to translate my Soul Language. Thank you.*

You also can invoke any saint and any spiritual father or mother in Heaven. You can directly invoke the Divine to help you to open your Soul Language translation abilities:

> *Dear Divine, I love you, honor you, and appreciate you. Please*
> *bless and assist me to translate my Soul Language. Thank you.*

Now, repeat the secret formula:

> *Dear soul, mind, and body of my Soul Language channel, I love*
> *   you.*
> *When I speak Soul Language, could you send the message from*
> *   my Message Center to my brain and mouth?*
> *Let me speak the exact meaning of my Soul Language.*
> *Thank you.*

Next, speak Soul Language for about one minute.

Then, begin to translate.

To begin translating, speak the very first word that comes to your awareness. It does not matter if that word is part of a sentence. It does not matter what that word is. For some, the first word received when they began translating was "the." Your willingness to say "the" and then allow whatever comes next to follow is vital. You need to be in a condition of trust when you are translating. When you are willing to trust whatever word you are given and to speak it out loud, that is the beginning of your ability to translate.

Some people will go through the whole process of feeling silly or being fearful that their logical mind is making up the translation. Some people will not believe the translation. Be sure to avoid these pitfalls.

The process of developing your gift for translation will start slowly in most cases. Do not be anxious or upset. Allow yourself some time. Allow yourself the possibility of having only one or two words given to you. Receive whatever you get as a precious gift because that is exactly what it is. If you receive the word *love,* that one word is connected with volumes and volumes of wisdom. Do not be disappointed. Do not think, "I only got the word *love*" or "I got just one word." Think instead about going into the condition of unconditional universal love. Think about how honored you are to receive one word. Think about how privileged and chosen you are if the word you receive is "love." Think about how privileged and chosen you are if the word you receive is "the." This is true for whatever word you receive. It is your own personal message from the Divine and from the Soul World. Receive it as the priceless gift it is.

Continue to translate. At the same time, always continue to be relaxed, grateful, and trusting that whatever you receive is the correct translation and message for you at this time. Many of you will not gain full Soul Language translation abilities right away. Practice translating Soul Language every day, ideally more than once a day. Practice again and again. The ability will suddenly come.

As you speak Soul Language, some of you may simultaneously understand in your mind the meaning of your Soul Language. If this happens, you are very blessed. Some of you may be sitting there saying, "I didn't get anything. Not a single word came to me." You are also blessed. If you had this experience, pay close attention to how you feel. Even if you have not received a single word, your experience when you are attempting to translate is itself a certain level of translation. Put that experience into words.

Perhaps you felt great peace. Perhaps you felt a degree of calm. Whatever experience you had, name it. Say the name out loud. This, too, is the beginning of your ability to translate your Soul Language. Before you spoke Soul Language, perhaps you asked the Soul World, "What is your guidance for me today? What is your teaching for me today?" Pay attention to the response, even if it is not in sentences or even a word. If it is a feeling, put that feeling in the form of an answer. For example, your answer might be, "My dearly beloved, the teaching we have for you today is love" or "The teaching we have for you today is peace." Very often, another sentence will follow. This is the beginning of having your translation flow, to have one sentence followed by another. Similarly, if you continue to receive single words, put them into a sentence.

Another possible sentence would be, "My dearly beloved, our teaching for you today is to live peace, to experience peace." This, too, would be a completely accurate translation for your experience and a completely accurate answer to your question. If you asked for guidance or direction and you received a very strong *feeling*, then that feeling is your answer. If you experience anxiety or stress when you ask the question, then your sentence could be, "My dearly beloved, the message for you today is to release your anxiety, your stress, your fear," whatever your experience.

Following the process I have just described will greatly support your ability to translate Soul Language in the form of sentences. But some of you may be saying, "I didn't hear anything. I didn't feel anything, either." Well, perhaps you saw something. Perhaps it was light. Put that into a sentence: "My dearly beloved, the teaching for you today is to continue your journey to light" or "My dearly beloved, the teaching for you today is that you are in the presence of light." Putting your images into a sentence in this way is not making up a translation. It is a way to put those images into words. It is actually the beginning of a translation that will come in the form of sentence.

A few of you may be feeling really discouraged because you are saying to yourself, "I didn't receive a sentence, a word, a feeling, or an image." You are also blessed! You are very close to what can be translated as "emptiness." Just try to be sure that your feeling was truly "emptiness" and not nervousness, anxiety, stress, or fear. If you were in the condition of receiving nothing, then put that response into a sentence like, "My dearly beloved, our gift to you this day is emptiness." As you can see, *whatever* happens for you when you begin translating helps you in the process of translation.

Whatever responses you receive, accept them as a precious gift. Recognize that they are in fact a translation. As you continue to practice, your ability to translate in sentences will begin. If you can already do this, your abilities will improve and develop continually. As you increase your soul's standing, the quality and standing of your translations also increase.

For those of you who didn't receive any words, feelings, or images, reread these pages again a few times. As you reread this section, be very open to receiving the blessings from these teachings. Ask your Message Center and your Soul Language channel to be fully open. Continue to do this and you will soon begin to translate your Soul Language.

Receive a Divine Download to Improve Your Translation Abilities

Let me offer a Divine Download to open your Soul Language translation abilities now.

Prepare. Receive the Divine Download. Then practice. Your Soul Language translation abilities could open very quickly.

TOTALLY RELAX. Open your heart and soul. Sit up straight. Put the tip of your tongue as close as you can to the roof of your mouth without touching. Close your eyes for one minute to receive this preprogrammed permanent Divine Download.

DIVINE DOWNLOAD: *Divine Soul Transplant of Divine Golden Light Ball and Golden Liquid Spring of Divine Soul*

Language Translation Abilities from the heart and soul of
the Divine to your soul. Silent download!

If your Third Eye is open, you may see divine light pouring into your Message Center to clear the path of your Soul Language channel. You may see the Divine giving you flowers, which represent virtue. You may see Taoist saints, other holy saints, healing angels, ascended masters, lamas, buddhas, gurus, and other high-level spiritual beings suddenly come into your Message Center to offer all kinds of blessings.

Now, speak Soul Language. Do not question what it means. The meaning will come instantly to your mind. You will understand the meaning of the Soul Language because the message of the Soul Language flowed up from your Message Center directly to your brain.

How did this happen for you? The Divine sent you a permanent blessing in the paragraphs above to open your Soul Language translation abilities. We cannot honor and thank the Divine enough for this second Divine Download gift in this book.

To open and improve your Soul Language translation abilities, you must practice. Practice translating and practice as follows with your Divine Download:

> *Dear Divine Golden Light Ball and Golden Liquid Spring of*
> *Divine Soul Language Translation Abilities, I love you, honor*
> *you, and appreciate you. Please further open and increase my*
> *ability to translate Soul Language. Fully open my Soul Lan-*
> *guage and Soul Language translation channel. Thank you.*

Then, chant your Soul Language for three to five minutes. Do it now!

Close:

> *Hao. Hao. Hao.*
> *Thank you. Thank you. Thank you.*

Practice with sincerity and dedication. Practice every day. Your Soul Language translation abilities will open and improve quickly.

Benefits for Yourself

Developing your ability to translate Soul Language brings you many benefits. These blessings are without limit. The most obvious blessings are the teachings, wisdom, guidance, and lessons from the Soul World that you receive specifically for you. Stop to consider how extraordinary this is. It is almost like having your own private tutoring session with the Divine and the entire Soul World, available at any moment and anywhere. Could you have conceived that such a thing would be possible?

When you translate your Soul Language, you are receiving very pure messages. The purity of these messages is very helpful in your soul journey. They are also very helpful in your daily life. You can ask questions about almost anything. You can ask about your soul journey. You can also ask about situations in your physical life. You can ask about the best way to participate in a meeting you need to attend. You can ask how to solve problems in your work environment or other areas of your life. You can ask about anything that is important to you.

The answers you receive can be amazing. They will be answers you could never have reached by using logical thinking. At the same time, they will seem familiar. Many of you will recognize the answer as what your soul desired; you simply were not able to bring it to the level of conscious awareness. Receiving information like this is an extraordinary blessing. This information can facilitate, even directly create, profound transformation in every level of your life. Answers received to questions that are specifically connected to your soul journey will make a great difference to your soul and its journey. Answers to questions about your job or other aspects of your physical life also make a great difference to your soul journey. Whatever happens on any one level of your life has an impact on every other level of your life.

Receiving teachings from the Divine and from the Soul World is an extraordinary privilege and honor. The blessings connected with these teachings are of a very high quality. Your soul standing and soul journey will be greatly accelerated when you use and translate Soul Language. Although all of this is completely true, it is also true that the Divine and the Soul World are very busy. They must attend to many things. Because of this, be sure that you are respectful when you ask your questions. It is appropriate to ask about your daily life, but do not overdo it.

What I mean by this is that some decisions should be made using your logical thinking. For example, if you are shopping and want to choose between two types of incense, use logical thinking. Using Soul Language and translation for a small issue like this is similar to pestering the Soul World. It is important to maintain a balanced perspective. Ask about those things in your daily life that are going to help you in your soul journey. For example, you may have a request about a difficult experience you are going through, or you may ask for guidance to solve a significant life problem. Asking which kind of incense to buy does not fit into the same categories.

Some may say in response, "I think it is important to use Soul Language. After all, I use the incense for my altar. I want to have the kind of incense that the Divine and the highest saints would like to have." That statement may sound wonderful, as if the main focus is on the Divine and the highest saints. However, it actually is much more connected to ego. Using logical thinking to make such a selection is completely appropriate, and I strongly recommend it for all such decisions.

I believe you now realize and appreciate what an incredible blessing it is to translate your Soul Language. You can potentially access all the information in the universe. Moreover, that information can be brought from the level of your soul to the level of your conscious awareness. This will benefit your daily life but, above all, it will have profound effects on your soul journey.

Benefits for Others

As you develop your ability to translate, not only will you benefit in all the ways I have described, but others will also benefit. They will of course benefit by hearing your translation. What you may not realize is that as they listen to your translation, they receive blessings from the transformation in your soul journey and the increase in your light and love. The teachings and wisdom that you received can now directly become part of another person's soul journey. As people listen to you, they will listen from their level and from their soul's journey. That means that each person will receive your translation in slightly different ways. Your translation will be adapted and adjusted to the teachings that listeners need at this particular point in their lives. This is a wonderful service for you to offer.

You can also benefit others by translating their Soul Language, delivering to them the teachings, wisdom, and blessings that are specifically adapted to their soul's journey. They will know what it is specifically that the Divine and the Soul World want to tell them. It is such a precious treasure for them. It makes an enormous difference to their soul's journey. The changes that take place on every level of their existence will be profound.

When you are doing translations for others, you will be aware that the information given is always positive. The Divine and the highest saints will rarely tell you that you are doing a poor job. You will never get messages that you are not a good person. I emphasize this because there is the possibility of receiving a *false message* or a false translation. Do not worry about this. Recognizing a false message or translation is easy enough. If the translation brings greater love, peace, harmony, forgiveness, and all the other qualities of universal service, then you can be certain it is an accurate translation. However, if the translation is judgmental, divisive, or if it feeds your ego or the ego of another person, it is a false translation.

An example of feeding your ego would be a translation whose focus is to tell you how great you are. This is a clear signal that you have moved away from an accurate translation. Do not be alarmed if this happens to you; it is part of the process. It is part of your spiritual journey. If this happens, simply say, "Thank you. However, I know this translation is not accurate. I know it is a false translation and I am not going to pay attention to it." Then, start over with your translation.

Being aware that a false translation is possible is very helpful. Knowing this before you open your ability to translate, or before your ability reaches a new level, will make it much easier for you to avoid focusing on a false message. You will avoid wasting time and effort trying to implement a false message, one that is not truly connected to the Soul Language.

Even though these teachings have been directed to you, they apply equally when you are translating for others. Sometimes you will receive a false translation. Always ask the other person if the translation sounds correct to them. Does it make sense? Does it resonate with their spiritual journey? If the answer is "yes," then you know the translation is accurate. If it is "no," then you know it was a false translation.

At times your translation may cause some discomfort or unease because it will be a teaching that says certain ego attachments must be released. It may also be connected to a situation where unconditional universal forgiveness is needed. These situations may cause the person for whom you are translating to feel some lack of comfort. At the same time, however, the person will also experience a resonance deep within and a recognition that "Yes, this is what I need" at this particular moment in their soul journey.

There is a great difference between the discomfort connected with this type of teaching and discomfort connected with a false teaching. As you continue to practice your Soul Language and translation for yourself and others, you will recognize more and more clearly when the translation is accurate and when it is a false message. However, do not spend too much time thinking about this. Do not spend any time worrying about it. As you begin your practice, it is enough simply to know that false messages are possible. The Soul World wants to help you progress rapidly on your soul journey. It is not going to give you many false messages when you are just starting out. It will not give false messages to those for whom you are translating.

When I referred to messages connected with feeding your ego, I meant any message that tells you that you are the best or the greatest. These are ego statements, not statements from the Soul World at all. The Soul World's messages tell you that you are loved, that you are cherished, and that you have a special role in having divine light and presence become a greater and greater part of your life and the lives of others. These are statements of appreciation from the Divine and the Soul World—very different from those that simply feed the ego.

A very good indicator for you and those for whom you are translating is your response. For translations that are messages of love and appreciation from the Soul World, you and others will experience gratitude, love, devotion, and other positive qualities, such as peace, calm, and confidence. When the messages are from the ego, you will feel a certain level of discomfort. You will have a feeling that the message somehow simply does not fit your soul journey. When you or the other person experience this type of response, you can be certain that your translation is not accurate.

Translating Soul Language for others is a wonderful privilege. It will be very helpful to their soul journeys. It also makes an enormous difference for your own soul journey, because translating for others is an exquisite form of service. The benefits that you and those for whom you translate will experience will be profound.

Benefits for the Universe

Translating Soul Language also has great benefits for Mother Earth and beyond. It benefits the entire universe. Every time new teachings and new wisdom are released, all souls are present to listen to these teachings and receive the wisdom. The higher saints bless what is released. The souls who need this wisdom and these teachings in order to progress on their soul journeys receive everything that is released with such enormous joy and gratitude that it cannot be imagined. Some souls who are in darkness now will cross over to the light. Some souls who are in darkness will have their darkness transformed to strength. They will become companions and assistants to the light. To offer this kind of service is truly most extraordinary.

This type of service makes an enormous difference throughout all universes. Pause and allow yourself to reflect on the significance of this. By translating Soul Language—either your own or someone else's—you can release teachings that will benefit countless souls. All the souls who need that particular teaching or wisdom to progress on their soul journey will receive it. Their soul journeys will be accelerated. Their soul's standing will be raised. This is yet another example of the incredible generosity of the Divine. It is another example of the many ways to offer service. To bring gifts of a greater participation in divine light, love, forgiveness, and every other quality of the Divine by translating Soul Language is a very special honor.

Many of you who have been doing Soul Language and translation will be delighted and somewhat surprised to learn these teachings. By doing translations you are being a teacher, doing a kind of teaching that is particularly blessed because it is not public. The amount of yin virtue attached to this type of teaching is extraordinary.

When you translate your own or another's Soul Language, the levels of benefits are so numerous they cannot be counted. The higher your soul's standing, the more souls throughout the universe also benefit, and the greater the benefit they will receive. If you are at a very high standing, all the souls at a lower level and even some souls at the same level will benefit from your translations. To give the gift of wisdom and light to all souls throughout the universes is a very special honor. And imagine how your own virtue increases every time you do a translation. Your soul's standing increases at a much accelerated rate.

The quality of light you will experience on every level of your being will increase significantly. You will appreciate new wisdom. You will receive insights and understandings at higher and higher levels. All that you receive will also become part of your daily life. The wisdom and teachings, the frequency and vibration of light that are present within your soul, mind, and body become part of your being.

You will begin to notice in your conversations that what you say is often a surprise to you. You will wonder, "What is the source of these comments? Where did that idea come from?" They come from the increase in the wisdom and teachings that your soul has received. They also come from connecting with the greater wisdom and teachings now available and present on Mother Earth and in all universes.

Those who listen to you will have a greater ability to understand and receive what you express because of the greater source of wisdom and teachings now present throughout all universes. It's like walking into a room that is air-conditioned. As soon as you enter, you benefit from the pleasant environment. You are surrounded by this environment. You do not have to make any effort at all to receive the benefit. It is simply there for you to receive, enjoy, and appreciate.

All of the benefits throughout the universes become part of what you could call the "spiritual environment" of the universes. You receive the blessings and benefits of this more light-filled environment by simply being in it. This is an extraordinary and wonderful gift from the Divine and the entire Soul World.

From what I have taught in this book, I believe many of you have a new or a greater appreciation of the extraordinary generosity of the Divine. You will appreciate how each of us is assisted in our soul journey in many ways. After all, the Divine and the entire Soul World want to make it as easy as they can for each of us—for every soul—to accelerate our journey to light. They want each of us to become more and more in harmony with divine light and with the light of the highest saints. As you connect with these higher frequencies and vibrations of light, your own participation in divine light, love, forgiveness, and service grows. In turn, your connection to the Divine, to all of the highest levels in the Soul World, and to all of their qualities becomes closer and stronger.

At this point, you have received enough ideas to help you understand and appreciate how powerful it is for you to translate your own or someone else's Soul Language. The benefits are beyond words. The service that you offer is profound. The teachings and the wisdom you release are treasures that will be received with gratitude by countless souls. The gratitude of all these souls also increases your virtue. Every time a soul receives the teaching, the wisdom, and the light and expresses gratitude for it, your virtue increases. All those souls who receive these teachings and wisdom because of your translation will not only receive it. They will bless it and some will multiply it, and the Divine and the Soul World will return it to you. It is very touching indeed to realize how deeply loved you are and how much the Divine and the highest levels of the Soul World desire the acceleration of your soul's journey.

These gifts that are connected with translating Soul Language are profound and transforming. Doing the translation benefits you on many layers and levels. It is indeed a most extraordinary honor, privilege, and service for you to do these translations. I trust that those of you who are new to translating Soul Language now understand the importance of developing this ability, not only for your soul journey but for the journey of countless other souls.

Some of you may experience this as a responsibility that may feel overwhelming or even like a burden. That is wrong thinking. In fact, it is perfect evidence that you have moved into logical thinking. And by now you realize that the way to correct logical thinking is to go into the condition of gratitude. When you do this, you will experience a most profound gratitude, and the sense that "This is too big a responsibility" will melt.

I am including very special blessings for those of you who have opened your ability to translate Soul Language as well as for those of you who are now in the process of opening that ability. As you reread this chapter, your ability will continue to open more fully. I deeply wish each of you to be able to translate Soul Language, and then to translate at higher levels. You are most loved. You are very blessed.

Thank you. Thank you. Thank you.

Conclusion

Soul Language is a unique and particular gift from the Divine and the highest levels of the Soul World. The benefits connected with this most beautiful gift are extensive.

In the previous chapter, I made it clear that the benefits of translating Soul Language are also extensive—literally impossible to imagine. Soul Language and translation are gifts that are being given to many because Mother Earth is experiencing profound transformation and purification at this time. This transformation and purification extend beyond Mother Earth and beyond this universe. All the blessings and light released through your efforts will assist in this transformation and purification. You will not only participate, you will also offer service that heals and transforms others.

You will connect with the Divine. You will participate in aspects of the divine essence that transform you and countless other souls. You will participate in aspects of the higher saints, in their abilities and gifts that will transform you and countless other souls. The effect this will have upon your Akashic Record is truly magnificent. Those of you with Third Eye abilities will see the quality of light that becomes part of your record each time you use and translate Soul Language.

Opening or further developing your Soul Language is a very special form of service and blessing. The same is true for translating Soul

Language. If you read this book with an open heart, you will have a very different understanding than you had before you started reading. Moreover, your entire soul journey will be changed more than you can begin to imagine. The blessings you have received and will receive throughout this book are very gentle yet very powerful.

As I said at the beginning, *everything in this book is a blessing.* Not just the ideas, teachings, and, of course, the Divine Downloads, but the very book itself. The pages, the words, the letters, the punctuation, and even the spaces are all very powerful and gentle blessings. Every time you read any part of this book, you receive more blessings.

By now you also have an understanding and an appreciation of the idea that any blessing you receive is, at the same time, also service that you offer. That is quite amazing. When you offer service, you receive more blessings. This is a most magnificent and generous cycle given by the Divine. Whatever you do is increased and multiplied. Many spiritual traditions have the realization that the Divine cannot be outdone in generosity. After reading this book, I trust you will have a much greater understanding and appreciation of the truth of this statement.

It may be helpful for you to repeat to yourself: "The Divine cannot be outdone in generosity." What that means, in part, is that the more fully you enter into participation with divine light, the more generous you yourself will become. All that you have read in these pages is received, blessed, multiplied, and returned to you every time you practice what I have taught.

You have received the teachings, wisdom, and blessings. Now all you need to do is practice. The more you practice, the more your Soul Language and translation abilities will open. If your abilities have not opened yet, the more you practice, the more ready you will become. I encourage you to practice and to make your practice part of your daily routine. I want your practice of Soul Language and translation to become so much a part of your day that it will be similar to brushing your teeth—something that will happen automatically, without your having to set aside a special time. You are most honored and privileged to be able to use Soul Language and translate it.

You who are reading this book are also selected for the service that has been described throughout. It is no accident that you have chosen to read this book. After all, there are many other books you could have read instead. The fact that you have chosen this book or, in some cases, that it has chosen you, is a message about how important it is for you to develop and open your Soul Language and translation.

You are part of a divine team to create the presence of all that is described and taught in these pages. You are blessed indeed. You are held very tenderly in my heart, the heart of the Divine, and the heart of all the highest saints. You are blessed.

Thank you. Thank you. Thank you.

PART 2

Soul Song

The Song of the Heart and Soul

6

What Is Soul Song?

For thousands of years, spiritual beings in many traditions have chanted mantras to heal, rejuvenate, and purify their minds and bodies. Many ancient mantras are widely used to this day. Mantras are powerful spiritual treasures and tools to enhance one's spiritual journey.

Mantras are chanted from the mind, even if one of the purposes of chanting them is to free the practitioner from the mind, to enter into emptiness. Because the syllables and melody of a mantra are fixed, chanting a mantra is mind-guided. Soul Song is the song of one's soul. It is the song of Soul Language. It is soul-guided.

Soul Song is simply the songs that are held within your soul that are being released at this time. The songs that your soul releases may differ according to your actions or circumstances. On the other hand, your soul's song may not change much. You might have a combination of these possibilities. You may have one Soul Song that seems to be your particular song because it is often repeated. You may also have a variety of Soul Songs that differ according to the occasion. It doesn't matter how Soul Song is manifested through you. The only important thing is that you *can* release your Soul Song.

To release your Soul Song, you must avoid having expectations and attachments. Expectations and attachments will effectively close the possibility of releasing your Soul Song. I suggest you go back to the chapters on Soul Language, where I dealt with the topics of attachment and expectation thoroughly. Not only are my teachings there quite complete, but the blessings included to help you release attachments and expectations are also powerful.

The most important attitude for you to have as you read about Soul Song is an attitude of *enjoyment*. It is also important for you to have an open heart. With these two qualities, you will be able to benefit in a powerful way from the teachings and the blessings in these chapters on Soul Song.

Bring Out Your Soul Song

Because Soul Song is the song of Soul Language, to release your Soul Song, you must first bring out your Soul Language. Most of you have done so by now. If you have not, continue to practice and receive the blessings as I described in Chapter 2. After you can speak Soul Language, return to this chapter to bring out your Soul Song.

How do you bring out your Soul Song? Once you have brought out your Soul Language, it is very simple! Ask your divine treasures to help you:

> *Dear Divine Golden Light Ball and Golden Liquid Spring of Divine Soul Language, dear Divine Golden Light Ball and Golden Liquid Spring of Divine Soul Language Translation Abilities and dear my Soul Language, I love you, honor you, and appreciate you. Please bring out my Soul Song. Thank you.*
> *Dear my beloved soul, I love you, honor you, and appreciate you. I am honored and delighted to hear your Soul Language. I would be honored and delighted to hear your Soul Song. Please sing your song through my mouth. Thank you.*

Then, start to chant your Soul Language out loud. Let it turn into Soul Song naturally. This will be easier to do than bringing out your

Soul Language. For many of you, it will happen instantly. Do it now!

Do not think about the sounds you are making. Do not evaluate or analyze the syllables, melody, volume, or timbre. Just sing from your soul! Sing for as long as you like. You may be so delighted that you do not want to stop. Your Soul Song may be so beautiful that every soul around you is paying attention.

Congratulations! You have brought out your Soul Song. Don't forget to close:

> *Hao. Hao. Hao.*
> *Thank you. Thank you. Thank you.*

You truly have a wonderful new treasure to be thankful for.

Soul Song and Soul Language

As I said, Soul Song is the song of Soul Language. It is the further development of Soul Language. Everything that I taught in the first five chapters about Soul Language and its translation is also true for Soul Song. However, Soul Song can be considered a higher level of Soul Language. Soul Song is an exquisitely pure connection with the Divine, the highest saints, and the highest realms.

Many of you who release your Soul Song will do so as pure sound. Your Soul Song will be only melody. It will literally be beyond words, even the words of Soul Language. Some of you will release your Soul Song as both melody and lyrics. It does not matter. Whatever is given to you at the moment is an exquisite and powerful gift. Once again, it is very important to have no expectation or attachment as to how your Soul Song is manifested.

Soul Song is a connection with frequencies and vibrations of the Soul World, the highest realms, and the Divine that has not been released before in such an extensive way. While Soul Songs have existed throughout the ages, their presence has been limited. Now, Soul Songs

will be released by millions of people, which has never happened before. In the Soul Light Era, Soul Song is being given to all who are
ready. Those who are ready belong to every segment of society. Soul
Song will no longer be held by, or limited to, a few small groups.

Soul Song is being given to, and will be released by, those who
have a sincere desire to continue their soul journey. It is given to all
who are committed to the Divine. Some people have actually been
singing Soul Songs for several years but were not aware that their
songs were Soul Songs. Now, the receivers of Soul Song will sing and
use this gift in a conscious way. Conscious awareness will make the
experience and the use of this precious gift much more powerful.

Significance of Soul Song

As you sing your particular Soul Songs, you will be connecting with
the Divine, the highest saints, and the highest realms in a powerful
way. The significance of being able to make this connection is also
very powerful. It will be transforming in a way that you have never
experienced before. Your participation in divine light, love, forgiveness, compassion, and healing will be of an entirely different level. It
will be intense, but this intensity will be accompanied by great lightness and freedom.

The transformation that will take place through your Soul Song
will accelerate your soul journey in an extraordinary way. It will
also accelerate the journeys of others in an extraordinary way. The
blessings and healings that you give using Soul Song will be very
powerful. The increase of divine light and energy will be exponential.
You and all throughout Mother Earth and beyond will receive benefits of a most powerful kind. Because the connections with the Soul
World and the Divine are of a different quality when you use Soul
Song, the benefits received and the service given are also of a different quality.

It is difficult to express the significance of this gift adequately in
words. After all, it is difficult enough simply to describe song in

words. All of the teachings in this book could actually be given through Soul Song itself.

As you are reading these pages, you may hear in your soul, heart, and mind a melody that accompanies the words that you are reading. This will be a connection with the Soul Songs of this book and with your own Soul Song. If this is not your experience, that is quite all right. What I said earlier about no attachment and no expectation is important at this point also. Avoiding attachment and expectation will keep open the possibility that you will begin to hear a melody to accompany the words in this book. If you do not hear a melody at all, that is also quite all right. The melody is still there within your soul. At the correct time it will be released.

Another aspect of the significance of Soul Song is the exquisite harmony and unity that will exist when all Soul Songs are brought together. This "bringing together" can occur in many ways. It can occur on the soul level. People who are singing their Soul Songs, wherever they are, will immediately become part of this harmony and unity. There is no need for them to be in physical or even geographical proximity. At other times, groups will come together physically for the specific purpose of singing their Soul Songs, to release these precious treasures to Mother Earth and beyond.

When this "bringing together" takes place, a great balancing of energies occurs and a great release of light takes place. Each one's soul journey will undergo great transformation. Many will enter more fully into the light. Many will begin their journey to become light. Many will be transformed from darkness to light.

The transformation that takes place through Soul Song is very powerful yet at the same time very gentle. It will feel like the flowing of a clear stream of light throughout your entire being. This kind of transformation will take place on all levels for all those on Mother Earth and beyond. It is a particular gift that is being given by the Divine at this time. The combination of power and gentleness is very important, even necessary for Mother Earth and beyond. This combination will give great strength, but it is a strength that is softened by gentleness. It will frequently manifest as an integration of strength and compassion.

The transformation that occurs through Soul Song will also be a powerful experience of the universal law of yin and yang. This universal law has existed for thousands of years, but its presence in the Soul Light Era is different. In this era, it will be understood, experienced, and lived in a way that has not occurred before. Soul Song is a very important vehicle for this new way of experiencing the universal law of yin and yang. We could say that Soul Song is really going to introduce the universal law of yin and yang to all of Mother Earth and beyond. Soul Song will make this law present in a most powerful way that will allow it to be experienced fully in this era.

Those of you who release your Soul Song will understand what is meant by the new aspect of this ancient wisdom that is being revealed. Much that is experienced through Soul Song has existed throughout time and before time. However, it has been waiting for the proper moment to be manifested. The Soul Light Era is that moment and Soul Song is one of the most powerful ways of expressing and releasing these ancient teachings and wisdoms. Much more could be said about the significance of Soul Song. However, to truly appreciate its significance, you will need to be able to release your Soul Song.

If you are thinking "I cannot carry a tune," that is completely unimportant. Soul Song is released from your soul. It will come effortlessly. You may have never been able to stay on pitch before, but you will be delighted to discover that with your Soul Song, you can. It will be released to you in a most magnificent sound. The sound may be harmonious. It may be dissonant. It may sound like the songs of ancient cultures. It may be a combination of these or other possibilities. However it is released, you will be able to sing your Soul Song without effort, because it comes from your soul and shares the characteristics of Soul Language. So long as you allow your Soul Song to flow freely, it will come to you generously and abundantly.

Benefits of Soul Song

Singing your Soul Song will bring countless benefits. An obvious one is the transformation that will occur within you. This transformation will resonate throughout your entire being. It will resonate with the most ancient sounds, those from before time and before creation, when sound was all there was. Connecting with this quality of sound will introduce the most profound frequencies and vibrations throughout your entire being. These vibrations will penetrate the tiniest spaces and the tiniest bits of matter, and will bring them into resonance with the Divine in an extraordinary way. At this time, this resonance can only be achieved through Soul Song.

Soul Song is precisely the tool that we are given at this moment to be able to make these connections. Not only will the tiniest particles and tiniest spaces vibrate with these divine frequencies, but also the largest things—and everything in between. You will be able to hear your particular Soul Song melody with your ears. However, throughout your entire being there will be a variety of melodies, all of which will be in harmony with what you can hear with your ears. Every organ, every system, every cell, every part of every cell, and every DNA and RNA in your body has its own melody. When you release and sing your Soul Song, all of these "inner" Soul Song melodies will also be released. All the souls within you will begin to sing their songs in unison with the Soul Song from your soul and voice.

It is impossible to describe the benefits that will result. However, you can at least begin to imagine how extensive and extraordinary the transformation through your use of Soul Song will be. Furthermore, when you use your Soul Song for healing and blessing, transformation occurs for those receiving your healing and blessing. When you are simply singing your Soul Song, the benefits radiate out to others even if you are not specifically sending healing or blessing. If you are simply singing for the joy of the experience, the blessings, light, and transformation radiate far beyond you. In many cases, the entire universe will benefit. It is a tremendous privilege to participate in such an extraordinary gift and to be able to extend the benefits to many others.

Transformation will occur on the levels of the soul, mind, and body. Some of the difficulties, barriers, and blockages facing you will begin to melt away. They will be transformed to light. This will be true for blockages in your soul journey. This will also be true for your mind. Some of the mind-sets, attitudes, and beliefs that you have had difficulty releasing will begin to be transformed to light in an amazing way. The process will be very powerful but, as I have said before, it will also be very gentle. This will also be true for your emotions and your physical health.

Using Soul Song will bring about these changes in a highly accelerated way. Many of you will be very surprised at how quickly the changes occur. These transformations will be particular gifts. They will be especially appreciated by those who experience depression, anxiety, or a heavy heart. For those who have lived with these emotions, the release of Soul Song will be a particular blessing. Because it is simply not possible to be depressed and to sing with joy at the same time, Soul Song will be a very powerful healing tool for all of these blockages.

Those who are depressed may experience the release of their Soul Song as an anguished cry. That is completely all right. Whatever the sound, allow it to be expressed. Do not censor or revise it. As you allow it to be expressed and as you experience the transformation that will occur, your Soul Song will also experience transformation. Its expression will also transform. Keep this in your awareness as you release your song. Do not be afraid of what is expressed through your voice.

Remember that your Soul Song will sound different at different times. Allow for the full range of possibilities and know that there are extraordinary benefits regardless of how your song is manifested. The benefits that you will receive and that will be radiated out far beyond you will be of a most extraordinary quality. These benefits have not been available before this time. They are benefits of a new and higher vibration and frequency. However your song is expressed, receive it with gratitude and delight in the realization of the benefits on the deepest levels of your entire being.

Soul Song as Service

From my brief description of the benefits of Soul Song, it should not be difficult to appreciate that using Soul Song is great service. In thinking of service, you may immediately begin to think in terms of added activities. This thought can be overwhelming because you probably already have more than enough activities to fill your day. But when I speak of service, I am not talking about adding more activities to your day. You can perform the most extraordinary service while you are otherwise involved in your daily activities, responsibilities, tasks, or jobs. How? As you go about your day, use your Soul Song!

As you read these pages and simultaneously receive the blessings that accompany these teachings, many of you will hear a song within you. You will be reading these words and hearing the song silently. Because it is a Soul Song, it is being expressed and heard by your soul. It may be silent to your ears; nevertheless, a silent song is every bit as significant, as powerful, and as transforming as a song that you can hear with your ears. You may have a preference for either the audible song or the silent song. One may come to you much more easily than the other. Nevertheless, each one is important. Each one is very special. Each one offers its own unique service.

As you use Soul Song through the day, your surroundings may make it necessary to sing your song silently. At other times, you will be able to sing it out loud. It doesn't matter; the benefits and service will be the same. I do suggest that at times you allow your song to be silent and at times you express it out loud. Doing both maintains a balance, and you will extend service that is also balanced. All of the benefits of Soul Song for you personally will be received by those to whom you offer your song. The service that you give through your Soul Song will resonate throughout Mother Earth and often well beyond. This service will be the presence of a quality of vibration and frequency that is extremely powerful. Through your song, you will be able to give blessings and the gift of transformation to many.

Giving service through Soul Song will be especially delightful because of its quality of joy and light. There will actually be people throughout Mother Earth who will suddenly begin to feel the joy and light connected with your song, even though they will have no idea what the source of their joy and light is. It is quite all right that they will have no idea who to thank. It is enough to know that the benefits experienced by others will be extensive, powerful, and transforming.

The fact that many will not know who to credit for your Soul Song, much less know its full impact and benefits, is actually a great blessing for you. Extending the benefits to others in this "invisible" way gives you a huge amount of yin virtue, which is much more extensive than the virtue received when you do something that is public or publicly acknowledged. Soul Song is a wonderful gift to allow everyone to accumulate yin virtue, thereby increasing their virtue in an accelerated way.

At this time on Mother Earth, it is important to have great virtue. Your virtue is directly related to your soul standing. Those with a very high soul standing will have great abilities. These abilities will allow you to give service to all humanity, Mother Earth, and beyond. The purpose of gaining virtue is to be able to give more service. It establishes a wonderful cycle. The more service you give, the more virtue you have. The more virtue you have, the more service you will be able to give and the more quickly you will accomplish the purpose of your soul's journey. To be able to gain this virtue by using your Soul Song is a very generous gift of the Divine. You can sing your Soul Song continually and in any setting. You can give this service throughout the day no matter what else you are doing.

It is important to develop the practice of singing your Soul Song. After you have begun this practice, you will notice that everything you do becomes part of your song. If you spend most of your day working at a computer, as you silently sing your Soul Song, your computer work becomes part of the song. Many of you work at a computer because you must. It is not necessarily a task that you approach with great enthusiasm. If this describes you, it will be a special gift to transform your work by having it become part of your Soul Song.

At the same time, you can also send your song to all others who are working at their computers in the same way. This will bring great light and great transformation to all those who are doing similar work. As you sing your Soul Song and experience the joy and light that accompany it, the others will experience the same joy and light. Many will be amazed that their work, which had felt like a burden, is beginning to feel joyful and full of light. What a wonderful gift to be able to give to so many!

If you are fortunate enough to have a job that already fills you with joy and delight, you can increase the joy and light by using your Soul Song throughout the day. In so doing, the blessings and benefits of your job will increase significantly. Those who interact with you will become aware of this change and be able to enter into that joy and light themselves. Again, those who do similar jobs will also benefit from your Soul Song. Indeed, every person on Mother Earth, Mother Earth herself, and souls beyond Mother Earth will also benefit from your Soul Song. Not only will the vibrations of the sound of your song radiate out, the virtue connected with your song will also radiate out. This is a wonderful service to be able to offer.

It is especially wonderful at this time on Mother Earth when many are feeling a heaviness and an absence of deep, authentic joy. To be able to add your Soul Song to the songs of many others is a special honor. The service that is given in this way will bring a quality of light and a vibration and frequency that will heal many. It will help many on their soul journeys. The yin aspect of this service is very powerful. It is connected in a profound way with the Soul Light Era. There is a powerful resonance and great harmony between yin virtue and the Soul Light Era. Offering this type of service at this beginning stage of the Soul Light Era is more significant than you could ever imagine. It will accelerate the presence of light and all that is part of this era. To do this is a very special blessing, a very special honor, and a very special gift.

7

Soul Song and Joy

There is a very strong connection between Soul Song and the presence of joy. There is a popular saying that *joy is the most infallible sign of God's presence and the most perfect expression of the Divine.* When you are using your Soul Song, you are the presence of divine light, love, forgiveness, and compassion in a special way. And so you are also the presence of joy. You make this quality present on Mother Earth and beyond. This is a much needed service at this time, when there are many without joy and many situations with heaviness and stress. Releasing the presence of the Divine, which is also to release joy, is a wonderful gift to be able to give to humanity, Mother Earth, and beyond.

Divine presence includes much more than joy. However, in this chapter I will focus on the aspect of joy, which is completely appropriate for Soul Song. Those of you who have already experienced your Soul Song have experienced this joy. You have experienced a depth, a peace, and a delight that are associated with the joy expressed through your soul's song.

If you have not yet released your Soul Song, I suggest you read the first few pages of the previous chapter again. There are many blessings connected with reading that chapter as well as a simple practice that will help you release your Soul Song.

If you want additional specific "how to" teachings, go back to Chapter 2 on Soul Language. If you want to release your Soul Song, you will accomplish that by reading both of these sections. I have given the blessings needed. I have transmitted Divine Downloads to you. Read these sections as many times as necessary for you to release your Soul Song, keeping in mind the necessity of having no attachment and no expectation. Practice with your Divine Downloads. As a universal servant, it is my delight and my honor to be able to serve you in this way.

Soul Song as an Expression of the Divine

The Divine is present in countless forms. Soul Song is one of the expressions of the Divine for our time. It is a unique and special expression of the Divine, through your soul's expression. By now, you have an idea of why it is such a special expression, but this is only a small hint. The Divine cannot be expressed adequately in human terms, and Soul Song manifests that fact. Soul Song is without limit.

You may have a wide variety of Soul Songs. Your Soul Song may vary for the various healing blessings that you give. Your Soul Song may vary at different parts of the day. The one thing that your Soul Songs have in common is that they are all expressions of your soul. They are the way your soul gives voice to whatever is being experienced or blessed at that moment.

One person's Soul Song can give you an idea of the extraordinary variety of the Divine. Multiply the example of a single person by all those who have released their Soul Song and you will have an even better idea of how varied the presence of the Divine can be. Expanding the wisdom, also include the Soul Songs of everything in your surroundings at this moment. This will help deepen your understanding of the great variety of expressions of the Divine, of how extraordinary and, at the same time, how ordinary these expressions are. It is very easy to overlook these Soul Songs completely. They may not even touch your awareness or consciousness. The same is no less true for the presence of the Divine. So, this is one aspect of how Soul Song is an expression of the Divine.

Another aspect is the extraordinary power of Soul Song. This power is at once very great and very gentle. It can transform that which is very ready and that which is very resistant. Soul Song is able to enter into the tiniest and the largest spaces. All of these qualities are also expressions of the Divine. The Divine is present and active in the tiniest matter. The Divine is present in those places where there is no visible manifestation. The Divine is also present and active in the biggest spaces and matter. The "activeness" of the Divine includes all the qualities of the Divine. The qualities I have mentioned most often are those connected with universal service: love, forgiveness, peace, healing, blessing, harmony, and enlightenment. However, there are many more.

It is not possible to identify all of the qualities and aspects of the Divine. In fact, it is not possible to identify even the major qualities. But one of them is the quality of joy and delight. This is a very special quality that is expressed in a powerful and unique way through Soul Song. Both joy and delight themselves have many different aspects. I will discuss some of the aspects of joy to give you some idea of their breadth and depth. With these examples, you can reflect on both joy and delight yourself and become more aware that we can only scratch the surface. You can do soul communication to do this. You can use Soul Language. You can use your intuitive abilities. You may have other ways to learn more wisdom for each of these qualities.

The quality of joy as an expression of the presence of the Divine has a very special aspect of lightness. But it is not only a unique presence of light, it is a presence that also brings a buoyant freedom. This feeling of freedom is very different from the idea of freedom that you hold in your logical mind. The freedom that is experienced as part of divine joy is the freedom of having no attachment or expectation. The burdens of having attachments and expectations will quite literally weigh you down. Attachments and expectations are accompanied by worry, stress, and other burdensome qualities.

When you experience the freedom of divine joy, all that is associated with attachments and expectations is gone. What you are experiencing is deep, true freedom. This freedom is an aspect of divine joy. This freedom is what gives divine joy its wonderful feeling of lightness.

Another characteristic of divine joy is a sense of glee. This characteristic is often used to express or identify the experience of complete peace, tranquillity, and enjoyment that occurs when you truly enter into the condition of divine presence. The qualities of peace, tranquillity, enjoyment, and glee are all part of the experience of entering this condition. They are also part of your awareness of divine presence. Whenever you connect with a greater awareness of divine presence, you experience what can be called glee. It can also be called bliss. During these experiences, you have an awareness that you have experienced Heaven on Earth by connecting with an exquisite manifestation of the Divine and entering into that part of your existence.

The quality of divine joy also has great depth. Joy resonates within your being in a profound way. It is present in all the frequencies and vibrations throughout your physical, mental, emotional, and spiritual levels. This depth and this resonance remain with you even after the event that triggered this response has passed. In other words, this depth and resonance become part of who you are, part of your very frequency and vibration. Because it has come via your Soul Song, the vibration reaches all the way to your DNA and RNA. Joy becomes part of your DNA and RNA.

Because of this, you can say joy is part of who you are. This is quite an extraordinary and wonderful gift. It is a special gift and treasure if you experience depression, anxiety, worry, sorrow, grief, fear, or anger. The resonance and vibration of Soul Song will make a great difference in your soul journey. It will make a great difference in healing your mind, emotions, and physical body. Having this quality of joy resonating throughout your being is also great service.

If you experience depression or similar issues, I strongly recommend that you make every effort to release your Soul Song. I also recommend that you sing this song consciously throughout your day. It would be very helpful for you to sing your Soul Song out loud. This would manifest the joy and delight of the Divine, and accelerate the transformation of your depression. It is quite amazing to think that something so simple as singing can bring about such profound changes. But of course, this is not ordinary singing; it is the singing that is an expression of your soul.

All of these manifestations of the Divine are very powerful. When you experience them, you also radiate them not only to all around you but also farther beyond. This generous radiation is also a manifestation of the Divine. When you radiate these qualities, which is to say that you radiate their vibration and frequencies, it is great service. And service is a primary expression and manifestation of the Divine. In fact, one of the best ways to describe the Divine is to say that the Divine is an unconditional universal servant. So, every time that you are being an unconditional universal servant, you are a most exquisite expression of the Divine. You make the Divine present in a powerful and profound way. To be able to do this is a privilege and honor beyond our ability to imagine.

Some of you may find it overwhelming to hear the Divine described as an unconditional universal servant for the first time. This concept can be very challenging to all that you have learned. It can also be challenging to your logical thinking. Various traditions and teachings have given many different descriptions of the Divine. Many of you may have been raised and educated with a very different way of expressing the presence of the Divine. Because of all this "training," the description of the Divine as an unconditional universal servant may be a great challenge.

If this is true for you, you now have a wonderful opportunity to release those mind-sets, attitudes, and beliefs. The more you can accept and live the truth of this description of the Divine, the greater possibility you yourself will have to become the presence of the Divine as an unconditional universal servant. When this happens for you, you will see everything in your life as service. This in turn will make it possible for you to appreciate more and more the service aspect of your Soul Song. I could say much more about Soul Song as an expression of the Divine, but the teachings in this section will give you some ideas that you can use to develop your own understanding and appreciation further.

Soul Song Manifests Joy and Delight

Because of the great need that exists on Mother Earth at this time, I want to put more emphasis on the characteristics and qualities of joy and delight. As the purification process for Mother Earth continues, these qualities will be needed by more and more people. They will be needed by Mother Earth herself. They will also be needed beyond Mother Earth.

The qualities of joy and delight bring the possibility and presence of groundedness and centeredness. When you are living joy and delight, your energy is grounded. Your Lower Dan Tian can become very strong. The Lower Dan Tian is the energy center that is located about one and one-half inches below your navel and about three inches in. It is about the size of your fist. This energy center is extremely important. Many people on a spiritual journey do not pay enough attention to it.

The Lower Dan Tian is the foundational energy center for stamina, energy, vitality, and long life. For most human beings, it is also the seat of the soul. The Lower Dan Tian is the foundation of physical health. It is the energy center for the immune system. This will give you an idea of its importance. It is vital that the Lower Dan Tian continually receive light and energy so that it will be replenished, boosted, and developed. When you experience joy and delight, the associated energy is experienced first in the Lower Dan Tian. It is also experienced in your Message Center, which is your heart center or heart chakra. However, it is experienced in the Message Center because of the powerful presence of energy and light in the Lower Dan Tian.

A powerful Lower Dan Tian helps to ground and center you.

This is necessary support for all aspects of your physical life. When you have a strong Lower Dan Tian, your major organs can also receive the energy and light needed to become healthier. And when you are grounded and centered, your emotional life has a much greater possibility of being balanced. There are numerous benefits to having a strong Lower Dan Tian.

The Lower Dan Tian is also the postnatal energy center. The prenatal energy center is the Snow Mountain Area. To locate the Snow Mountain Area, imagine a line going through your body from your navel to your back. Go along this line about one-third of the way in from your back. Then go down about three inches from your navel level. This is the center of the fist-sized Snow Mountain Area, essentially just above and in front of your tailbone. The Snow Mountain Area feeds energy to the kidneys and the brain. The Lower Dan Tian and the Snow Mountain Area are the two vital foundation energy centers for your physical existence, but I will focus on the Lower Dan Tian at this time.

When you sing your Soul Song, you are strengthening your Lower Dan Tian. The light and energy it receives are of a very special quality. As a practice, I recommend sometimes thinking specifically of strengthening your Lower Dan Tian as you sing your Soul Song. This will accelerate the development of your Lower Dan Tian. This one aspect of your Soul Song will help bring groundedness and centeredness to every aspect of your being. This will help your soul journey in many ways.

The mind-sets, attitudes, and beliefs that have sometimes led you to think things over and over without resolution, to have thoughts spin around in your head repeatedly, can be transformed as you increase the strength of your Lower Dan Tian. Using your Soul Song to help you will accelerate the process and turn it into a joy and a delight. You can consider the aspects of joy and delight and a strong Lower Dan Tian to be part of the yin and yang of your soul journey and your physical journey. Looking at things in this way may help you to understand and appreciate how they work together.

Being grounded and centered is the fastest way available to most people to experience joy and delight. Conversely, experiencing joy and delight is a very fast way to help you become more grounded and centered. It is wonderful to know that these qualities and the Lower Dan Tian assist and reinforce one another in this way. Using your Soul Song to promote this is a very special blessing and gift. In many ways, it makes this task easy. At this particular moment in the history of Mother Earth, staying grounded and centered is essential. Having Soul Song as an effective tool for this is an incredible blessing given to humanity at this time.

Soul Song Heals and Soothes

Soul Song has an extraordinarily powerful ability to heal. It is able to touch areas of life that have not been reached before. Those areas that are most resistant can be reached through the vibration of Soul Song. Soul Song can travel to great depths. It can set in motion a series of vibrations that will bring about healing in amazing ways. These healings will be accompanied by the experience of being soothed. When you think about it, this makes quite a bit of sense. Having healing vibrations begin to reach, touch, and transform those things that have been most resistant would result in a very soothing response.

When the stiffness and the pain that are associated with resistance begin the healing process, an initial response is relaxation. When you are relaxed, you will have the experience of being soothed. This is a very special blessing and gift of Soul Song. And what can happen for you on the finest level can happen on every other level as well. Soul Song can also heal and soothe the most resistant mind-sets, attitudes, and beliefs. You can imagine how extraordinary it would be to have the firmest resistance begin to be touched and transformed.

The benefits will reach the emotional level and the physical level. This transformation takes place throughout Mother Earth and beyond. When you use your Soul Song, all that I have described takes place. Even if you are using your Soul Song without a specific healing intention, the vibrations and frequencies of all levels within you will benefit. Of course, having a conscious intention will strengthen the benefits. It is important, however, to realize that all the benefits I have mentioned will accrue whenever you are using your Soul Song.

If you have learned *Love, Peace and Harmony*, the Soul Song given to me by the Divine on September 10, 2005, you will have all of these benefits multiplied in a most extraordinary way. *Love, Peace and Harmony* is a very special message for our time. I will discuss it in the next chapter. Using this and other Soul Songs I have been given will make a great difference in your soul journey. The Soul Song's ability to heal is so powerful that you must experience the benefits to truly appreciate how extraordinary Soul Song is for the healing process. Use your Soul Song for yourself and others. Begin to experience its effectiveness. This experience will be a very powerful teacher.

Pay attention to all aspects of the healing process. Each aspect holds within it profound wisdom. The teachings you will receive are unique to you. However, you will be able to make a connection to the healing process for others, for Mother Earth, and beyond. The healing process itself is a special wisdom teacher. Both Soul Song and the healing process will help you enter into great wisdom, wisdom that will assist you in many ways on your soul journey. The teachings you receive are connected with the particular healing that you are experiencing. You will be able to use these teachings to assist others in their healing process.

Receiving these teachings will make it possible for you to become a powerful healer. It will release even stronger healing abilities through your Soul Song. Receiving these teachings is like being taught personally by the Soul World. This is a most extraordinary blessing. The benefits from receiving these teachings will make all that you do much more powerful. Your healing process will accelerate. Your soul journey will accelerate at a most amazing rate.

When you pay attention to the teachings you receive, your spiritual channels will also open further. The more you pay attention to the teachings, the more open your spiritual channels become. The more you pay attention to the teachings of your healing process, the deeper and faster that healing becomes. As I said, the healing is accompanied by the experience of soothing relaxation. All of these gifts and benefits take place every time you use your Soul Song.

Every benefit you have read about in this book takes place when you use your Soul Song. The benefits are for you. They are also radiated beyond you. Mother Earth and beyond also benefit. Everything that I have presented in this section is equally true for the healing blessings that you give to others. If the other person is ready to receive the information, you can suggest that they pay attention to their healing process. Let them know that the process is a wonderful wisdom teacher. Some of those who receive your healing blessings will be ready for this information.

Others will not be ready. For them, it is best to simply offer a healing blessing. Do not suggest to them that they can receive wisdom teachings from their healing process. It will only confuse them. It will actually slow down their healing process, because their logical thinking will become so active that it will block part of their process. If you feel a strong desire to let these people know about the wisdom teachings in the healing process, you can speak to their souls. Give the teachings on the level of their souls. After you have done this enough times, you will notice their "openness" for you to give the teaching directly to them. The direct teaching will be received through their logical thinking. This will make it possible for them to implement the teachings in their daily lives.

There are many benefits connected to receiving the wisdom teachings from your healing process. Because these teachings are specific to you, the benefits for your soul journey and your healing journey are also specific to you. The ways in which these teachings will transform your being on all levels and transform your soul journey will be unique to you. The wisdom teachings that you receive will intensify and accelerate the entire healing process. The transformation, healing, and soothing that you experience will be profound.

These are special gifts being given to humanity at this time. Each person will benefit in an extraordinary way. And these benefits will radiate to others, to Mother Earth, and beyond. Receiving and using the wisdom teachings is also a very high level of service. Offering this service to others will have powerful blessings connected to it. It is amazing to realize that Soul Song brings with it such extraordinary and powerful blessings and abilities. We are very blessed to release Soul Song at this chapter in the story of Mother Earth.

Soul Song as a Very Special Gift for Our Times

This book gives you many teachings about Soul Song. Many of the teachings so far have pointed out how Soul Song is a gift for our times. Keep those teachings in your awareness. They are all true and the various gifts connected with Soul Song are all very special. Putting all of those aspects of Soul Song together creates a most powerful and extraordinarily beautiful pattern, frequency, and vibration. Although this realization is important, to say that Soul Song is a very special gift for our times means even more than that.

This special gift is a unique connection to the extraordinary generosity of the Divine. It is best described as divine generosity, for no other description would be adequate. The Divine has given this gift of joy, delight, and profound healing ability at this particular moment because there is such need for these qualities. Soul Song is also a powerful manifestation of divine compassion. The purification of Mother Earth is necessary, but it will be extraordinarily difficult for many people. Knowing this, the Divine has given us a tool that will assist and serve in a way that other tools cannot. In fact, the Divine wants to do more than assist. The Divine also desires to be present with us as humanity experiences this purification process. Soul Song is a very powerful yet tender and gentle way for the Divine to be present with us and for us to become the presence of the Divine.

The compassion manifested in the Divine's desire to be with us is beyond our ability to comprehend. Soul Song is also a very powerful manifestation of divine mercy and forgiveness. Giving humanity this most beautiful and extraordinary gift at this time will allow many to experience the forgiveness that is greatly needed on an individual level as well as on the level of groups, nations, and even Mother Earth as a whole. The presence of divine forgiveness through Soul Song will make it possible for each one to become aware of those areas that need to request and receive forgiveness. It will be possible for events in past lives to be forgiven in a most powerful and gentle way. This process of forgiveness will bring about an amazing peace, a peace that will be experienced by the individual and that will also radiate out to others.

All of these may seem like individual gifts; however, they are all manifestations of the Divine. To say that Soul Song is a very special gift for our times is a way of saying that Soul Song makes the presence of the Divine with us and through us a powerful transforming reality. It is not possible to adequately explain in human words what an extraordinary gift this divine presence is. Everything that I have said about Soul Song will give you an idea of how profound this gift is, and what an amazing manifestation of service it is. When you have in your conscious awareness the reality of this gift of Soul Song, it is easier to understand and appreciate that the Divine is an unconditional universal servant.

I cannot say too many times how special it is to know that the gift of Soul Song is the very presence of the Divine. The Divine desires to be with us at this time to assist us in the purification process of Mother Earth. Use and enter into the experience of your Soul Song to receive further teachings that will help you grow in your understanding and appreciation. Use your Soul Song to experience divine presence. Use your Soul Song to become divine presence. The more you do this, the better you will understand this unique gift for our times.

You could say that the Divine is heard by and among humanity in a very special way through Soul Song. The Divine has chosen to use human voice and human sound to be present in this magnificent way. The Divine has chosen song for all the reasons I have mentioned already. As you use your Soul Song, you will become aware of even more reasons. The ones that I have explained form the very essence of Soul Song. We are very privileged to be given this most amazing and extraordinary gift. Use it often. Use it well. Use it with the most profound gratitude, love, appreciation, and respect. We are very blessed.

8

Soul Song and the Song of the Universe

There is a continual melody and song that is being sung throughout the universe. Your Soul Song is a manifestation of part of this song of the universe. Your Soul Song is also a unique contribution to the song of the universe.

The range of sounds that exist is extraordinary. Your Soul Song will manifest many of these frequencies and vibrations. It will manifest a certain combination of sounds and it will be in harmony with the range of sounds that includes sounds beyond the ability of the human voice to express. To bring this resonance into physical form through your Soul Song is very powerful. It connects with the very essence of energy that exists in all matter. It connects with the very core of life. Manifesting this resonance through your Soul Song is very healing. It brings into human form, and into the yang world, a powerful presence of divine light and divine energy.

Those of you who have experienced energy as vibration have a deep appreciation of what it means to be able to manifest these vibrations as Soul Song. The variety of songs gives us an appreciation of the extraordinary variety that exists throughout the universe. Being able to connect with this incredible range of sounds is a blessing that is greatly needed on Mother Earth at this time. There are many souls throughout the universe who are able to help Mother Earth in her time of purification. Your Soul Song is a powerful way to make the help of these souls present on Earth. Through your Soul Song, you are able to connect with their vibration and frequency. You are able to manifest their assistance on Earth.

Possibilities for Harmony on Mother Earth

As you sing your Soul Song, the harmony of all the sounds on Earth will increase. Think of experiences you have had when you started to hum and then others around you also started to hum. If you work with children, you will be especially aware of what happens when one child in a group begins humming. Very often, several others in the group will immediately join in. And after just a few seconds, the entire group of children will participate. This example will help you to understand what happens on Mother Earth when you sing your Soul Song.

I have already explained what happens within your body when you sing your Soul Song. Ancient wisdom teaches that *what happens in the small universe happens in the big universe.* What happens within your body also happens for Mother Earth. You will advance the process of harmonization for Mother Earth. You will be able to bring into harmony the vibrations of your immediate surroundings. Appreciate for a moment how extraordinary that is. At this moment, you are sitting as you read this book. Look at the immediate area around you. Think about the many parts of the chair that you are sitting on. Think about the area of the floor below your chair.

The chair—every part of the chair—has numerous souls, including the soul of the entire chair, the soul of the legs of the chair, the souls of the back and of every other part of the chair. There are also the souls of each molecule in the chair. The chair has a countless number of souls. Each one has its own frequency and vibration. Each one has its own sound. As you sing your Soul Song, you will connect with the songs of your chair. In so doing, you will help every part of the chair come into greater harmony within themselves and with each other.

The song of the chair will come into greater and greater harmony with your Soul Song. The song of the chair will also experience a greater harmony within itself. It will experience a greater richness, strength, power, and light. It will be able to add all of these qualities to the song and the harmony of Mother Earth. Now multiply this example by all of the objects in your immediate surroundings. Look around the room you are in.

All of the things in your room will be singing their own songs. They have their own vibration and frequency. As you sing your Soul Song, you are bringing all of these songs into greater harmony within themselves and together. You are bringing all of them into greater harmony and resonance with the Divine. As you do this, the benefits for harmony on Mother Earth will be extraordinary. The harmony that exists within Mother Earth will also become extraordinary. Facilitating all of this by singing your Soul Song is such a simple and effortless way to offer service. It is a most enjoyable way to help bring about the transformation of Mother Earth.

When thousands of people are participating in this type of service, the transformation of Mother Earth is increased and accelerated more than you can imagine. The sounds and the songs of Mother Earth and all of her children will become a most beautiful symphony. Their sounds are echoed in the Soul Songs of all who have released this precious gift. When those who have manifested their Soul Songs come together in groups of even as few as two or three, the participation in the symphony of Mother Earth will increase significantly. The more people who manifest their Soul Song, the more powerful the participation in this symphony will be.

It is important that you always be aware that your Soul Song is an expression of your soul, so that you allow it to flow forth from your soul. At times it may be expressed very softly and gently. At other times it may be louder. Follow nature's way and always allow your Soul Song to be expressed in the way it desires. The most important aspect of bringing about greater harmony within and among all that exists on Mother Earth is the soul-to-soul connection that

Soul Song establishes. It is this connection and not the volume of the song that confers great power. It is this connection that is the link to the Divine. When you allow your Soul Song to be expressed as it desires, you are making a soul-to-soul connection with the Divine and with the entire Soul World that is utterly profound, powerful, and transforming. The possibilities for transformation are without limit.

As you sing your Soul Song, it is most important that you keep this soul-to-soul, heart-to-heart connection in your awareness. The very moment that you move to logical thinking and attempt to direct your soul singing, you have moved away from a soul-to-soul, heart-to-heart connection. It is important to keep this aspect of soul singing in your awareness. Many people in this society have the impression that more is better. When it comes to singing, that would mean the greater the volume, the greater the benefit. This is definitely not the case. There may be times when your Soul Song will be expressed with great volume. There may be other times when it will be very gentle and very soft. It doesn't matter.

The soul-to-soul, heart-to-heart connection is the most important aspect of your Soul Song. When you keep this connection in your awareness and allow it to guide your Soul Song, the power and ability to transform will be most extraordinary. The connection with the Divine will be profound. Your ability to manifest this connection will also be profound. You will become the presence of divine sound. This is a very special aspect of the Divine that is at the very essence and core of all that exists. It is an aspect of the Divine that is present in a special way throughout Mother Earth and beyond.

The special sound of Soul Song exists beyond time. To be able to use your Soul Song to manifest the presence of the realms beyond time is an extraordinary privilege and honor. It is a blessing of the most powerful kind. The light that becomes present and the transformation that occurs will bring blessings to all humanity, Mother Earth, and beyond. The healing that will take place is of the deepest quality. The healing, quite literally, is from the inside out and also from the outside in. This combination will bring about healing to those parts of life that have not been touched before this time.

The healing will take place on all levels. The depth of the healing will reach beyond this lifetimes and the many past lifetimes your soul has experienced. Those most ancient areas that still need to be touched by healing will begin to resonate and vibrate with the Soul Song. There will be transformation and healing that are, once again, beyond your ability to imagine. This healing will take place on the individual level and also on the level of groups, societies, and nations. It will take place on the level of our entire planet and it will reach beyond Mother Earth.

Here is a comparison that will help you appreciate the power of Soul Song. If you have had major surgery, you know it typically takes months for complete healing and recovery. The depth of healing that can take place through the beautiful gift of Soul Song reaches areas that have needed healing for not only months, but for years, decades, and lifetimes. These areas may not have been touched before in any other way. Just as a surgery takes time to heal completely, these areas that have needed healing for a very long time may also require significant time to be healed. However, there is a great difference between medical, or physical, healing and healing that occurs on the soul level.

Through Soul Song, the healing process is accelerated significantly. The very ancient areas where healing is needed can experience this accelerated healing process, which is both powerful and gentle. As these ancient areas are healed, a song of comfort and joy emerges. This song becomes part of the harmony of Mother Earth.

When there is a need for healing in an area, the vibration and frequencies of that area are ones of yearning. The area yearns for transformation, greater light, and greater resonance. It is a wonderful service to be able to bring these qualities to areas that have yearned for them for a very long time—for lifetimes in some cases. When this yearning is transformed to a harmonious resonance, the benefits for our planet are extremely powerful. And the new quality of harmony that is born has a strength and beauty that is uniquely its own. When these ancient areas are healed, the harmony that comes into being has all the richness, wisdom, and light from these very ancient times. This gives a depth to the harmony Mother Earth will experience, a depth that can only be given by healing these very ancient areas.

Is it not extraordinary to realize that we can reach back through time and even forward to what is called the future with the healing of our Soul Song? And as we do this, we help bring about a greater harmony on Mother Earth. Keep in mind that this harmony resonates with the sounds we know but it is not limited to those sounds. There will be a time in the Soul Light Era when we will be able to more fully experience and manifest the full range of sounds that exist. At this time that is not very important, but there will be a time when the range of sounds is greatly expanded.

Soul Song is a possibility for everyone. Even though some of you may respond to this by saying, "Not for me, I simply cannot carry a tune," know that if you can speak, you can sing. The ability to carry a tune is irrelevant. Soul Song does not come from what is external to you, from what you have been taught or learned, or from what you have listened to. The song that you will sing is from your soul. When you allow your Soul Song to simply flow, you will be delightfully surprised at your newfound ability to stay on pitch and to carry a tune. Soul singing is a completely different way of singing that will always produce exactly what is needed at the moment.

As I have said, each person's Soul Song will be different from that of others. Your own Soul Song will also be different according to what you are doing or what is happening around you. That is part of the delight of this special gift. As you allow your soul to release its song, you are making a precious and unique contribution to Mother Earth and to all who dwell upon Earth. You are making a precious and unique contribution to the entire universe and to all times. You are also making an extraordinary connection with the Divine, the entire Soul World, and beyond. You are the manifestation of sacred sound.

Possibility for Harmony Throughout the Universe

All that I have said about Soul Song bringing greater harmony to Mother Earth is also true for the universe. Every part of the universe has its own song, its own vibration, and its own frequency. Think of the stars, the planets, the asteroids, and the space between them. Think of all the clutter in the space around Mother Earth. All of these things have their own song and their own vibration. All the souls that exist throughout the universe have their own song. With some of these songs, there is great harmony and resonance. With others, there is great clashing and dissonance. For some parts of the universe, there is also a need for deep and profound healing.

As you sing your Soul Song, the benefits extend out to the universe. It would be helpful for you sometimes to offer love and light to the universe through your Soul Song. The power and energy that exist in the vastness beyond Mother Earth are extraordinary. There are many souls beyond Mother Earth who are eager to add their strength, light, and service to assist Mother Earth at this time. They are also eager to assist throughout the universe. Through your Soul Song, you can connect with these souls. You can participate in their efforts. You can assist them in their efforts.

Soul Songs will bring all aspects of the universe into greater harmony. This will take some time. The universe is vast. The healing that is needed in the universe is also vast. But beginning that healing process is most important, and knowing that the process will be accelerated through the use of Soul Song is very important. The light and frequencies that will be sent to the universe are very powerful yet very gentle. This beautiful gift of Soul Song will be able to touch the areas of deepest blockage within the universe.

These areas will begin to experience the beginning of light, like the glimmers at the first moments of dawn. This is the light beginning to crack through the darkness. Something similar happens in the universe with Soul Song. The light that is released, along with the energy, the vibration, and the frequency, begins to move and vibrate those areas that previously resisted the presence of light and love. As this begins to happen, the most amazing transformation will begin.

There will also be the most amazing resistance. But as Soul Song continues to be sung consistently, little by little the resistance will be transformed. This is a most wonderful service to offer. The song of the universe is a bit muted at the present moment. As the vibration and frequency of the universe are transformed through your and others' Soul Songs, the song of the universe will become much more vibrant. It will become fuller, richer, and more harmonious.

The resistance that Soul Song will encounter also has its own song. However, it is a song of dissonance and discord. As the Soul Song of the universe is transformed, it will become rich and full and the quality of the song of resistance will also be transformed. The dissonance will become part of the song in a way that is truly beautiful. It will enhance the harmony because it will complement what is there. The dissonance will make it possible to appreciate and fully enjoy the harmony. Each will be a foil to the other. The harmony will make it possible to appreciate the transformed dissonance. The transformed dissonance will make it possible to hear and enjoy the harmony completely. They will blend with one another in a most extraordinary way.

As this happens, the vibration and frequency of the universe will become more and more attuned to the Divine and to the highest levels in the Soul World. The Soul Song of the universe is exquisitely beautiful. It has the most extraordinary potential and even now it has the most amazing power. As your Soul Song joins with this aspect of the song of the universe, it becomes more and more powerful. Just as your Soul Song brings about the most amazing transformation within yourself and just as it radiates out to others, so, too, does the song of the universe. The song of the universe is also able to transform itself.

You can offer great service by using your Soul Song to send love and light to the universe. It is important that you send blessings only to heal. Do not send blessings to stop the clashing in the universe. You do not have enough virtue to do that. If you attempt to stop the clashing, you may experience great discomfort. You could end up with a very serious illness. It is very important to follow this guidance.

I repeat: do not attempt to stop the clashing. It has accelerated beyond your level. It is very appropriate, however, to send love and light. Love and light will help heal the hurts and injuries that result from the clashing. Sending and asking your Soul Song to bless what has occurred is appropriate.

Even though this caution is very important and must be kept in mind and observed, know that whenever you sing your Soul Song, the universe will benefit. Your Soul Song is of a quality and connection with the Divine that extends beyond Mother Earth. It will be part of the process of bringing harmony throughout the universe even if that is not your conscious intention. Your Soul Song is so minute that it touches the tiniest matter and the tiniest space within you, while at the same time it extends far beyond you. The vibrations and frequencies radiate out and join the vibrations and frequencies throughout the universe.

All of this is possible because of the unique connection that Soul Song has with the sounds that exist throughout the Soul World. Your Soul Song connects with the Divine and the highest levels in a unique way. Amazingly, your Soul Song has the ability to participate in the sounds of the highest levels in the Soul World even if your own soul standing is not on that level. Think in terms of a concert. All of the instruments blend together. A particular instrument may have a very high frequency and vibration. Another instrument may have a solo for part of the concert. Another instrument may have the loudest part for part of the concert. However, all of the instruments are important because they blend with and complement one another. They all contribute their unique frequencies and vibrations to the overall beauty of the concert.

This is similar to what happens with your Soul Song. Even if your standing is not as high as the highest saints, your frequency and vibration add to the overall sound and the entire concert. This is how your Soul Song helps to bring about the possibility of harmony throughout the universe. The ranges of sound in this harmony are truly beyond imagining. To say that their beauty and power are extraordinary is not enough.

That your Soul Song can resonate with all of this is a very special gift. It is a gift for you. It is also a gift *from* you. As each person releases his or her Soul Song, the process of realizing a greater harmony throughout the universe is accelerated. Of course, it will take some time for the process to reach fruition. It will take some time for the transformation to be completed. Moreover, what is happening in our universe is also happening in other universes. Each one assists the others. We are blessed that something as delightful and enjoyable as singing your Soul Song can be so powerful, so transforming, and of such great service. This is indeed a very special blessing and gift.

Heaven's Song

What is happening through the release of Soul Song is that human voice is able to express parts of Heaven's Song. As you sing your Soul Song, you connect with an aspect of the highest realms that has not been available before. This is the proper time in Mother Earth's history to literally bring Heaven's Song to Earth. Each person who releases his or her Soul Song is a privileged messenger, the privileged singer of that part of Heaven's Song which is revealed through them.

Heaven's Song is beyond our human capacity to contain and imagine. Each person who releases a Soul Song brings a bit of Heaven to Earth and manifests it as song. It is ineffably great kindness, generosity, and mercy of the Divine to give us this exquisite gift at this time.

To know that you are quite literally the voice of Heaven when you are singing your Soul Song is a very special honor and privilege. This realization will help greatly to transform those aspects of ego that may still be strongly entrenched in your mind-sets, attitudes, and beliefs. It is difficult to approach life from the stance of ego when you have the conscious realization of being the voice for one part of Heaven's Song—to not only have been gifted with this little bit of

Heaven, but also to have the opportunity to make that bit of Heaven present on Earth.

Many who release their Soul Song also release great joy. For many, the soul's singing is accompanied by a smile. And so it is possible to say that Heaven's Song is also the presence of Heaven's smile. When you sing your Soul Song, you are making Heaven's smile present upon Earth. What another wonderful gift to be given to those who release their Soul Song.

You can have other experiences as you sing your Soul Song. You may be moved to tears without knowing exactly why. Sometimes those tears are simply a release. Sometimes they are healing. Sometimes they touch a great sadness. All of this is part of what exists within the highest realms and so, as with Heaven's smile, you have the privilege of making that present on Earth also.

It may surprise you to hear that there is sadness in the highest realms. But this sadness is quite different from what we as humans experience here on Earth. It is similar to the sadness experienced by parents who see their child choosing to do something harmful, but it is a sadness with no attachment. When this aspect of Heaven is brought to Earth, it is powerfully healing and transforming for all of the sadness that exists within human hearts. And so, if it is your experience sometimes to be moved to tears because of your Soul Song, realize that this, too, is a gift. Whatever your experience, you are bringing that aspect of the highest realms to Earth by giving it voice. This is a privilege, an honor, and a responsibility that are beyond words.

The more you use your Soul Song, the more you will be able to enter into the power and the extraordinariness of what it means to bring Heaven's Song to Earth. However you experience your Soul Song, it is always filled with light, love, forgiveness, peace, healing, harmony, and blessings. No matter how you feel as you sing your Soul Song, you are connecting with all of these qualities, because these qualities are part of Heaven's Song no matter how it is expressed and experienced. Heaven's Song is also an expression of service. It is one of the highest forms of service that has manifested on

Earth at this time. Every aspect of soul singing is an expression of this magnificent service.

Heaven's Song is the sound that exists in the highest realms at all times. Indeed, it is the sound that has existed from before time. The sound that exists in each realm is of a different quality. At this moment, we are connecting with Heaven's Song as it exists in Jiu Tian. This is a most extraordinary gift. It is a magnificent honor and privilege to be the messenger of your part of Heaven's Song.

Know that Heaven's Song is a song of light. When you sing your Soul Song, you are releasing not only sound but also light. The ability to give this powerful service is a new gift from the Divine for you at this time. Just by singing your Soul Song, you fill your entire setting with light. And the light radiates far beyond you. Remember, too, that your Soul Song also connects with the songs of everything in your surroundings, so that the possibility of increasing the presence of divine light is huge. This possibility is truly beyond imagination. Even those with Third Eye capabilities will not be able to see the full extent of this possibility.

This is yet another facet of the extraordinary nature of this gift and of the service it allows you to offer every time you sing your Soul Song. Singing your Soul Song throughout your day will create powerful transformation. You will be able to bring that part of Heaven to Earth and surround your activities and yourself with it. How wonderful it is to know that Heaven is on Earth with you in this special way, especially when so many people feel very stressed, discouraged, or overwhelmed.

When you sing your Soul Song and bring part of Heaven to Earth, you are surrounded by and radiating divine light. This will be transforming. When you allow yourself to really enter into that experience, you will realize that your stress, your discouragement, or your feeling of overwhelm have shifted dramatically. The blessings that are part of Heaven's Song are beyond limit. Make your requests for blessings and then sing your Soul Song. You will receive incredible blessings that are filled with light.

At the same time, you must keep in mind the necessity of having no attachment and no expectation. Only then can you fully receive what is given to you through your Soul Song as the exquisite gift it is. When you are grateful for whatever response you receive, the Divine will in turn respond extravagantly. The generosity of the blessings you will receive is far beyond what you can imagine.

There is a saying that can illustrate what I mean. Frequently, people use the cautionary statement, "Give him an inch and he will take a mile." With the Divine, the statement becomes "Give the Divine an inch and you will receive much more than a mile." Whatever you give to the Divine is returned to you in extravagant abundance. Give gratitude through your Soul Song and it is returned to you with the most extraordinary abundance and generosity.

All of this is part of making Heaven's Song present on Earth. The qualities of love, forgiveness, peace, healing, harmony, blessing, and light that you will experience and that you will radiate will increase in a most extraordinary way. The benefits connected with Heaven's Song will become very powerfully present on Mother Earth. It is very important for this to happen at this time. It will assist greatly in the purification and transformation of Mother Earth. To be able to participate in this process is great service.

Heaven's Song is also present on Mother Earth in a silent way. This may sound puzzling, but it is completely true. You may have already experienced this by hearing music within yourself. Sometimes you will hear a melody and sometimes you may also hear words to go with the melody. This experience is the presence of Heaven's Song. Some of you may have had this experience for a number of years. If so, you are honored and very privileged to have been part of the readiness to release Heaven's Song at this time.

Heaven's Song is present in all those who dwell upon Earth. At times, you may feel or even hear parts of your surroundings singing in harmony with your Soul Song. These parts could even be singing what sounds like your Soul Song but in a different register. You may also hear their own Soul Songs, and their songs and yours will blend together to make a most magnificent sound. All of these experiences are part of making Heaven's Song present on Earth.

As this happens, deep transformation will be taking place on all levels—physical, mental, emotional, and spiritual. It is no understatement to say that extraordinary changes will result from the coming together of all of these Soul Songs. The process of blessing, purification, and transformation will be greatly accelerated. More and more people will experience the presence of the Divine in a powerful way. The recognition and reality of the primacy of the soul in all aspects of existence will increase greatly. All of these blessings are part of the wonderful combination of Soul Songs.

These changes will occur at the tiniest subcellular levels. They will also occur at the level of the body's organs and systems. Even the structures that have been built by humanity will experience this transformation. They will also participate in the increase of divine light and divine presence. Of course, the process will take some time, but it has already started.

This process will be of great benefit to Mother Earth as she goes through her time of purification. It will be of great benefit to the entire universe and beyond. The highest realms are giving the gift of their particular song. Each realm has its own special sound. The sounds of Jiu Tian and the sounds of Tian Wai Tian are different. The sounds beyond Tian Wai Tian are different again. All realms will be in synchrony and harmony. When Mother Earth eventually is resonating fully with the song of Jiu Tian, she will then be ready to resonate with Tian Wai Tian and beyond. There is no limit to the possibilities.

What is possible for Mother Earth and all her creatures is completely beyond our ability to imagine. At this moment, there is no one who actually knows in detail how this process will develop, how it will look, or how it will be manifested. What we do know is that the transformation will continue. The generosity of the Divine and the highest saints will continue. The presence of light and of all aspects of the Divine and the highest saints will be manifested in a greater and greater way. We are very privileged. We are very blessed.

Healing, Rejuvenation, and Transformation from Divine Soul Songs

By now you understand that Soul Song is a precious treasure that the Divine is generously giving to us at the beginning of the Soul Light Era. I received my first Soul Song directly from the Divine on September 10, 2005, while I was enjoying the redwoods in Marin County, California with three of my advanced students.

My first Divine Soul Song is entitled "Love, Peace and Harmony." It was transmitted to me from the heart of the Divine with lyrics in Soul Language. I then translated the Soul Language, first into Chinese and then into English. Here are the original lyrics and the English translation:

> *Lu La Lu La Li*
> *Lu La Lu La La Li*
> *Lu La Lu La Li Lu La*
> *Lu La Li Lu La*
> *Lu La Li Lu La*

> *I love my heart and soul*
> *I love all humanity*
> *Join hearts and souls together*
> *Love, peace, and harmony*
> *Love, peace, and harmony*

Visit mastershasoulsong.com to hear me sing this Soul Song. Today, thousands of people around the world sing this Soul Song every day for healing, rejuvenation, life transformation, and service. Since late 2005, I have also taught thousands of students around the world to sing their own Soul Songs, as I have taught you in this book.

Your Soul Song carries your own Soul Power, but it connects with the Soul Power of high spiritual beings in the spiritual world. Your Soul Song also connects with divine love and light. Your Soul

Song is a soul treasure for healing, prevention of sickness, rejuvenation, and prolonging life, as well as for transformation of relationships, finances, and other aspects of life. In less than three years, Soul Song singers have shared thousands of heart-touching stories of the healing and transformation created by their own Soul Songs.

In early 2008, the Divine guided me further: "Zhi Gang, this is the time for you to sing Soul Songs for healing and rejuvenation for humanity. Because you are my servant, vehicle, and channel, your Soul Song carries my love, light, and compassion. I will also download many divine souls to your soul. When you sing a Soul Song, these souls will come out to serve humanity and other souls." I was deeply touched and moved. After receiving transmissions of new divine souls from the Divine every day for a week, I invoked these new Divine Downloads and recorded a number of Soul Songs for Healing and Rejuvenation of various organs, systems, parts of the body, and emotional imbalances.

The Divine guided me to offer Soul Songs for Healing and Rejuvenation to all humanity. You can sample them at mastershasoulsong. com. In less than two months, people have reported hundreds of heart-touching stories of remarkable healing and life transformation that they have received by listening to my Soul Songs. My heart is deeply moved. I cannot honor the Divine enough for his guidance, blessing, and Soul Power.

As a special gift for you, I am including a CD in this book of my Soul Song for Healing and Rejuvenation of Brain and Spinal Column. I recommend you listen to this often, even repeatedly. You could have it playing constantly at low volume in your home or office. This Soul Song could offer you healing for many health challenges, because the brain and spinal column include the central nervous system, which connects with every system, every organ, and every cell of the body.

When you listen to this Soul Song, do not forget to Say Hello first:

Dear Soul Song for Healing and Rejuvenation of Brain and Spinal Column, I love you, honor you, and appreciate you. Please give me a healing and a blessing for (state your health challenges or the blessings you wish to receive). *Thank you.*

A soul healing wave of divine love, light, compassion, vibration, and frequency will pour into your body and soul to serve you. My Soul Song is your servant. I wish you will receive great healing results from this Soul Song.

Conclusion

his section on Soul Song is a special treasure. I believe you will find its teachings very helpful for our time. The blessings contained within this section and in the entire book are very powerful. Use this book (and the included CD) as a tool. Use it as a very special wisdom teacher and respond to it with great respect. The teachings in this book could change your life significantly. These teachings will assist you during the transformation of Mother Earth. You can participate in and accelerate this healing process using what you have learned in this book.

The subsection on "Soul Song as a Very Special Gift for Our Times" will help you appreciate that this book is much more than simply a book. It is a tool of divine presence. Carry this book with you throughout your day, if possible, so that it will be physically present with you wherever you go and whatever you are doing. This book has the ability to radiate the blessings that are described in its pages. It also makes present the wisdom and the teachings given in these pages.

Knowing this makes it possible for you to appreciate the importance of having this book with you. It will help you understand the amazing and extraordinary blessings you will receive from doing so. Those blessings will radiate out far beyond you. Follow my suggestions and you may be delighted to observe the changes in your work environment. These changes can come about just by keeping the book with you at all times.

Carrying the book will also give you a wonderful reminder to use your Soul Language and Soul Song throughout the day, either silently or out loud. You will offer great service simply by having the book with you. This service can be increased as you use your Soul Language and Soul Song. Many changes will take place within you and around you. Pay attention to those changes. There will be an opportunity to say "thank you" and to use your Soul Language and Soul Song to bless the changes. I cannot tell you enough how important it is to follow these suggestions. As you do, you will be amazed at what you experience and observe.

Everything I have said is just a hint of the possibilities available to you and through you to Mother Earth and beyond. Your experiences as you follow these suggestions will help you to understand more and more how limitless the possibilities are. It is an extraordinary and humbling blessing to be able to offer this service and to participate in this extraordinary aspect of divine presence.

You are very blessed. It is my honor and my privilege to serve you in this way.

PART 3

Soul Movement

*Ancient Practice to Energize, Heal, Rejuvenate,
and Enlighten Soul, Mind, and Body*

Introduction

In the thousands of years of recorded history, there have been innumerable energy and spiritual practices. China, India, Egypt, Hawaii, and many other places have been the source of these practices, which include the sacred and often secret teachings of Taoism, Buddhism, yoga, tai chi, and qi gong, to name a few that have continued to evolve to this day. These teachings offer wisdom, knowledge, and practices to boost energy, vitality, stamina, and immunity. These practices can heal, prevent illness, rejuvenate, and prolong life. They can transform lives.

Much of this ancient wisdom, knowledge, and practice has not been widely spread. In fact, many of these sacred teachings have been kept very secret, given to only one or two lineage holders in each generation. All of this wisdom is extremely precious because of its truth and power, which have been tested and refined over time. These teachings can improve health. They can heal illnesses. They can make people younger. They can prolong human life. They can bring inner joy and inner peace to those who follow and practice the teachings. They can transform humanity.

My Training

In this life, I was honored and privileged to start my tai chi training at the age of six, and my qi gong training at the age of ten. I also studied feng shui, I Ching, Buddhism, Taoism, and Confucianism, as well as Shaolin kung fu using sticks, swords, and knives. I am very blessed to have had China's most renowned tai chi masters, qi gong masters, I Ching masters, and feng shui masters as my personal teachers. I studied Western medicine, becoming an M.D., and traditional Chinese medicine, becoming an acupuncturist and herbalist. In 1986, I began to study Zhi Neng Medicine. *Zhi Neng* means "the intelligence and capabilities of the mind and soul." In 1996, I began to study Body Space Medicine from my most beloved spiritual father and mentor, Master and Dr. Zhi Chen Guo, who had also created Zhi Neng Medicine. All of my masters and teachers, and Master Guo above all, have empowered me to build a solid foundation for energy, vitality, stamina, and spiritual development. They have taught me much sacred and secret wisdom and knowledge, including many secret practices.

In 1993, Master Guo, who has five wonderful daughters, adopted me as his only son and selected me as his sole worldwide representative to teach and spread Zhi Neng Medicine and Body Space Medicine. The top masters of Taoism and Buddhism who have taught me do not allow me to share their names because they want to be quiet, pure servants for the universe. However, I would very much like to acknowledge their teachings. I want to honor all of my master teachers deeply for all of their training in the ancient wisdom and practices of tai chi, qi gong, I Ching, and feng shui, as well as in sacred Taoist, Buddhist, and Confucian teachings. I honor all of them from the bottom of my heart. Without their teachings, I could not have created the Soul Movement teaching presented in this book.

In 2003, I was chosen by the Divine as a divine servant, vehicle, and channel. The Divine gave me the greatest honor and ability to transmit permanent divine healing and blessing treasures to humanity. In a few short years, I have offered countless divine permanent healing and blessing treasures to humanity and all souls in the universes. I am extremely blessed that my teachers have included not only several of the greatest masters in the physical world, but also my spiritual fathers and mothers in the Soul World, as well as the Divine directly. With their sacred training, I have been able to integrate all the wisdom, knowledge, and practices that I have learned to create this teaching on Soul Movement.

Simple and Practical

Soul Movement is very simple and very practical. It may be too simple to believe. But I want to share one key insight: *The simplest teaching is the best teaching. The simplest practice is the best practice.* You do not need to go running around for thirty to fifty years to try to figure out how to master something. I myself have already spent nearly fifty years trying to figure out the best wisdom. Save yourself thirty to fifty years. Grab the wisdom, knowledge, and practice in this book. Soul Movement can serve your health well, improving your energy and vitality, offering healing and rejuvenation, and prolonging your vital, healthy life. Soul Movement can also transform every aspect of your life.

A human being consists of soul, mind, and body. The body is one's temple. The mind is one's consciousness. The soul is one's essence. A human being cannot exist without a soul. The soul is your spirit, your message, and your life's essence. If your Third Eye is open, you can actually see your beloved soul. It is a small golden light being that resides in your body. This being has a head, body, arms, and legs. This being has emotions, likes, and dislikes. This being has consciousness, dreams, and desires. This being has its own existence, spanning hundreds and thousands of lifetimes.

Your soul has huge potential powers to transform your life. You may not have thought about or realized the importance of your small golden light being. Do not forget that this small golden light being has huge power and huge potential. It can dramatically change your life much like the difference between Heaven and Earth. Pay attention to your small golden light being. Nourish that small golden light being. Your soul can heal; prevent illness; boost your energy, vitality, and stamina; rejuvenate your soul, mind, and body; and prolong your life. Your soul can transform every aspect of your life.

Soul Movement uses the power of soul, including the power of your own soul. It also uses the power of "outer" souls, including the souls of nature, the souls of your spiritual fathers and mothers, and the soul of the Divine. All of these souls have great power to heal, bless, rejuvenate, and transform every aspect of your being. You only need to learn how to access that power. The power of soul is the key to Soul Movement. The power of soul is the power of Soul Movement. The power of soul is the reason Soul Movement works.

There are various forms of Soul Movement. This book will teach you how to do Soul Movement while lying down, sitting, standing, or walking. Each of these ways of doing Soul Movement serves its own specific purposes. Each of these ways is important. A complete practice of Soul Movement is one that integrates all forms. This book will explain this concept and offer you some simple practice protocols to empower you to receive complete and maximum benefits from this ancient and, up to now, secret practice.

The benefits of Soul Movement are many. Among other things, this book will teach you how to do Soul Movement to:

- boost energy and stamina
- heal
- rejuvenate
- enlighten your soul, mind, and body.

Soul Movement integrates thousands of years of ancient principles, laws, and practices for energy development and the spiritual journey. I will give you specific guidance on how to do Soul Movement. I will explain its purpose and why it works. Although simple, practical, and easy to learn, Soul Movement is profoundly and powerfully effective.

A Gift for Humanity

This teaching is a practical treasure for humanity. It is a gift for everyone who is searching for ancient wisdom and practice, for optimum health, and for healing of chronic and life-threatening conditions. Use Soul Movement to rejuvenate, to prolong your life, and to fulfill your spiritual journey. Soul Movement is a flower that is blossoming to serve and nourish your soul, mind, and body. It is a special flower, a rainbow lotus flower that carries universal light and universal liquid, the yang and yin aspects, respectively, of universal nourishment. It carries all ancient sacred wisdom, knowledge, and practice. Its principles can be distilled into a few sentences.

I am greatly honored to bring this teaching to humanity in the twenty-first century. Soul Movement is based on many ancient secrets. I am honored to have received these secrets. To receive is to give. The ancient secrets cannot be kept secret anymore. They must be revealed. They must be updated for our time. They must be shared. They must be spread as widely as possible. They must be allowed to serve. Allow the gift of Soul Movement to serve you well.

To give is to receive. I know that in sharing these secrets with you wholeheartedly and with no reservations, I am making more room in my warehouse of intelligence for new wisdom and secrets. I hope you will follow this principle by sharing the gift of Soul Movement with your loved ones and friends. Serve others as well as yourself with this divine treasure and your generosity will be returned to you many times over. May you also use the gift of Soul Movement to serve others well.

Soul Light Era

As I write this, we stand near the beginning of the Soul Light Era. This fifteen-thousand-year-long cycle of Mother Earth and the universe began on August 8, 2003. In this era, the power of soul will come to be widely recognized, fully developed, and totally relied upon. Soul will guide every aspect of life and culture, including science, education, economics, and politics. Soul will be paramount. Soul will be the leader. Soul will be the boss.

My total life mission is to bring the Soul Light Era to fruition. I want to help transform the consciousness of humanity and souls in the universe. I want every being to recognize the importance of the soul, to acknowledge the importance of the soul, to deeply trust and believe in the wisdom of the soul, and to be guided by the soul in all aspects of life. Why? Because the soul has great wisdom, acquired through its many lifetimes of existence. The soul has great power. The soul has great love and care. The soul wants to serve, to benefit others rather than benefiting itself. The soul wants love, peace, and harmony. Ultimately, the soul wants to return to its source, to the heart of the Divine. Only when the consciousness (or mind) of humanity and all souls is transformed to these realizations can minds and souls be in harmony. Only then can all souls be together in love, peace, and harmony. Only then can all souls join hearts and minds as one.

My total life mission includes three empowerments to help achieve *wan ling rong he* (all souls joining as one). My three empowerments are to:

- empower people to be unconditional universal servants;
- empower people to heal themselves and others;
- empower people to use Soul Power to transform every aspect of their lives and enlighten their souls, minds, and bodies.

The mind, and the logical mind in particular, is great. It has led humanity to many great discoveries and creations. Without the logical mind, life as we know it could not exist. However, total reliance on the mind is not enough. In health and healing, for example, the mind-body connection is well known and has been thoroughly studied. The intention of the mind, concentration of the mind, focus of the mind, affirmation of the mind, imagination of the mind, flexibility of the mind, creativity of the mind, visualization of the mind, inspiration of the mind, manifestation of the mind—all have been demonstrated to offer real, tangible benefits to our health and healing.

Mind over matter is great, but it is not enough. In my book, *Soul Mind Body Medicine*, I explain that *soul over matter* is greater than mind over matter. The mind is powerful, but the soul is *much more* powerful. The soul can work wonders that are beyond the abilities of the mind to comprehend.

Because Soul Movement is *soul-guided* movement, it uses the power of soul above all else. Through the power of soul, Soul Movement supports all three of my empowerments and, in this way, my total life mission. Through the power of soul, Soul Movement can serve, heal, transform lives, and enlighten souls, minds, and bodies. Soul Movement will be a very important teaching and method for transforming consciousness in the Soul Light Era.

Before the Soul Light Era can flourish, humanity, Mother Earth, and all who dwell upon her must undergo a transition to provide the impetus for the mass transformation of consciousness. This transition will be a major wake-up call for all beings on this planet. Natural disasters, tsunamis, hurricanes, earthquakes, floods, drought, extreme temperatures, famine, disease, political and religious wars, terrorism, and other such upheavals are part of this transition. Millions more people will suffer from depression, anxiety, fear, anger, and worry. During this transition, the need for service, for healing, and for soul wisdom and enlightenment will be great. How great? These needs will be universal. Humanity needs help. The consciousness of humanity needs to be transformed. The suffering of humanity needs to be removed. Especially for the transition period, I need this treasure of Soul Movement. You need this treasure. Humanity needs this treasure.

Soul Movement is a universal servant. Allow it to serve you all. Practice Soul Movement for three to five minutes at a time. It will boost your energy and refresh your soul, mind, and body. Practice for fifteen minutes to a half hour to receive great rejuvenation to prolong your life. I wish you will receive great benefits for your soul, mind, and body from this universal servant. I wish you will receive great benefits for your life.

Open your heart and soul. Practice Soul Movement. Experience the benefits. You will receive its nourishment. You will receive its blessings. You will receive transformation for every aspect of your life. Learn the wisdom, knowledge, and practice of Soul Movement to boost your energy every day, to rejuvenate, and to have true inner energy and great inner joy and peace. If we all were to do Soul Movement, our families would be transformed. Society would be transformed. Every city, every country would be transformed. This ancient secret practice will benefit millions of people worldwide. Let us practice together. Let us receive the benefits together. Let us thank all the teachers who trained me. Let us appreciate divine nourishment. Let us honor universal wisdom and knowledge. Let us be universal servants to serve others, and to join our hearts and souls together to bring harmony to Mother Earth and the universe.

> *I love my heart and soul*
> *I love all humanity*
> *Join hearts and souls together*
> *Love, peace, and harmony*
> *Love, peace, and harmony*

Accompany your Soul Movement with my Soul Song, "Love, Peace and Harmony." Please visit www.mastershasoulsong.com to listen to this song. When you sing this Soul Song, you are giving total love to yourself, to others, and to the universe. This service of divine love will deeply transform your soul, mind, and body. Singing this Soul Song while you practice Soul Movement will accelerate and enhance the benefits. You will rapidly energize, heal, rejuvenate, transform, and enlighten your soul, mind, and body.

Soul Movement takes only three to five minutes per practice session. You can do Soul Movement in any position—lying down, sitting, standing, or walking. You can do Soul Movement anytime, anywhere. No boundaries. No time, no space. Soul Movement can bring you to emptiness. In the "empty condition," you will meld with the universe to receive unimaginable spiritual blessings. You will receive amazing benefits for your soul, mind, and body, and for your life.

I wish Soul Movement will serve you, humanity, and all souls in all universes well.

Thank you. Thank you. Thank you.

9

Basic Formula for Soul Movement

Everyone understands movement. When you go for a walk in the morning, that is movement. When you jog or swim, that is movement. When you work out in a gym, that is movement. Yoga, tai chi, and qi gong are all forms of movement.

Human beings move. Animals move. Plants move. Insects move. Bacteria and viruses move. Cells move. Cell units move. Even inanimate objects are full of movement; you need only look at the atomic level. Rivers move. Trees move. Oceans move. Glaciers move. Mountains move. Souls move also. Movement is life. When the heart or the lungs cease to move, life ends. Movement is existence.

What is the purpose of movement? It is to promote energy flow. Vigorous physical exercise like walking and jogging moves energy. Ancient practices using "slow" movement like tai chi and qi gong also promote energy flow. Fast movement is yang movement. It accelerates cellular vibration, causing large amounts of energy to radiate out from the cells. This energy then flows quickly through the energy channels, increasing metabolism and stimulating and warming the body. That's why vigorous exercise or fast movement induces sweating. When you do slow movement such as tai chi, or when you meditate with some gentle movement, your blood circulation and heart rate could also speed up significantly. Equally, slow movement and meditation practices could also slow down your blood circulation and heart rate significantly.

If your heart rate is slower than normal, your heart is more efficient than normal. Fewer heartbeats are enough to circulate blood for the body's needs. Endurance athletes typically have a slow resting heart rate. "Slow" movement techniques can yield similar benefits and more. They can increase the potential abilities of your heart, your brain, your circulatory system, your respiratory system—all systems and all organs.

Slow, gentle movement such as tai chi, combined with meditation, is yin movement. Yin movement can be very powerful. In fact, for optimum health, slow yin movement is better than fast yang movement. It is well known that high-performance athletes often have major health challenges later in life. This is precisely because they do such fast, vigorous exercises. They run, jump, and weight-train. They do lots of fast exercises to reach and expand the limits of their body's potential. However, they force themselves too much. They push themselves too hard and strain themselves too much, overextending their own abilities. In the end, all of their intense training and competition doesn't help their health. In fact, it *hurts* their health. Many competitive athletes have major health challenges after they are forty years old.

I suggest that all athletes also practice slow movement techniques such as tai chi and Soul Movement. Combining fast movement with gentle movement balances your abilities. It balances your soul, mind, and body. You will receive great benefits.

Soul Movement is unique. It isn't necessarily fast or slow, yang or yin. Your beloved soul knows best! At one moment, it may be fast. At the next moment, it may slow down. It might be generally slow for a half hour, but at times you may find yourself compelled to speed it up. Who controls the speed of your movement? Your *soul* controls it.

Tao Fa Zi Ran—Follow Nature's Way

One of the highest Taoist philosophies is *tao fa zi ran*. *Tao* is universal law and universal principles, the Way. *Fa* means method. *Zi ran* means natural. *Tao fa zi ran* can be translated as: *follow nature's way for your life*. The idea can be illustrated in many ways. For example, often the more you want something to happen, the less likely it is to happen. When you take it easy and let go, the thing often happens. You are following nature's way by surrendering to the course of nature. When you plant a seed, water it, and fertilize it, it will grow naturally. When you educate your children, you need to teach them basic principles of behavior. You need to teach them how to offer respect and how to give love. Then your children will blossom naturally.

There are always natural principles to be followed, whether in a human being's life or in nature. In the winter, you must wear enough clothes to keep warm. On the other hand, if you wear a heavy jacket in the summer, you are not following nature's way. If it's raining, you carry an umbrella. To follow nature's way is to follow nature's changes. In the workplace, yelling at people and using force and coercion are not nature's way. Loving and caring guidance is nature's way. For health, you have to practice. You have to move, meditate, prevent illness. It is not nature's way to exhaust yourself, to work without breaks or rest. It is not nature's way to be emotionally unbalanced—upset, sad, unable to let go of something. Sometimes in your spiritual journey as well as in your physical journey, you know that you are doing something that is not nature's way, not the correct way. Yet you do not want to change. You persist in the wrong behavior, which is the wrong path for your physical or spiritual journey. That is not following nature's way.

Soul Movement can be summarized in one sentence: *Soul Movement follows nature's way*. How does it do this? Your beloved soul knows nature's way better than your mind does. Your spiritual fathers and mothers in Heaven know nature's way better than your soul does. The Divine knows nature's way best of all. There are two ways to invoke souls when doing Soul Movement. First, you can invoke your own soul to guide your movement. Second, you can invoke your spiritual fathers and mothers in Heaven or the Divine to guide your movement. You can also combine these two invocations.

When you do Soul Movement, how is it that you can invoke your own soul *and* your spiritual fathers and mothers in Heaven at the same time? *The universe is one.* We are all one. Ask that oneness, that unity, to guide your movement. The practice is very simple.

Basic Formula for Soul Movement

Dear my beloved soul, dear my beloved spiritual fathers and
mothers in the physical world and in the heavens, dear Divine,
I love you.
Could you please guide me to do Soul Movement?
I am very grateful.
Thank you.

After this invocation, just let your body move naturally. It doesn't matter if you are lying down, sitting, standing, or walking.

In the following chapters, I will explain in more detail how to practice Soul Movement for boosting energy, for healing, for rejuvenation, and for enlightenment. Finally, Chapter 14 summarizes all the wisdom, knowledge, and practice.

This ancient wisdom and practice is in front of you. Grab it. Absorb it. Receive nourishment from it. Enlighten your soul. Receive the service of Soul Movement. This is the honor of Soul Movement. Thank you for reading this book and for practicing Soul Movement. May Soul Movement be a pure servant for you.

10

Boosting Energy, Stamina, Vitality, and Immunity

One word, one concept underpins traditional Chinese medicine: *chi*. *Chi* is vital energy or life force. *Chi* moves through the meridians, the pathways of energy used by Chinese acupuncturists. The purpose of tai chi is to produce and move *chi*. Where does *chi* come from? It comes from the vibration and radiation of matter. In human beings, *chi* comes from cellular vibration. Our cells are constantly vibrating, contracting, and expanding. Energy radiates out from this cellular vibration. This energy is *chi*. Similarly, trees and flowers radiate their energy, or *chi* from the vibration of their matter. It is no different for an ocean or a mountain; for the sun or the moon; for every planet, every star, every galaxy, and every universe. Everything radiates its energy, or its *chi*, from the vibration and resulting radiation of its matter.

Everything in the physical world has matter. Matter vibrates and radiates energy. In turn, energy itself vibrates and radiates. Everything has a soul. A soul radiates and also vibrates. Soul Movement applies soul vibration, soul radiation, and soul resonation. Your cells are constantly vibrating, constantly radiating energy. If you are tired or lack vitality and stamina, it is because your cellular vibration is impaired. To boost your energy, stamina, vitality, and immunity, use Soul Movement. Soul Movement will direct the soul of your cells to vibrate normally. Once normal cellular vibration is restored, *chi* will be produced normally and radiate and flow smoothly. This will boost your energy, stamina, vitality, and immunity.

Soul Movement to boost energy, stamina, vitality, and immunity can be done in any of four positions—lying down, sitting up, standing, and walking. I recommend incorporating all four positions in a daily practice to begin each day, as described in the rest of this chapter. Of course, any one of these positions can be practiced alone at any time.

Lying Down

The day belongs to yang. The beginning of the day, dawn, is the beginning of yang. Throughout the morning, until noon, the sun continues to rise, gaining in power and intensity. That's why the beginning of the morning, right after you wake up, is a perfect time to do Soul Movement for boosting energy, stamina, vitality, and immunity. Here's how to do it. As soon as you wake up, say *hello* to your soul; invoke your soul. Do not get up. Remain lying in bed.

> *Good morning, my beloved soul.*
> *Good morning, all of my spiritual mothers and fathers in all*
>   *layers of the heavens.*
> *Good morning, soul of nature.*
> *Good morning, Divine.*
> *I love you.*
> *Could you guide my arms, legs, internal organs, systems, cells,*
>   *DNA, and RNA in movement?*
> *I'm so grateful.*

Then add this request:

> *Dear soul, mind, body of the Soul Song "Love, Peace and*
>   *Harmony,"*

I love you.
Please offer healing, blessing, and boosting for my energy, stam-
     ina, vitality, and immunity.
I'm so grateful.

Start to sing "Love, Peace and Harmony" silently. Singing or chanting aloud when you are lying down can drain your energy. Free yourself so your movement is not impeded. You may want to do this
practice lying down on top of your bed. Then start to move your
arms and legs gently. You can also play the CD of this Soul Song.
Play it just after you wake up and sing along with it silently. Then,
start to move.

Do this Soul Movement for three to five minutes. Because you
just woke up, you are in a very deep yin condition. With this very
gentle movement to start, your body, systems, organs, and cells will
resonate and vibrate more and more, bit by bit. Energy will be produced. Energy flow will be promoted. Yin will begin to transform
into yang.

After five minutes of Soul Movement lying in bed, you are ready
to do Soul Movement in the second position, sitting.

Sitting

If you can, sit up on your bed. You may sit in a full lotus position, a
half lotus position, or simply with your legs crossed naturally. For
greater comfort, sit on a cushion or a pillow. Continue to sing the
Soul Song and start to do Soul Movement. Follow nature's way. You
may be able to see in your mind's eye how your hands and body are
going to move. Bend and stretch your back by soul guidance. You
may feel or sense how you are to move. At times you may sit up
straight. At times you may almost be reclining on your back, side, or
face. Just move naturally, according to your soul's and the divine
souls' guidance.

If you are not able to sit up in bed due to some physical limitations, sit beside your bed in a chair. Then begin your Soul Movement. Practice in the sitting position for only about three minutes. Three minutes is enough to expand, resonate, and vibrate your cells and your being further. Your movement could be a little faster than it was when you were lying down. Yin continues to recede and yang continues to expand. On the other hand, your movement could be even slower than it was. The key is not to have any intention or expectation. Follow your soul's guidance. Practicing in the sitting position will activate your cells more, producing more energy and better energy flow. After three minutes of sitting Soul Movement, you are ready to do Soul Movement in the third position, standing.

Standing

Stand up. Start to do Soul Movement in a standing position. You do not need to move around, but you can bend your back, stretch your arms, and bend your knees. Follow nature's way. You can sing the Soul Song "Love, Peace and Harmony." You can sing along with the recording if you wish. Spend another three minutes practicing in the standing position to further boost your energy, stamina, vitality, and immunity. After three minutes of standing Soul Movement, you are ready to do Soul Movement in the fourth position, walking.

Walking

Now you are ready to move and walk. You can walk in your bedroom. You can walk to your living room. Best of all, walk outside in nature. Continue to sing the Soul Song as you do Soul Movement. For this step, I suggest you practice for at least fifteen minutes. If possible, practice for a half hour or even longer. Fifteen minutes will make a big difference in your energy, vitality, immunity, and stamina. It will really boost your life force, fully awakening the yang. If you don't have fifteen minutes, do what you can. Even three minutes would be beneficial, but practicing while walking for fifteen minutes will give you a big boost.

A fundamental principle set forth in *The Yellow Emperor's Classic of Internal Medicine*, the first authority textbook in traditional Chinese medicine, states, "If *chi* flows, one is healthy. If *chi* is blocked, one is sick." When you do Soul Movement in sequence (lying down, sitting up, standing, walking), your energy will develop rapidly. You will feel comfortable, vibrant, fresh, and energetic. You may actually feel warmth, tingling, vibration, radiation, expansion, or movement within your body. You may have not only great energy and vitality, but also great mental clarity—perhaps visual clarity as well. This Soul Movement practice will greatly benefit every aspect of your day and your life.

11

Healing

Soul Movement can heal. You may suffer from poor health, dis-ease, or dis-ease in your physical body, including pain, inflammation, tumors, cancer, AIDS, or communicable diseases. You may suffer from depression, anxiety, fear, anger, worry, grief, or guilt in your emotional body. You may have confusion or mind-sets that you cannot release in your mental body. You may have confusion or lack clear direction for your spiritual journey in your spiritual body. Soul Movement can be done for healing the physical, emotional, mental, and spiritual bodies. Here is the simple formula:

> *Dear soul, mind, body of my beloved body soul, system souls, organ souls, cell soul, cell unit souls, DNA, and RNA souls, I love you.*
> *Dear souls of my spiritual fathers and mothers on Mother Earth and in the spiritual world,*
> *Dear souls of all nature,*
> *Dear souls of the Divine, I love you all.*
> *I cannot honor you enough.*
> *Please guide me to do Soul Movement to give me total healing for my physical, emotional, mental, and spiritual bodies.*
> *I am very grateful.*

Thank you.

Dear Soul Song of "Love, Peace and Harmony," I love you.

Could you give me a total healing for my soul and for my physi-
cal, emotional, mental, and spiritual bodies?

I am so grateful.

Thank you.

Then, do Soul Movement for three to five minutes. If you suffer from a chronic or life-threatening condition, try to practice for fifteen to thirty minutes. This extended Soul Movement practice can offer great benefits for chronic and life-threatening conditions. Three minutes alone can offer great healing, but fifteen minutes can offer major healing that can make a big difference for your health. Always continue to sing the Soul Song "Love, Peace and Harmony" as you are doing the Soul Movement.

You can do Soul Movement for healing whether you are lying down, sitting up, standing, or walking. Total flexibility. No limitations. Whatever position you use, Soul Movement can offer you total healing of your soul, mind, and body.

Soul Movement works for healing because the soul has great power to heal. The essence of the teachings in my book *Soul Mind Body Medicine* is that *soul can heal.* We know mind can heal. Medicines can heal. Other remedies can heal. However, soul can heal and, in fact, soul is the most powerful healer. Everything has a soul. The brain, heart, lungs, shoulders, knees, back—each has a soul. If you have a health problem in those areas, you can ask and invoke those souls to heal themselves. When you give this a try, you will learn that they have great power. Add the "outer" souls of nature, your spiritual fathers and mothers, the Divine, Soul Song, and Soul Movement, and the power is multiplied many times.

One key to all soul healing, including soul healing with Soul Movement, is to show appreciation, love, and gratitude to the souls you are requesting help from. Always give love. Even if your back is hurting, even if you are suffering from excruciating pain in your back, always give love. Never express dissatisfaction, anger, upset, or frustration with your own back no matter how it feels. If you do not show appreciation and love, how can you expect your back to give you healing in return? The more love you give to your back, the more healing you will receive from it. That's why the basic formula includes "I love you" several times. Say that with total sincerity and total gratitude. Even if you have a serious or chronic condition, even if you've suffered from back pain for ten years or migraine headaches for twenty years, even if you have cancer, never be upset. Never fight with the souls of your sickness. Always give love to your sickness. Always give love to all souls. Love is absolutely the foundation of Soul Mind Body Medicine, of soul healing, and of Soul Movement. Love melts *any* blockage.

Soul Movement is such a simple healing treasure. You can do it anytime, anywhere. Soul Movement is your servant. It will offer healing service for your physical, emotional, mental, and spiritual bodies. Do it. Practice it. Enjoy it. Receive the benefits from it.

Thank you. Thank you. Thank you.

12

Rejuvenation

Several major antiaging conferences are held around the world. A number of research institutions are dedicated to studying the processes of aging, including the connections among aging, disease, genetic factors, nutrition, and lifestyle. Stem cell research and regenerative medicine are two very active areas of biomedical inquiry on aging.

I thank the many researchers, teachers, and practitioners for their great efforts and contributions to our understanding of aging and its counterpart, rejuvenation. However, what I offer is a unique way to do rejuvenation: soul rejuvenation. Soul power is, of course, the key to soul rejuvenation. The underlying principle of soul rejuvenation is:

> *Rejuvenate your soul first; then rejuvenation of your mind and body will follow.*

How can your beloved soul be rejuvenated? Your beloved soul has been with you for many lifetimes, but it *can* become younger and younger. Rejuvenate your body soul. You can also rejuvenate the souls of all your systems, organs, cells, cell units, even the souls of your DNA and RNA.

What is the secret? Say *hello*. Invoke the souls of your body, systems, organs, cells, cell units, DNA, and RNA. When you do, these souls will be very excited. They will tell you, "I am grateful. I am excited. You've never asked me to rejuvenate. I know I can do a lot for you there. I've been here waiting for you to ask me. Now, finally, you are asking me. I will do a good job."

Then, your beloved soul will start to vibrate, shine, and radiate light. This soul light will begin to remove the dark, gray and black spots and areas in your systems, organs, and cells. These dark areas represent energy blockages in your systems, organs, and cells. When they are removed by the soul light, your sicknesses will be removed. Your systems, organs, and cells will be rejuvenated. This is how soul rejuvenation works.

Rejuvenation from Any Soul

Everything has a soul. An ocean has a soul. A river has a soul. A swimming pool has a soul. When you swim, say, "Dear soul, mind, body of the water, would you give me nourishment while I am swimming?" The soul of the water will respond, "I am delighted to nourish you. I am delighted to rejuvenate you." If you're sitting on a beach, say *hello* to the ocean. If you're sitting at the foot of a mountain, say *hello* to the mountain. When you're walking through a forest, say *hello* to the forest: "Dear soul of the forest, souls of the trees, the leaves, the earth, could you give me nourishment? Could you give me healing? Could you give me rejuvenation?"

Expanding the wisdom, in fact you do not need to be near an ocean or a mountain. You do not need to be in a forest or a garden. You can be anywhere and invoke anything you want, at any time! At this moment, I am teaching a workshop in a conference room as I flow this book. All of my students are sitting here with me and listening to my flow. Practice together with us as you read this book.

Sit up straight.

Grasp your left thumb with your right palm and fingers.

Grip firmly, with about 80 percent of your maximum strength.

Place this "Yin/Yang Palm" in front of your lower

abdomen, close to but not touching your body or your
clothing.
Keep your back straight.
Tuck your chin in a bit.
Put the tip of the tongue as close as you can to the roof of
your mouth, without touching.
Contract your anus slightly.
Completely relax.

Except for your hands, your entire body is relaxed. The Yin/Yang
Palm combined with total relaxation is the secret to boosting your
energy quickly.

Now, repeat after me silently:

Dear my beloved body soul,
I love you.

Dear my beloved system souls,
I love you.

Dear all my beloved organ souls,
I love you.

Dear souls of my cells,
Dear souls of my cell units,
Dear souls of all my nuclei,
I love you.

Dear souls of all my DNA and RNA,
I love you.

Please guide my Soul Movement.

Dear souls of Mother Earth near us,
Dear souls of the water outside of my window,
I love you.

Dear souls of the trees near my home,
Dear souls of my garden,
I love you.

Dear soul of the sun,
Dear souls of the stars,
[It doesn't matter if it's overcast or clear, day or night,
    you can invoke the sun and the stars anytime.]
I love you.

Dear souls of the planets, galaxies, and universes,
I love you.

Dear spiritual fathers and mothers in all layers of Heaven,
I love you.

Dear soul of the Divine,
I love you.

Could you boost my energy,
Heal my physical, emotional, mental, and spiritual bodies and
    rejuvenate my soul, mind, body?

I am so grateful.

Dear soul of the Soul Song "Love, Peace and Harmony,"
I love you.

Could you give me a blessing to rejuvenate my soul, mind, and
    body?
I am extremely grateful.

Thank you. Thank you. Thank you.

Now sing the Soul Song as you start to move your arms.

After two or three minutes, stand up. Don't stand in a fixed position. Bend your knees and rotate your body as you are guided. Follow nature's way. Continue for two or three minutes.

Now start to walk around and continue your Soul Movement. Your movements could be broad and expansive. They could be more restrained and gentle. Follow nature's way. Follow the soul's way.

As a direct divine servant, vehicle, and channel, I have downloaded a Soul CD of this Soul Song to every soul in all universes. In particular, every cell of your body has this Soul CD. Let's invoke these Soul CDs.

> *Dear soul, mind, body of Divine Soul CD of "Love, Peace and Harmony" in all my cells with any blockages, I love you, honor you, appreciate you.*
>
> *Turn on, please, to remove the blockages.*
>
> *Dear soul, mind, body of Divine Soul CD of "Love, Peace and Harmony" in all my unbalanced systems, organs, and cells, I love you, honor you, appreciate you.*
>
> *Turn on, please, to bless me with divine healing.*
>
> *I am so grateful.*
>
> *Thank you. Thank you. Thank you.*

Continue to sing as you continue to move. It doesn't matter if your movements are grand or gentle. Alternate if you can between yang and yin. Soul Movement will enhance your cellular vibration, removing energetic and spiritual blockages. You will receive healing. You will receive rejuvenation.

The Soul CD is a golden divine soul. The moment you say *hello*, everything shines. Turn it on for every cell. You could receive amazing results. *Dear soul of every cell, every DNA and every RNA, sing with me. While I am sleeping tonight, please continue to sing.*

This is how to do Soul Movement (and to use your Soul CD) for rejuvenation. Connect with the souls, both inner and outer, as we did at the beginning of the practice. Let the souls guide you in Soul Movement for a few minutes as you sit, then for a few minutes as you stand, and finally for a few minutes as you walk. It will give you great benefits for healing of all imbalances and illnesses of the physical, emotional, mental, and spiritual bodies. It works by promoting *chi* flow and by using Soul Power. It rejuvenates by promoting *chi* flow and by giving your soul, your mind, your systems, your organs, and your cells the nourishment of soul light and soul liquid, and of universal light and universal liquid. When you connect with the souls of the universe, as well as with the souls of your spiritual fathers and mothers in Heaven, and when you communicate with these souls as well as with all of your inner souls (body, systems, organs, cells, DNA, RNA) at the same time, you will receive all kinds of soul nourishment from within your own body, from nature around you, and from the entire universe. First and foremost, you will receive rejuvenation for your soul.

Rejuvenate your soul first; then rejuvenation of your mind and body will follow.

With this short practice, you will feel comfortable, peaceful, and alert. You will feel great because your internal energy or *chi* will flow better. Your cells will be vibrating actively and be in balance.

Energy flow is the foundation of rejuvenation. This Soul Movement practice also gives you blessing from your own soul's light and liquid, from the soul light and soul liquid of nature, your spiritual fathers and mothers, and the Divine. Soul light is a yang blessing. Soul liquid is a yin blessing. Only by receiving both yin and yang blessings in harmonious balance can you receive the benefits of rejuvenation for your soul, mind, and body. You only need to practice. The more you practice, the more benefits you will receive. Great benefits will fly to you. I wish you will do a good job. Practice Soul Movement to receive more benefits.

Thank you. Thank you. Thank you.

13

Enlightenment

As I have taught in other books, soul enlightenment means that your soul's standing has reached a certain high level. There are nine layers of Heaven (Jiu Tian, which literally means "nine heavens"). Where your soul resides in your body reflects your soul's standing. If your beloved small golden being resides in your Message Center, or heart chakra, you have reached soul enlightenment. If your Third Eye or medical intuitive channel is open, you will be able to see your own or someone else's soul, the small golden light being. If this golden light being sits in the Message Center, you know that the person has reached soul enlightenment.

If you have not yet reached soul enlightenment, Soul Movement can help you get there. How? To do Soul Movement is to serve. To serve is to accumulate virtue. The more virtue you accumulate, the better it is for your soul. When you have accumulated enough virtue, the Akashic Records will uplift your soul to sit in your Message Center. You will become enlightened by a single divine order.

"Love, Peace and Harmony"

As you do Soul Movement, also sing the Soul Song "Love, Peace and Harmony" constantly. This Soul Song is a divine mantra and a divine code. It is a divine message of service. Let's look more closely at this Soul Song, the better to decode it.

The first line of the song is *I love my heart and soul.* This is service through love. You have to love your own heart and soul first; otherwise, how could you offer unconditional love to others? To love your heart and soul is to purify your heart and soul, to energize your heart and soul, and to transform the quality of your heart and soul. You are initiating the transformation, putting yourself in the process of enlightenment.

The second line of the song is *I love all humanity.* You are still offering love through your thoughts, as well as from your soul, by singing this song. Your voice will carry the frequency of love to others—to all humanity and to all souls in the universe. Simply to truly *feel* that you "love all humanity" is to offer service at the moment you are singing this line. This service will credit you with large amounts of virtue from the Akashic Records. As you accumulate more and more virtue, your soul will prepare to be uplifted. When you have gained sufficient virtue from service, your soul will be given a spiritual order from the Akashic Records. Your soul will move from its current residence, perhaps around your navel, to a higher location. Suddenly, your soul will sit in your Message Center. It is a spiritual "aha!" moment. It is a soul enlightenment moment.

The next line of the song, *Join hearts and souls together,* describes nothing less than the purpose of life. We are to serve, to join as one with the hearts and souls of others, to unite our own hearts and souls with every heart and soul, and to align all with universal consciousness and divine consciousness.

The Soul Song ends with *Love, peace and harmony.* This is the goal, the end result of our service. Offer love, peace, and harmony to ourselves, to our surroundings, to all humanity, all souls, and all universes. Create love, peace, and harmony for humanity, Mother Earth, and all souls.

Singing this Soul Song is a great service at the soul level. It is also a great service at the level of consciousness. That's why this Soul

Song is a vital part of Soul Movement practice. As you move and sing together, you are purifying, you are cleansing, and you are removing the dark and gray areas at the soul, mind, and body levels. When you sing this Soul Song as you do Soul Movement, you receive blessings from the souls of nature, from your spiritual fathers and mothers in Heaven, and from the Divine. You receive blessings from your own soul. All of these spiritual blessings will help you to energize, heal, and purify. They can help you prevent illness; rejuvenate; prolong life; transform your soul, mind, and body; and accumulate great amounts of virtue. Finally, you can reach that "aha!" moment of receiving soul enlightenment.

A Spiritual Calling

Soul Movement is a spiritual calling for humanity. It gives you and all humanity the simplest practice for energy and healing; for boosting your vitality and immunity; for becoming more youthful, beautiful, or handsome; and for enlightening your soul, mind, and body. The benefits you can receive are limitless.

Soul Movement will give you the greatest blessing for enlightenment of your soul, mind, and body. In fact, Soul Movement can offer this blessing to other souls. Those of you with open Third Eyes will be able to see clearly that when you do Soul Movement, there are many souls who come to dance and move with you. They join you because of the third line in the Soul Song: *Join hearts and souls together.* Through your Soul Movement and Soul Song, you are offering universal service. Countless souls are joining you. That's why this universal service will help bring love, peace, and harmony to humanity, to Mother Earth, and to all planets, stars, galaxies, and universes.

The more you do Soul Movement and chant "Love, Peace and Harmony," the more you give love to yourself, to humanity, and to all souls and the universe, the more love, peace, and harmony there will be—for yourself, your family, your organizations, your city, your country, Mother Earth, the planets, stars, galaxies, and universes, and even for Jiu Tian (the nine layers of Heaven) and Tian Wai Tian (the Heaven beyond the nine layers). Do a good job!

You can help enlighten the universe. What incredible potential for such a "simple" practice! Soul Movement is a spiritual gathering for all souls in Jiu Tian, Tian Wai Tian, and beyond. Soul Movement also gathers souls in Hell. There is no difference; light side, dark side—we are one family. Let us join hearts and souls together to create love, peace, and harmony for all. We *will* achieve this divine goal through our universal service. We are honored to be of service. We are honored to do Soul Movement.

Thank you. Thank you. Thank you.

14

Putting It All Together

In the previous four chapters, I described Soul Movement for energizing, for healing, for rejuvenation, and for enlightenment, respectively. In this chapter, I will reveal the secret of how to receive all of the major benefits of Soul Movement in one practice.

This practice can be done anytime, anywhere, and in any physical position—lying down, sitting, standing, or walking. Soul Movement is a practice for life—every day. Practice during a break at work. Practice when you feel a little tired at home. Three minutes of Soul Movement can give you healing benefits. In three minutes, you can boost your energy, stamina, vitality, and immunity. In three minutes, you can rejuvenate your soul, mind, and body. In three minutes, you can offer universal service to accumulate virtue and to advance yourself toward soul enlightenment.

Practice the Tao

In Chapter 9, I taught you an early-morning Soul Movement practice to do just after you wake up. The practice progressed from Soul Movement while lying down, to movement while sitting, to movement while standing, and ended with Soul Movement while walking. This progression fits natural law. From dawn to noon, the sun is rising and gaining intensity. Starting in yin, the day becomes more and more yang. Lying down, then sitting, standing, and walking mirrors the natural progression of the morning and the day. It follows nature's way.

The evening is yin time. The yin advances further and further. If you have trouble falling asleep or cannot sleep well, due to stress or other blockages at your soul, mind, or body level, Soul Movement is one of the best ways to enhance the quality of your sleep. Here is a specific Soul Movement practice for the evening, before you go to sleep.

Prepare for bed as you normally do, but then start to do Soul Movement in the walking position for three minutes. Follow that with three minutes of Soul Movement in the standing position, and then three minutes in the sitting position. Finally, lie down in bed and do three final minutes of Soul Movement.

This twelve-minute practice will move you from yang to yin, facilitating the transition of your soul, mind, and body from the stimulation of yang to the tranquility of yin. This, too, is natural law. This is the Tao (the Way, the method, the universal principle and law) for sleep. The combination of the evening practice before going to sleep with the morning practice upon walking follows the Tao. It follows the law of yin and yang.

There is a famous ancient statement: *tian ren he yi. Tian* means "Heaven." *Ren* means "human being." *He* means "join as." *Yi* means "one." *Heaven and human being join as one.* Because Heaven represents big nature and a human being represents small nature, this saying teaches us that big nature and small nature are one. What happens in big nature is what happens in small nature. To understand big nature, understand your small nature first. Once you understand the small nature of a human being, then you will understand the big nature of Heaven and the universe. Big nature and small nature must be harmonized. When you wake up, do Soul Movement from yin to yang to follow the law of big nature. Before you go to sleep, do Soul Movement from yang to yin to follow the law of big nature also. This is the practice of the Tao. This is the practice of *tian ren he yi.*

Universal Soul Movement

Now let me reveal the sacred and secret practice of Universal Soul Movement. You have learned all the wisdom in the preceding chapters of this book. Many of you may have also studied qi gong, tai chi, energy healing, and spiritual healing. Do you realize that all of the essence of these various practices and teachings is contained within the wisdom and practice of Soul Movement? Soul Movement is a great example of *soul over matter.* It is a very practical treasure of the application of soul over matter. The soul can heal, prevent illness, rejuvenate, prolong life, and transform any aspect of life, including relationships and business. This is soul over matter.

How can you do Soul Movement to improve your relationships? Do Soul Movement with your partner. Do Soul Movement with your colleagues at work. Even if you are home alone, you can call the souls of those with whom you want to improve your relationship and do Soul Movement with their souls. You will all receive the benefits of improved relationships.

Here's a secret for improving your business. Call the souls of all the people in your business. Call the souls of all the people associated with your business. Call all the organizations, cities, and countries that are connected with your business. Say to them, "Let's do Soul Movement together. Let's sing the Soul Song 'Love, Peace and Harmony' together." Your business will benefit. If you really understand the wisdom of the soul, you can do anything you want by working at the soul level. Apply Soul Power with your Soul Movement. Soul Power has no limitations; it is boundless. Soul Power can give you all kinds of benefits for any aspect of your life.

Finally, let me give you one "formula," one method for invoking Soul Movement to receive boundless benefits. Say *hello* as follows:

Dear all souls of my body, systems, organs, cells, cell units,
   DNA, and RNA

Dear all souls of my spiritual fathers and mothers in all layers
of Heaven
Dear all souls of my loved ones
Dear all souls of my colleagues
Dear all souls of my business team members and all my associates
Dear all souls of nature
Dear soul of the Tao
Dear soul of the Divine
I love you all.
I honor you all.
Please come join me to do Soul Movement together.
Dear soul, mind, body of the Soul Song "Love, Peace and Harmony"
I love you and honor you.
Dear every soul whom I have called
Let us sing this Soul Song together.
Let us do Soul Movement together.
Please energize, heal, rejuvenate, and enlighten me and every
soul here.

This is far greater service than energizing, healing, rejuvenating, and enlightening yourself. This is service for humanity. This is service for all souls in the universes. Then you could further request:

Please give me a total healing.
Give a total healing to others.
Give me a blessing for my relationships and business.
Give others blessings for relationships and business.
(Request anything you wish to receive.)

Then start to sing and move:

Lu La-a Lu La Li
Lu La-a Lu La La Li

Lu La-a Lu La-a Li Lu La
Lu La-a Li Lu La
Lu La-a Li Lu La

I love my heart and soul
I love all humanity
Join hearts and souls together
Love, peace and harmony
Love, peace and harmony

This is the method. Invoke all souls to join you. Sing the Soul Song "Love, Peace and Harmony" together to serve. To serve is to receive. To serve is to heal. To serve is to energize. To serve is to rejuvenate. To serve is to enlighten soul, mind, and body. Imagine if one hundred people were to do this. One hundred people and more would benefit. If one hundred thousand people were to do this, one hundred thousand people and more would benefit. If millions of people were to do this, millions upon millions of people would benefit. If all souls were to do this, the entire universe would benefit. Soul Movement is a divine calling and gathering. It is a universal calling and gathering to serve humanity during Mother Earth's transition period and beyond. It will offer great service to energize, heal, rejuvenate, and enlighten soul, mind, and body for humanity, Mother Earth, and all universes.

Soul Movement is a practical treasure built upon ancient wisdom and practice. We thank all the teachers of Buddhism, Taoism, Confucianism, tai chi, qi gong, I Ching, feng shui, and yoga. We thank gurus from India, all spiritual teachers, and all spiritual practices. We thank all the spiritual fathers and mothers in Heaven. We thank the Tao, the Way. We thank the Divine. We thank the millions of people who will practice Soul Movement to receive great benefits for their lives. We thank every soul of the universe. We thank the Soul Song, "Love, Peace and Harmony."

Lu La Lu La Li
Lu La Lu La La Li
Lu La Lu La Li Lu La
Lu La Li Lu La
Lu La Li Lu La

Wo ai wo xin he ling
Wo ai quan ren lei
Wan ling rong he mu shi sheng
Xiang ai, ping an, he xie
Xiang ai, ping an, he xie

I love my heart and soul
I love all humanity
Join hearts and souls together
Love, peace and harmony
Love, peace and harmony

Let every human being and every soul in the universe join hearts and souls together to create love, peace, and harmony in ourselves, our families, our organizations, our cities, our countries, Mother Earth, every planet, every star, every galaxy, every universe. From the Divine through Tian Wai Tian, Jiu Tian, and Hell, let us join the light side and the dark side. Let us join our hearts and souls together to create love, peace, and a harmonized and enlightened universe. Blessings from the Divine. Blessings from every soul.

Hao! Thank you. Thank you. Thank you.

PART 4

Soul Tapping

Advanced Soul Healing for Ages 8 to 108

Introduction

In the morning of August 3, 2006, I began to teach my first Soul Mind Body Medicine Retreat. My book *Soul Mind Body Medicine* had been published less than three months earlier. I suddenly received a divine inspiration: the divine wisdom, knowledge, and practice of Soul Tapping must be released to humanity! I spent the morning explaining the basic concepts of Soul Tapping and teaching all the participants how to do Soul Tapping.

After a simple lunch, I lay down for a moment. Immediately, the Divine told me, *Zhi Gang, write this book now. Create Soul Tapping Practitioners worldwide starting today.* In my decades-long spiritual journey, whenever I receive a divine calling and divine inspiration, it doesn't matter what my circumstances are. I am honored to follow Divine Guidance. I am honored to do what the Divine asks me to do. Then, I received the entire contents of this book in one brief transmission or "download" from the Divine. When I say the entire contents, I mean not just the words and the information, but also the wisdom, the practices, the blessings, the healing potential—everything that is part of this book. This came through purple light, which was the highest level, frequency, and vibration of divine light available at the time. The transmission, which remains with my soul permanently, is a direct connection to the soul, heart, and mind of the Divine. As such, this book is exactly what the Divine wants to tell humanity at this time. This book carries divine love, compassion, mercy, and forgiveness. It carries many messages from the Divine through the avenue of healing. For many of you, it may be the starting point for a deeper and more conscious soul or spiritual journey.

When I continued the workshop in the afternoon, I told the participants *I am going to flow this book today.* It has been an incredible divine honor to do this, because this book offers you the simplest divine wisdom, knowledge, and practice of divine healing, prevention of illness, rejuvenation, prolongation of life, and transformation in any and every aspect of your life.

The fundamental teaching of Soul Mind Body Medicine is that the *soul* can heal, prevent illness, rejuvenate, prolong life, and transform every aspect of life. Soul Mind Body Medicine also teaches the Four Power Techniques: Body Power, Sound Power, Mind Power, and Soul Power. Soul Power is the key. Unconditional love, forgiveness, compassion, and light are the essence of Soul Power. Love melts all blockages. Forgiveness brings peace. Compassion boosts power, vitality, and immunity. Light heals, blesses, prevents illness, rejuvenates, and prolongs life.

Soul Mind Body Medicine offers many practical treasures to humanity. I am grateful for the incredible worldwide response to this book. Now the Divine has asked me to deliver an even simpler technique, and another practical treasure to humanity: Soul Tapping.

Soul Tapping is soul-guided tapping for healing, preventing illness, rejuvenating, prolonging life, and transforming every aspect of life. You have a hand. I have a hand. Everybody has a hand. A hand can tap. But this is not ordinary tapping. This is soul-guided tapping. There are two levels of Soul Tapping. The first level is using your own soul to guide your hand to tap. The second level is using a Divine Download for Soul Tapping. During the lunch break at my retreat, the Divine told me, *Zhi Gang, offer my download to practitioners so that they can use my power to serve.* That is Divine Soul Tapping. Just learn first-level Soul Tapping first. If you decide you want to become a Divine Soul Tapping Master Healer, start by joining my Divine Soul Healer Training Program. Divine Soul Tapping Master Healer is actually the fourth level of this program, which will give you an idea of the extraordinary power and abilities a Divine Soul Tapping Master Healer carries. Start by trying first-level Soul Tapping. Experience its power. Move gradually to Divine Soul Tapping Master Healer later when you are ready.

My Mission

In 2006, the Divine also guided me to create the International Healing and Peace Movement. Since then I have committed to travel at least three weeks per month around North America and the world to teach healing, Soul Power, and universal service, which are the three empowerments of my total life mission, which is:

> *To transform the consciousness of humanity and all souls in the universe, in order to join all souls as one to create love, peace, and harmony for humanity, Mother Earth, and the universe.*

Mother Earth is in a major transition period. Climate changes from global warming; hurricanes; drought; floods; famine; diseases; volcanoes; tsunamis; earthquakes; economic stresses; religious conflicts; civil wars; nuclear threats; torture; trafficking in human beings, body parts, and animals; terrorism; extinction of species; and other problems are intensifying and proliferating. Mother Earth and all humanity are struggling with all of these problems and more, including emotional imbalances such as depression, anxiety, fear, and anger. How can we help humanity get through this difficult transition period? We have to offer divine treasures to humanity for self-healing, prevention of illness, rejuvenation, prolongation of life, and transformation of every aspect of life. We have to bring divine love, forgiveness, compassion, and light to humanity. We have to join our hearts and souls together to serve all humanity.

"Love, Peace and Harmony"

In September 2005, I went to the forest and seashore in Marin County, California. One of my Assistant Teachers asked, *Master Sha, can you ask for a song from the Divine?* I thought that was a great idea. I held out my hand, pointed at Heaven, and connected with the Divine. I said, *Dear Divine, could you download a song to me?* Divine purple light came shooting down, into and through me. The light flooded through my whole body. Then I opened my mouth. Soul Language flowed out, sung to a simple but beautiful melody:

> *Lu La Lu La Li*
> *Lu La Lu La La Li*
> *Lu La Lu La Li Lu La*
> *Lu La Li Lu La*
> *Lu La Li Lu La*

Because I am Chinese, I asked the Divine for the exact meaning of this Soul Language in Chinese. The translation came to me right away:

> *Wo ai wo xin he ling*
> *Wo ai quan ren lei*
> *Wan ling rong he mu shi sheng*
> *Xiang ai, ping an, he xie*
> *Xiang ai, ping an, he xie*

Then I said, *Dear Divine, translate this Soul Language into English:*

> *I love my heart and soul*
> *I love all humanity*
> *Join hearts and souls together*
> *Love, peace and harmony*
> *Love, peace and harmony*

The Soul Light Era began on August 8, 2003. This was the dawn of a new century and a new era for the entire universe. This era will last fifteen thousand years. The Soul Song I received is a song for the Soul Light Era. It is named "Love, Peace and Harmony." Read the lyrics to the song again. Its essence is love—only one word, *love*. Love melts any blockage. Love heals, prevents illness, rejuvenates, and prolongs life. Love transforms every aspect of life including relationships, business, and communities. Love transforms soul, heart, mind, and body. Love is the essence of the Soul Light Era.

On August 3, 2006, not even three years into the Soul Light Era, the Divine asked me to flow this teaching on Soul Tapping. As a medical doctor from China, a doctor of traditional Chinese medicine in China and Canada, a spiritual master, and, above all, a universal servant, I am so blessed to offer service to humanity through the divine wisdom of Soul Tapping. This teaching offers divine love, peace, and harmony. My Soul Song teaches you to offer love to your heart and soul, to offer love to all humanity. Join hearts and souls as one to create love, peace, and harmony. Soul Tapping is a universal servant that will offer love, peace, and harmony to you and to all humanity. I wish that Soul Tapping will serve you, your loved ones, all humanity on Mother Earth, and all souls in all universes well. It is my great honor to be a universal servant. It is my great honor to offer Soul Tapping, an unconditional universal servant to serve you forever.

Love, Peace and Harmony

Love, Peace and Harmony

15

What Is Soul Tapping?

Everyone knows how to tap. You can tap your fingers. You can tap your feet. With your fingers, you can tap your desk. You can tap your leg. You can tap your heart. When you feel pain or stiffness in some part of your body, you may spontaneously do a little bit of tapping there. It will help release a bit of the pain. But you probably don't realize the potential power of tapping. You probably don't know that tapping is a huge, advanced soul healing treasure for self-healing and for healing others. Soul Tapping can heal, prevent illness, rejuvenate, and prolong life. Soul Tapping can transform any aspect of life.

Ordinary tapping is guided by your mind. *Okay, I have some pain in my shoulder, let me tap a little there.* Or, *my knee hurts, let me tap it a bit.* Soul Tapping is different and unique. **Soul Tapping is soul-guided tapping.** If you have knee pain and you do Soul Tapping, your fingers may not go to your knee. Your fingers may go to your abdomen and start tapping there. Why? Because in Soul Tapping, your fingers will go to the area where the root energy blockage is located. In the case of your knee pain, yes, pain in the knee indicates an energy blockage there, but the root blockage or source blockage could be in your abdomen.

You have pain in the knee. You want and ask for healing of your knee pain. But because Soul Tapping is soul-guided, your fingers may not go to your knee. They will go to the exact area of the root blockage, which may be in your abdomen. This may feel or seem strange to you at first. *I asked for healing for my knee. Why are my fingers tapping my abdomen?* The answer is simple. *Your soul guided your fingers* to go to the area where they should go and need to go to give you healing. This is the unique characteristic of Soul Tapping. To summarize, the secret of Soul Tapping is that the soul guides and directs the tapping to the area of the root energy blockage in order to remove that blockage. If the root blockage is removed, you will recover five times, ten times, even twenty times faster than if you had tapped the painful area directly.

Expanding the wisdom, Soul Tapping can be used for all kinds of sickness, including all pains, all inflammations, all cysts, all tumors, and all cancers in the physical body. It can also be used for emotional imbalances, including depression, anxiety, anger, sadness, fear and worry. It can be used for mental conditions, from lack of clarity and concentration to confusion and serious mental disorders. Finally, it can be used for some spiritual blockages. Specifically, when you offer Soul Tapping for an organ, bodily system, or part of the body, the spiritual blockages for that organ, system, or part of the body can be removed on the spot. However, Soul Tapping doesn't give you the ability to clear all the spiritual blockages that are caused by bad karma. The ability to perform this kind of total karma cleansing requires a special divine order. Very few people on Mother Earth have received this divine order to offer karma cleansing for all of one's lifetimes.

Nevertheless, Soul Tapping can definitely clear some spiritual blockages to create heart-touching stories. It can serve you, your loved ones, and humanity with great results.

Significance of Soul Tapping

Soul Tapping has many significant capabilities and benefits. They are beyond our imagination and are almost limitless.

SOUL TAPPING IS ADVANCED SOUL HEALING

Soul Tapping is a direct divine self-healing treasure for self-healing, healing others, group healing, and remote healing. Through Soul Tapping, you can offer healing to yourself, to another person, to thousands of people, even to millions. There is no difference. Soul Tapping is soul healing. Soul healing is quantum healing, which is not limited by space or time.

SOUL TAPPING CAN PREVENT SICKNESS

The five-thousand-year-old canonical text of traditional Chinese medicine, *The Yellow Emperor's Classic of Internal Medicine,* or *Huang Di Nei Jing,* states: "The best doctor is not one who treats sickness, but one who teaches people how to prevent sickness."

If we can prevent sickness, why would we have to wait until we get sick to be healed? It is very important for us to learn how to offer prevention. Soul Tapping is a great method for prevention. Soul Tapping is soul prevention.

SOUL TAPPING CAN REJUVENATE

Many doctors, scientists, and others specialize in research and practice for rejuvenation. They study and use vitamins and minerals, herbs, diet, exercise, hormone therapy, along with time-honored practices such as tai chi, qi gong, yoga, meditation, chanting, and various energy practices. They hold major antiaging conferences worldwide. Soul Tapping can rejuvenate. Soul Tapping offers unique soul rejuvenation.

SOUL TAPPING CAN PROLONG LIFE

How can Soul Tapping prolong life? Soul Tapping can rejuvenate the soul.

Rejuvenate the soul first; then rejuvenation of the mind and body will follow.

SOUL TAPPING CAN TRANSFORM EVERY ASPECT OF LIFE

How do you transform a relationship? If a couple, whether husband and wife or lovers, has a conflict, call their souls to come before you. Use Soul Tapping to tap their souls. Give them love. Give them care and compassion. Offer forgiveness. Their souls will be loved, cared for, and moved. They will offer forgiveness to each other. When their souls are transformed, their relationship will instantly be transformed as well.

How do you transform a business by Soul Tapping? Call the soul of business to come before you. Use Soul Tapping to tap the soul of the business. If you have advanced spiritual abilities, you are able to see the soul of the business. A healthy soul is a golden light being. If the soul of the business appears small, gray, and dark, you are guaranteed that it is not a good, successful business. If the soul of the business is huge, shining, golden, rainbow-colored, or purple, you don't need to know any thing more. You are guaranteed that the business is successful.

This is an example of a true soul reading. When you see a business with a small, gray, dark soul, use Soul Tapping. Remove the dark and gray areas. That business will be transformed. Why does it work?

Transform the soul first; then transformation of the mind and body will follow.

This is advanced soul wisdom. Transform the soul first, then every part of your life will be transformed. A business has a soul. If the soul of the business is transformed, the mind and the body of the business will follow.

Remember this technique. It is very simple. It may be too simple to believe. But remember further that the simplest wisdom is the best wisdom. This is the twenty-first century. This is the Soul Light Era. Throw out the old ways of thinking. Eliminate mind-sets, attitudes, and beliefs that no longer serve you. Open your heart and soul to learn the simplest wisdom. There is a famous ancient saying: *If you want to know whether an apple or pear is sweet, you have to taste it.* If you want to know whether Soul Tapping works, you have to experience it. Fully open your consciousness, your heart, and your soul to experience Soul Tapping wisdom, knowledge, and practice. Apply Soul Tapping wisdom, knowledge, practice, and techniques to heal yourself and others, to group heal and remote heal, to prevent illness, rejuvenate, prolong life, and transform every aspect of your life. You could experience an "aha!" moment. You could say *Wow, aha!, why didn't I know this before?* Many "aha!" moments, many inspirations, many surprises could appear in seconds in front of your eyes. My wish is that you receive maximum benefits from Soul Tapping wisdom, knowledge, and practice.

16

Key Areas for Soul Tapping

S oul Tapping can be done anywhere on one's body, but there are several areas with special significance.

Soul Tapping of the Hand

Practitioners of traditional Chinese medicine and others know that the hand represents the entire body. The palm side (bottom side or front side) of the hand represents the front side of the body from head to toe, including internal organs. The other side (top side or back side) of the hand represents the back side of the body from the back of the head to the back of the heels. Consequently, the hand is a very important place to do Soul Tapping. For example, if you have pain in your back, neck, or behind a knee, use your right fingers to tap the back of your left hand. Soul Tapping your hand is powerfully effective.

Here's how to do Soul Tapping of your hand if you have lower back pain. Hold your left hand in front of you, with the back of the hand facing you. Hold your right hand in front of you in the prayer position. Then say: *Dear soul, mind, body of my hands, please do Soul Tapping following the guidance of my soul. Dear my soul, could you guide my right hand to do Soul Tapping of my left hand? I am very grateful.* Then let the fingers of your right hand tap the top side of your left hand. Continue to tap for a few minutes. As you do this soul-guided tapping, say: *Perfect lower back, perfect lower back. Love, heal, thank you. Love, heal, thank you. Love, heal, thank you. Love, heal, thank you. Perfect back, perfect back, perfect back, perfect back. Love, heal, thank you. Love, heal, thank you. Perfect back, perfect back, perfect back.*

To end this practice, say *hao* (pronounced "how") three times. *Hao* is Chinese and means "perfect," "get well," "fantastic." It is an affirmation *and* a command. Then say *Thank you. Thank you. Thank you.* The first "thank you" is for the Divine. The second "thank you" is for all the spiritual fathers and mothers, all the spiritual beings in Heaven. The third "thank you" is for your own soul, mind, and body.

Ancient wisdom about the hands and the body is great and deep. For example, the middle finger represents the neck. Because the hand represents the entire body, there is hand acupuncture and hand massage. There are numerous reflexology points that connect with specific parts of the body. This is all great wisdom. For Soul Tapping, however, we do not need to know any of this wisdom. We do not use this wisdom at all. Just follow the method in the example above and let your soul direct the tapping. The basic steps are as follows:

1. Prepare: Put your left hand in front of you. Put your right hand in front of you in the prayer position.

2. Say Hello: Silently say: *Dear soul, mind, body of my right hand, I love you, honor you, appreciate you. Can you do Soul Tapping of my left hand to offer a healing to my organs and systems?* You could ask specifically: *Please offer a healing to my heart. Please offer a healing to my liver.* Simply make your request for any system, any organ, any part of the body, any cells, cell units, DNA, and RNA.

3. Apply Soul Power: Say: *Dear my soul, I love you, honor you, appreciate you. Please guide my right hand to do Soul Tapping of my left hand to serve my request.*

4. Tap: Let your tapping fingers (the fingers of your right hand) go where they may. Sometimes they will go to the fingertips of your left hand. After a few seconds, they may move to the palm of your left hand, to the thumb, to the baby finger. The only principle you have to remember is that if you have a problem on the back side, tap the back of your left hand. If you have a problem on the front side, tap the palm of your left hand.

No expectations, no thinking, no "square," no limitations! This is soul-guided tapping. Wherever your fingers go, just let them go. You have to follow your soul! *The soul is the boss.* If, for example, you asked for healing for your stomach, say *perfect stomach* or *heal my stomach* while you are tapping. Just continue to say *perfect stomach, love my stomach, love, heal, thank you. I love my stomach. Perfect stomach, perfect stomach, perfect stomach.* Tap for three to five minutes.

5. Close: Say *Hao. Hao. Hao. Thank you. Thank you. Thank you.*

As long as you can raise your hands, you can do Soul Tapping of your hand to offer healing for any area or part of the body. Even very sick people who can only lie in bed can do Soul Tapping in this way to serve themselves and others. If you practice Soul Tapping while you are lying down, remember to say everything silently to conserve your energy.

Soul Tapping of the Ear

The ear is another part of the body that represents the entire body. Just as with the hands, there is ear acupuncture and ear massage. Through Soul Tapping of the ear, you can offer all kinds of healing. You do not need to know which part of the ear represents which part of the body. The soul knows which part of the ear should be touched.

Let's start. Put your hands beside your ears. Say: *Dear soul, mind, body of my hands, I love you, honor you, appreciate you. Please do Soul Tapping to my ears following the guidance of my soul. Dear my soul, could you guide my fingertips to tap my ears to give me a healing?* You can request any healing—for pain, inflammation, a tumor, cancer, degenerative changes—anything.

For example, if you have arthritis in the knees, as you do Soul Tapping you can say silently: *Perfect knees, perfect knees, perfect knees, perfect knees. Love, heal, thank you. Perfect knees, perfect knees, heal my knees, heal my knees, perfect knees. Love, heal, thank you.*

If you have breast cancer, say *Heal my breast, heal my breast, heal my breast, heal my breast, perfect breast, perfect breast, perfect breast, perfect breast.* Cancer can connect with many different parts of the body, many systems, and many organs. The ear represents the entire body, including all of its systems, organs, and cells. Soul Tapping of the ear will guide you to touch exactly those parts of the ear that represent the various systems, organs, and areas of the body related to your cancer. This is soul healing, which is healing of souls and also healing by souls. All the healing is guided by souls. All the healing is happening first in the soul realm. Then, healing of the mind and body will follow.

As your Soul Tapping stimulates different parts of the ears, energy will flow in the corresponding parts of your body to remove the energy and spiritual blockages related to your illness. Your health can be restored quickly.

Hao. Hao. Hao. Thank you. Thank you. Thank you. Do not forget to say *thank you* after you offer Soul Tapping service. At the end of your healing, sincerely offer your thanks three times. The first "thank you" is for the Divine, the Creator and Source. The second "thank you" is for all the spiritual fathers and mothers, all the divine beings in all layers of Heaven. The third "thank you" is for your own soul, mind, and body, including your ears and your hands.

Soul Tapping of the Foot

Put one foot on the opposite knee. If you have an illness in the front part of your body, tap the bottom of your foot. If you have a problem in the back side of your body, tap the top of your foot. Again, you do not need to know more about which part of the body is represented by which part of the foot.

For example, if you have a heart problem, say: *Dear soul, mind, body of my hand, please offer Soul Tapping to the sole of my foot to offer healing to my heart. Dear my beloved soul, can you guide my fingertips to do Soul Tapping to the sole of my foot to offer healing to my heart?* Then, start tapping. At same time, chant *perfect heart, perfect heart, perfect heart, perfect heart.* Why do you say this? Because it is a direct soul command. Say *Perfect heart, love, heal, thank you. Love, heal, thank you.* Love melts all blockages. If you offer love, healing will occur. If healing occurs, give appreciation to the soul, mind, and body. *Love, heal, thank you* is love and appreciation — a command and a mantra — that can be offered for any sickness.

You can request healing for any organ, any system. *Please heal my liver. Perfect liver, perfect liver, perfect liver, perfect liver; love, heal, thank you, love heal, thank you, love, heal, thank you, love, heal, thank you.* Tap for a few minutes. *Please heal my brain. Perfect brain . . . Love, heal, thank you . . . Please heal my stomach. Perfect stomach . . . Love, heal, thank you . . . Please heal my uterus. Perfect uterus . . . Love, heal, thank you . . .* Just remember two phrases: (1) *perfect organ* and (2) *love, heal, thank you.*

Now let me give you a very secret and sacred teaching. *Dear soul, mind, body of all ten of my fingers, please do a Soul Tapping of the soles of my feet to offer a total healing for my soul, mind, and body.* It doesn't matter which organs, joints, or cells are sick. It doesn't matter whether you have a physical, emotional, mental, or spiritual illness, blockage, or imbalance. Simply ask for a total healing of your soul, mind, and body. When you do this, any part of your body that is sick will automatically open by itself. Just tap! You do not need to think. Say *love, heal, thank you* over and over, or *soul light* over and over, or *God's light* over and over. *Hao! Hao! Hao! Thank you. Thank you. Thank you.*

Soul Tapping of the Body

You can do Soul Tapping directly to your body. You can do Soul Tapping to the entire front side of your body and to any part of the back side of your body that you can touch. For example, if you have a stomachache or digestive problems, put your hands in front of you and say *hello* to make a soul connection: *Dear soul, mind, body of my fingers, I love you, honor you, appreciate you. Please do Soul Tapping to my abdomen according to my soul's guidance.* Then say: *Dear my beloved soul, could you guide my fingers to do Soul Tapping to heal my digestive system? I am very grateful. Perfect digestive system, perfect digestive system, perfect digestive system, perfect digestive system . . .* Continue to tap for a few minutes.

Here is an example for healing the immune system. *Dear soul, mind, body of my fingertips, please boost my immune system by tapping my body following my soul's guidance. Dear my beloved soul, please guide my fingertips to do Soul Tapping on any part of my body to boost my immunity. I am grateful. Perfect immune system, perfect immune system, perfect immune system, perfect immune system . . .* You do not know where you are going to tap. Just let your hands go freely. It doesn't matter whether you tap your legs, arms, or body. The immune system connects everywhere.

You can do this after a meal—stand up, walk around, say *Please boost my immune system,* and tap. You can do this even if you have a strong immune system and your *chi* flows well throughout your body. If your *chi* is blocked anywhere, this Soul Tapping will awaken your immune system. Your immunity will be strengthened wherever you do the tapping. You could also jog slowly at the same time. *Perfect immune system, perfect immune system, perfect immune system, perfect immune system . . .*

MANAGING YOUR WEIGHT WITH SOUL TAPPING

Soul Tapping offers a simple, practical, and powerful technique for losing weight. Here's how to do it:

Dear soul, mind, body of my fingers, I love you and honor you. Could you do Soul Tapping for losing weight according to my soul's guidance? Dear my beloved soul, I love you and honor you. Please guide my fingertips to do Soul

Tapping to my body to adjust my endocrine system, digestive system, cardiovascular system, immune system, nervous system, metabolic system, and metabolism—all systems, all organs. Thank you. Thank you. Thank you. Lose weight, lose weight, lose weight. If you have too much fat in particular areas—abdomen, buttocks—tap that area. *Lose weight, lose weight, lose weigh, lose weight. Burn fat, burn fat, burn fat, burn fat. Lose weight, lose weight, lose weight, lose weight. Burn fat, burn fat, burn fat, burn fat. Fire, fire, fire, fire . . . Lose weight, lose weight, lose weight, lose weight. Fire, fire, fire, fire.* Do this Soul Tapping practice fifteen to thirty minutes twice a day. You will hardly believe the results. Add a little bit of jogging to the mix.

If you need to *gain* weight, use the mantra *gain weight.* If you are neither overweight nor underweight, use the mantra *perfect weight.* The key wisdom is that *gain weight, lose weight,* and *perfect weight* are spiritual commands, soul commands, or soul orders. When you give a soul order, the mind and body listen. This is a very advanced piece of soul wisdom, knowledge, and practice that I am releasing for the first time. It is a total secret for doing soul healing, including prevention of illness, rejuvenation, prolonging life, and transforming every aspect of life. You do not need anything one bit more complicated. Just directly say what you want. *Gain weight. Lose weight. Perfect weight. Perfect heart. Perfect liver. Perfect immune system. Perfect endocrine system. Rejuvenation. Younger. Beauty. Handsome. Attractive.* Any of these can be used as a Soul Tapping mantra. Come to the point. Whatever you want, just ask. This is the simplest, most direct, and most powerful soul healing treasure for humanity. Give a soul command. Things will happen. Your mind and body will respond. This is a soul order. This is soul health. This is soul healing. This is soul prevention. This is soul rejuvenation. This is soul prolongation of life. This is soul transformation for relationships. This is soul transformation for business. This is soul transformation for any aspect of life.

17

Healing Emotional, Mental, and Spiritual Imbalances and Blockages

In the last chapter, you learned a few important areas of the body for doing Soul Tapping. Ultimately, there is no standard and no limitation in Soul Tapping. You can tap any part of the body. Even though the hand represents the body, the ear represents the body, and the foot represents the body, you are not limited to these areas.

For example, you can tap your inner forearm. You can say: *Dear my right fingers, please do Soul Tapping to heal my heart, to heal my liver, to heal my kidneys.* Then, tap your left forearm. *Heal my heart, heal my liver, heal my kidneys. Heal my heart, heal my liver, heal my kidneys. Heal my heart, heal my liver, heal my kidneys.* Areas of your forearm also represent your heart, your liver, and your kidneys. In fact, any part of the body, any inch of the body can represent the whole body. Expanding the wisdom, every inch and every cell can represent the entire body. This is twenty-first-century medicine, twenty-first-century healing, twenty-first-century health.

Any part of the body can represent any other part of the body. Tap your thigh and say *Heal my heart, perfect heart* . . . Tap your shoulder and say *Heal my liver, perfect liver* . . . Tap your head and say *Heal my toes, perfect toes* . . . It works!

Now, let's examine in turn Soul Tapping for healing of the emotional body, mental body, and spiritual body.

Healing the Emotional Body

In traditional Chinese medicine, the liver connects with the emotion of anger. The heart connects with anxiety and depression. The spleen connects with worry. The lungs connect with grief and sadness, and the kidneys connect with fear. If you are angry, tap your liver and say *Perfect liver, perfect liver, perfect liver . . . love, heal, thank you . . .* You are offering a healing for your anger.

Organs are the physical body. Emotions are the emotional body. They are interconnected. But what if you don't know how they are connected? How can you heal your anger? Even if you do not know that the liver connects with anger, you can still use Soul Tapping to heal your anger. For example, you can tap your thigh. Whatever area you are tapping can also represent emotions. Say *Heal my anger, heal my anger, love, heal, thank you.* This soul command will automatically connect with your liver. You will receive healing for your anger even without knowing that your anger is connected with your liver.

The wisdom is that any area of the physical body that you are tapping can represent any emotion in the emotional body. I have known this for a long time, but I could not release this wisdom before the appropriate time. Now, I offer this deep healing secret to you. Now I can tell you that the knee, for example, can represent any system, any organ, any cell, any DNA and RNA, and any emotion. Furthermore, it can represent any spiritual center. It can represent Mother Earth. It can represent entire universes.

In summary, you can do Soul Tapping of the liver to remove anger, Soul Tapping of the heart to remove depression and anxiety, Soul Tapping of the spleen to remove worry, Soul Tapping of the lungs to remove grief and sadness, and Soul Tapping of the kidneys to remove fear. But in fact you can do Soul Tapping of any part of the body to remove any emotional imbalance.

How does it work? If you tap your knee and say *heal my anger,* soul light will flow right away from the area you are tapping to your liver. Because you have given the soul command *heal my anger,* this light will radiate to the liver, helping to clear energy and spiritual blockages in the liver. Say *heal my grief* and light will flow to and through your lungs. Say *heal my depression* and right away the heart chakra or Message Center will resonate with light. Say *heal my fear* and the kidneys will resonate.

Healing the Mental Body

You understand that the brain causes mental blockages. You may not understand that any system, any organ, any cell could cause mental blockages. To heal the mind is to heal the brain and its functions. But, expanding the wisdom, to heal the mind is to heal the consciousness of every system, every organ, every cell, every cell unit, and every DNA and RNA. To heal mental blockages and disorders, use Soul Tapping in this way:

Dear soul, mind, body of my fingers, please do Soul Tapping following my soul's guidance. Dear my beloved soul, please guide my fingers to do Soul Tapping to heal my mental disorder or to heal my mental blockages. I'm very grateful. Then gently tap—soul tap—your Message Center. Say *Heal mental disorders* (be specific if you can with the name of the disorder), *heal mental disorders, heal mental blockages, heal mental blockages.*

In fact, as discussed above for healing the emotional body, you can do Soul Tapping to any part of the body to heal the mental body.

Healing the Spiritual Body

To remove spiritual blockages is to clear the record of your spiritual journey through your previous lives and this life. The record of your service in all your lifetimes is your accumulated virtue, karma, deed, or, in Chinese, *te* (pronounced "duh"). These terms are used by different cultures and different belief systems, but they have the same meaning: the record of service. There are two kinds of service. Good service includes love, care, compassion, forgiveness, kindness, purity, generosity, integrity, and so on. Unpleasant service includes killing, harming, taking advantage of others, stealing, cheating, power struggles, and so on. If one offers good service, the Akashic Records note that by colored dots and colorful small and large flowers in your Akashic book and upon your soul. These dots and flowers are red, golden, rainbow-colored, and purple. Unpleasant service is recorded by dots, small flowers and large flowers that are dark, gray, and black.

For the mistakes (bad virtue, bad karma, bad deeds, or bad *te*) you made in previous lives, you received dark gray and black dots, small flowers, and big flowers. To clear karma is to remove these dark gray and black dots, small flowers, and big flowers. How can you remove these dark parts of the records? There is only one way: offer universal service to humanity and souls in the universe. When you serve well, you receive red, golden, rainbow-colored, and purple dots and flowers. These good dots and flowers can erase the dark dots and flowers.

To offer good service is to clear your bad records. Many people do volunteer work or donate time or money to do good service for humanity, animals, the environment, or world peace. All of these good services are great ways to remove your karma. I would like to share a secret and sacred way to clear your karma, which will transform your life. Simply chant the Soul Song "Love, Peace and Harmony."

> *Lu La Lu La Li*
> *Lu La Lu La La Li*
> *Lu La Lu La Li Lu La*
> *Lu La Li Lu La*
> *Lu La Li Lu La*
>
> *I love my heart and soul*
> *I love all humanity*
> *Join hearts and souls together*
> *Love, peace and harmony*
> *Love, peace and harmony*

Sing this song repeatedly, silently or aloud, as you would chant a mantra. Sing it for five minutes, fifteen minutes, thirty minutes, or more. This song *is* a mantra. To sing it is to give its message to humanity. To sing it is to give its message to all souls. To give its message is to transform the consciousness of minds and the consciousness of souls. When you sing this song sincerely, you are going into the condition of love, peace, and harmony. You *are* love. You *are* peace. You *are* harmony. In this condition, you are offering great spiritual service for humanity and souls in the universe. It is one of the greatest services you can perform. You will gain many red, golden, rainbow, and purple flowers. Through this service, your dark dots and flowers will be removed. This is the secret, sacred method. It is one of the fastest ways to clear your own karma: chant "Love, Peace and Harmony."

Consider the English translation:

> *I love my heart and soul*
> *I love all humanity*
> *Join hearts and souls together*
> *Love, peace and harmony*
> *Love, peace and harmony*

Imagine if everyone were to sing this song from their hearts. If everyone were to know love, experience love, share love, spread love, and apply love in our consciousness, in our thoughts, in our activities, and in our behaviors, then love, peace, and harmony would truly be a reality.

KARMA

Bad karma is the root blockage of life. Bad karma can block your health, your relationships, and your business. It also blocks your capacity for love, inner joy, and inner peace. It blocks harmony between companies, between religions, and between countries. If everyone were to chant "Love, Peace and Harmony" and apply love, peace, and harmony, they would not have conflicts. The barriers between religions and between nations would crumble. Everyone would have inner peace and inner joy. In this condition, soul, mind, and body will be balanced. Organizations will be balanced. Cities will be balanced. Countries will be balanced. Mother Earth will be balanced. The planets will be balanced. The stars will be balanced. The galaxies will be balanced. All universes will be balanced. The Soul Song "Love, Peace and Harmony" is a divine mantra for the twenty-first century for the entire Soul Light Era, the fifteen-thousand-year era that began on August 8, 2003.

To chant this song is to serve. To serve is to accumulate good virtue recorded as red, golden, rainbow, and purple flowers. These flowers will erase the dark gray and black dots and flowers in your Akashic Records. Your soul, mind, and body will be purified. Your thinking will totally transform. You will see the world with different eyes. You will be much more loving and much more loved. You will be able to forgive. You will have incredible tolerance, even for the people and things that bothered you the most before. You will be a good example of a pure servant.

Life is about service. The purpose of life is to serve. The purpose of your physical life is to serve your spiritual life. Physical life is limited; spiritual life is eternal. We are here on Mother Earth, a place of "red dust," to learn lessons in order to purify our souls, minds, and bodies. We learn lessons, repay our karmic debts, and purify further and further to advance on our spiritual journey by uplifting our soul's standing. To be a human being is to continue to purify your soul, mind, and body, especially your soul. On the spiritual journey, your soul wants to be enlightened. Your soul wants to have its standing uplifted. Lifetime after lifetime we struggle to accomplish this.

In the spiritual world, there is Jiu Tian, the nine layers of Heaven. There is Tian Wai Tian, the Heaven beyond Heaven. Tian Wai Tian has countless layers. At the top of Tian Wai Tian sits the Divine. A spiritual being strives to move onward and upward by climbing

Heaven's staircase. It takes great effort. The only way to do it is to offer unconditional universal service. There is no second choice, no second way to climb Heaven's stairs. While I was teaching a soul retreat in 2003, I received direct teaching from the Divine. I was taught a universal law, a law that applies to all physical life on Mother Earth and to all spiritual life for the entire Soul World. This Universal Law of Universal Service states:

> *I am a universal servant.*
> *You are a universal servant.*
> *Everyone and everything is a universal servant.*
> *A universal servant offers universal service including universal love, forgiveness, peace, healing, blessing, harmony, and enlightenment.*
> *Offer little universal service, receive little blessing from the universe.*
> *Offer more universal service, receive more blessing from the universe.*
> *Offer unconditional universal service, receive unlimited blessing from the universe.*

Some people offer unpleasant service, such as killing, harming, taking advantage of others, stealing, cheating, and more. If one offers a little unpleasant service, one will learn a little lesson. If one offers more unpleasant service, one will learn more lessons. If one offers huge unpleasant service, one will learn huge lessons. These lessons include poor health, broken relationships, business failures, emotional struggles, and more. Every aspect of life could be a struggle.

I met a doctor who has suffered from brain cancer three times, first when he was three years old, again in his twenties, and now in his forties. When he met me recently, he said, "Master Sha, I have been trying to figure why I've suffered from brain cancer three times. I've concluded that it is a spiritual issue, karma issues. Is this correct?" I responded, "Yes, I think so," because I saw the blockages. I saw the bad deeds that he did in his previous lives. In my book *Soul Mind Body Medicine*, I taught that bad karma or spiritual blockage is a major root blockage underlying sickness and all blockages in life, including relationships and business. To clear bad karma, one must offer unconditional universal service. "Unconditional" means that you offer service *without expectations*. You simply give pure love, pure service. Do not misunderstand me. Everyone has to make a living in our physical world. Your normal fee for your normal service is totally correct. By unconditional universal service, I mean that you do not have extra expectations when you serve others. Serve to make others healthier and happier. Serve to transform other people's lives. Serve to bring joy and inner peace. Serve to unite all humanity to create love, peace, and harmony for Mother Earth. Serve to join all souls together to create love, peace, and harmony in the universe. Let us all join hands together as human beings. Let us join our hearts together with all souls to create a loving, peaceful, and harmonized Mother Earth and universe. Divine, bless all of us. Universe, bless all of us.

Thank you. Thank you. Thank you.

18

Group Healing and Remote Healing

Soul Tapping is quantum healing. It is not limited by numbers, distance, or time. Let me explain how you can use Soul Tapping to heal ten, a hundred, ten thousand people; to heal remotely; and to heal past lives and future lives.

Group Healing

A human being has a soul. A system has a soul. An organ has a soul. A cell has a soul. A cell unit, such as the nucleus, has a soul. DNA and RNA have souls. An animal has a soul. A tree has a soul. An ocean has a soul. A mountain has a soul. Everyone and everything has a soul. To do Soul Tapping for group healing, the secret is to call the souls of those to whom you want to offer healing to come before you. Then, connect with your hands:

> *Dear soul of my fingers, I love you, honor you, and appreciate you.*
> *Can you offer Soul Tapping for group healing according to my soul's guidance?*

Next connect with your own soul:

Dear my beloved soul, could you guide me to do Soul Tapping to offer a group healing? I'm very grateful.

Then start your Soul Tapping, while chanting silently at the same time:

Love, heal all of you.
Love, heal all of you.
Love, heal all of you.

You can serve thousands of people at the same time in this way. Start by simply calling their souls to come together in front of your chest. Then follow exactly the same procedure. You can ask each person to make one specific request or ten specific requests for healing. The requests could be for healing of the physical body, emotional body, mental body, or spiritual body. After the group has made their requests, call the souls of all the systems, organs, and joints for which a request has been made to come in front of your chest. Then do Soul Tapping for all the souls, chanting silently:

Love, heal all of you.
Love, heal all of you.
Love, heal all of you.

Do not forget to say *thank you* after you offer service. At the end of your healing, sincerely offer your thanks three times.

Healing a group of thousands in this way takes only two or three minutes. The results can be beyond your comprehension. This is a top spiritual secret. It may be very hard to believe, very hard to accept by many people, perhaps by you. But I am very confident. I am totally honored to give this top secret to humanity. May you open your heart and soul to learn, apply, and benefit from this healing secret.

Remote Healing

Soul Tapping, like Soul Mind Body Medicine and Body Space Medicine, is quantum medicine. Soul Tapping can offer healing without regard to or limitation by time and space. You can offer healing by Soul Tapping anytime, anywhere—to anyone. You can offer healing for one's past lives, present life, and future lives. The large majority of healers on Mother Earth know how to heal one's present life. How can you heal someone's previous lives? How can you heal someone's future lives? You must have enough spiritual wisdom. You must truly and deeply understand that there is no time, no space. You must understand that past, present, and future are one. Then you will be able to offer any healing for past, present, and future. To heal the future is to prevent future sickness. When you do Soul Tapping, you can offer healing for the future by preventing a sickness that was supposed to come next year or in ten years.

With soul healing, space and distance are also no barrier. Soul travel is instantaneous. It doesn't matter whether the people you want to help are in Asia, Europe, Africa, or America. Just call the souls who need healing to come before you. One second is too conservative an estimate of how long it takes for souls in Asia, Europe, Africa—anywhere—to come before you. To offer remote healing to people anywhere in the world, simply call their souls to come before you. Then connect with your fingers:

> *Dear soul, mind, body of my fingers and my hands, I love you, honor you, appreciate you.*
> *Could you offer a Soul Tapping healing to all the souls who have come from different countries and different parts of the world?*
> *Follow my soul's guidance to do this healing. Thank you.*

It is very important to say: *Follow my soul's guidance to do this healing.* After you have connected with your hands and fingers, tell your hands and fingers not to do the job by themselves. Command them to do the job by following your soul's guidance. That is the essence of Soul Tapping. Now you are ready to communicate with your soul:

> *Dear my beloved soul, can you guide my hands, my fingers to do Soul Tapping to heal all the souls who are in front of me? I'm very grateful.*

Then start to do Soul Tapping for two or three minutes. All the souls who have come in response to your call will receive instant healing results, no matter where their physical bodies are. Many of them will receive instant miracle healing. Many will receive significant healing and improvement. Some will receive a little improvement. Some will not notice any change at all. Remember that even though a recipient of a Soul Tapping healing may not notice any benefit, that doesn't mean that there was no healing. It doesn't mean that Soul Healing doesn't work. It simply means that healing for that person may take more time. After all, you've offered only two or three minutes of healing. The recipient could have major energetic or spiritual blockages. It could take more time to see results.

Why am I releasing this top spiritual secret now? Because Mother Earth is in a major transition period. There's no time to wait anymore. This wisdom must be delivered to as many people as possible on Mother Earth to save people, to save humanity, to help Mother Earth and all who dwell upon her to pass through a most difficult time. No secrets should be kept. We should release all the divine wisdom, knowledge, and practice we have to offer pure service to humanity and to souls in the universe. This is a very urgent task. I wish each of you will understand this urgency and understand my pure service. I am a total GOLD servant for humanity and for all souls in the universe. What do I mean by total GOLD? *G* is gratitude. *O* is obedience. *L* is loyalty. *D* is devotion. I am a total GOLD servant for humanity, for souls in the universe, and for the Divine.

Grab this wisdom, knowledge, and practice. Use them for humanity. The more you serve, the more the Divine will bless you. The more you serve, the more you will fulfill your physical life. The more you serve, the more you will fulfill your spiritual life. The more you serve, the faster world peace will be attained. The more you serve, the faster love, peace, and harmony will become universal. The more you serve, the faster every soul will join as one.

The more you serve, the more easily Mother Earth and all who dwell upon her will pass through this major transition. This is our immediate task. It is most urgent. It is a divine calling. It is a universal calling. Treasure the wisdom and the knowledge—the sacred and secret knowledge—that I reveal in these pages. Do not treat this treasure lightly. Be honored to read this book. Use the wisdom, knowledge, and techniques presented to serve. The more you honor this divine wisdom, the more powerful you will be. Always remember, though, that the more humble you are, the more growth and progress you will make. Always remember there are human beings above human beings. Always remember there is Heaven above Heaven. Wisdom is unlimited. Power is unlimited. The moment you have ego is the moment you will block your own journey. You won't move further. You will go backward.

Serve with a pure heart. Serve as much as you can. Serve unconditionally. You will be blessed beyond your imagination.

Everyone's Soul Tapping Power
Is Different

Every human being has a soul. Every human being's soul standing is different. Your soul could stand at an ordinary human being's level. Your soul could stand at a saint's level. Your soul could stand at a spiritual father's level. Your soul could stand at the highest spiritual father's level.

When some people offer Soul Tapping for healing, it may not work. Other people may get incredible results when they offer Soul Tapping. Someone else's results may fall anywhere between these two extremes. What accounts for these differences? Because Soul Tapping is guided by one's soul, the major difference lies in one's soul standing. Where does your soul stand? The higher your soul stands in the spiritual world, the more power and abilities you are given. Soul standing is especially important when it comes to the ability to clear spiritual blockages. As I discussed in Chapter 17, many illnesses are related at their root with spiritual blockages, which are due to bad karma. If your soul stands at a very high level, you are given the ability to clear part of the bad karma. If you are given a Divine Order, you are given the ability to clear karma for one's entire life. Soul standing is usually determined by the Akashic Records. The highest levels of soul standing are determined directly by the Divine.

Your soul has probably gone through hundreds, even thousands, of lifetimes. Your soul standing has probably gone up and down, down and up throughout those lifetimes. In some lifetimes, you may have done a good job, and been a good servant to uplift your soul standing. In other lifetimes, you may have gotten lost, or offered bad service to lower your soul standing. Heaven has nine main layers. That's why I call Heaven *Jiu Tian,* which literally means the *nine heavens*. An animal's soul stands at level five or six. Most human beings' souls stand at level three or four. A saint's soul stands at level one or two. There are souls that stand above level one, which is beyond Jiu Tian, in Tian Wai Tian, the Heaven beyond Heaven If your soul stands at the saint level, when you do a gentle tapping, amazing healing will result. If your soul stands at the Tian Wai Tian level, you do not even need to do Soul Tapping! With only a *thought,* you can get a miraculous result. In summary, Soul Tapping yields different results for different people. This is determined primarily by the soul standing of the person doing Soul Tapping. Different levels of soul standing have different levels of power that are given by Heaven and by the Divine.

If you want to be a better servant, you must uplift your soul standing. The higher your soul standing, the better the results you will achieve. If you use Soul Tapping without getting much in the way of results, there is only one explanation: your spiritual standing is not high enough. Do not be disappointed. Purify your soul. Make a major commitment to serve. Even if your results are wonderful, they could be much better. To achieve even better results, to acquire a higher ability to serve, you have to pay attention to purification.

Pass spiritual tests and uplift your soul standing. There is no second way. There is only one way. Open your heart and soul to offer universal service. Selfishness and ego won't bring you one step further. You must be humble, offer unconditional service, and climb Heaven's stairs. You will move higher and higher. You will understand that wisdom is unlimited and power can be immeasurable. You will have healing results that are beyond your comprehension and understanding.

This is the Soul Light Era. I am not teaching healing with *chi* or energy healing. I am teaching soul healing. Soul Tapping is soul healing. Soul healing is based on *Soul Power.* I honor mind over matter, but I'm not talking about mind over matter. I am talking about *soul over matter.* Soul over matter means soul can make things happen. Soul can heal, prevent illness, rejuvenate, prolong life, and transform every aspect of life. Uplift your spiritual standing to increase your Soul Power. Uplift your spiritual standing to fulfill your physical life and your spiritual life. Uplift your spiritual standing to be a better servant of humanity and souls in the universe.

20

How to Uplift Your Soul

Now you know that the secret to being a powerful Soul Tapping healer is your soul standing. How can you uplift your soul?

Clear Your Karma

To purify your soul, mind, and body, first be sure your karma is cleared. If you carry bad karma, there is no way you can have great soul power. You are blocked by your bad karma. If you carry bad karma, when you offer healing, many souls will come to block you, not to support you. The souls to whom you owe a karmic debt from your misdeeds will come and say, "Why are you are offering soul healing? Pay me back first!" They will be upset, even angry. They want you to pay them back because you hurt and harmed them in past lives. They won't support you. They will block your healing. You won't get great healing results, much less miraculous healing results.

Clear karma by offering unconditional service and giving your total love. The key is to remove selfishness. If you remove a little selfishness, you will make a little progress. If you remove more selfishness, you will make more progress. If you are totally selfless, you will grow very fast, beyond comprehension. I shared with you earlier that one of the best ways to clear your personal karma is to sing and chant the Soul Song "Love, Peace and Harmony." Why? *I love my heart and soul* melts the blockages in your own heart and soul. *I love all humanity* is to offer service. When you chant *I love all humanity* with true love and great will, you *are* offering great service. The Akashic Records will pour red, golden, rainbow, and purple flowers into your Akashic book. Your dark records will start to be erased. Some people have huge karma issues. It could take ten, twenty, thirty years of chanting to clear your lifetimes of karma. But isn't even thirty years of this effort worth it for your hundreds and thousands of future lifetimes?

Pass Spiritual Tests

Trying to clear your own karma can be a very challenging experience. You want to serve? Your own selfishness can block you. Your spouse or partner can block you. Other family members and relatives can block you. Your best girlfriend or boyfriend can block you. They may believe you are brainwashed. They may tell you that you got lost. You may start to wonder about all these messages you are getting from those who are closest to you, those whom you most love. You may think: *Maybe I really did get lost.* You start to doubt your spiritual journey. You start to doubt the whole idea of service. You could also feel disappointed and depressed. You could go through physical suffering, emotional imbalances, broken relationships, or business failures.

Let me share a secret with you: this is all perfectly normal! If you have studied high-level spiritual teachings, if you have learned about the lives of great spiritual masters and teachers, this will be no secret to you at all. No spiritual master, not one single true spiritual master and leader, has had an easy life. They suffer more than ordinary beings. They want to purify completely. This is a long and intense process, one that ordinary human beings do not experience. The more successful a spiritual master is, the higher the level of attainment, the more bitter fruit he or she has eaten.

This is a serious spiritual law. *No pain, no gain. No drain, no gain.* The Divine will present serious spiritual tests to a true spiritual master or leader. The Divine requires them to taste all the bitter fruit, all kinds of serious suffering to understand deeply the suffering of humanity and souls in the universe. To be a spiritual master and leader, you must have total love, care, and compassion to serve humanity and souls in the universe. This is why the process of purification, including severe spiritual testing, is very important. If you cannot pass the spiritual tests from Heaven and from the Divine, you cannot progress.

Total Purification of Soul, Mind, and Body

On Mother Earth, millions, perhaps billions of people are consciously on their spiritual journey. Yet very rare is the being who has divine abilities. Why? Because most spiritual beings cannot go through the purification required by passing their spiritual tests. They may stop near the beginning of their journey. They may stop halfway through. Some will almost reach a successful end to their journey, but then they stop. They back off. They give up. Very unfortunately, they lost all their years, all their lifetimes of effort.

How difficult is the journey? It is not easy at all. If you wish to become a divine being, the Divine will train you for one-third of your life with divine tests. For example, if you are sixty years old, you can expect twenty years of serious testing. Can you pass serious test after serious test for twenty years? If not, you cannot be given divine power. You can only receive limited power and abilities.

How can you pass spiritual testing? How can you totally purify your soul, mind, and body? The golden key is total love and total GOLD—to the Divine, to humanity, to service. *G* is gratitude. *O* is obedience. *L* is loyalty. *D* is devotion. To go through the process of purification, to pass spiritual tests, it doesn't matter how difficult it is. It doesn't matter how much suffering you go through. It doesn't matter if your loved ones say you are crazy, if they tell you that you went in the wrong direction, that you are lost. You must understand that you are undergoing spiritual testing. If you really want to accomplish your spiritual journey, you must keep your mind very clear. You must trust your spiritual journey.

Guidance from a True Spiritual Master

If you are serious about your spiritual journey, I strongly suggest that you absolutely need a true spiritual master to guide you. Sometimes you may think you are correct, but you could make a big mistake. You could take the wrong direction. A true spiritual master, one with total love and total experience in training spiritual students, will give you great and essential guidance.

There are many true spiritual fathers and mothers on Mother Earth. There are true spiritual fathers and mothers in Heaven. How can you tell if a teacher or a master is a true master? After all, some "masters" are not true masters. The standard of evaluation is simple. Is the spiritual teacher or master selfless or not? Is the spiritual master totally committed to serve or not? A "yes" to both questions is clear guidance that you have found a true master to guide you.

Heaven's Stairs

The first goal in climbing Heaven's stairs is to reach soul enlightenment. What is soul enlightenment? You may think, "I have great love, care, and compassion. I feel I am enlightened." I must tell you that, no, this does not mean that you are enlightened. You may not have reached enlightenment. In my understanding, soul enlightenment is a high soul standing (spiritual standing) that is granted directly by the Divine. Upon receiving this high spiritual honor, the Akashic Records transfer the record of your soul to a special place reserved exclusively for enlightened souls.

To reach soul enlightenment is a great accomplishment in the soul's journey but, as I have taught, there is Heaven beyond Heaven. When you have entered the gate of enlightenment, you have actually only reached the first level or layer of enlightenment. There are seven levels of enlightenment in all. To reach the seventh and highest level is to have your soul standing uplifted to Tian Wai Tian, the Heaven beyond Heaven. When your soul reaches this level, it does not have to reincarnate anymore. Your soul will reside in the Divine's realm forever, to receive direct divine teaching and blessing every day. To reach Tian Wai Tian is the ultimate goal of one's soul journey.

The first level of enlightenment itself has four sublevels. Each sublevel can be identified by where the soul sits in the body. Those with open Third Eyes can see not only where their own souls, their small golden light beings, sit in their bodies, they can also see where anyone's soul sits.

There are seven possible "houses" in the body for one's soul. The higher your soul is in your body, the higher your soul's standing. A human being's soul resides in one of the following seven locations:

- the groin area
- the area between the groin and the navel
- at the "belt" or level of the navel
- the Message Center (also known as the heart chakra)
- the throat
- the brain
- above the crown chakra, just above the head

Most human beings' souls sit below the Message Center. If your soul sits in the Message Center, throat, brain, or just above your head, then you are an enlightened being at the first level of enlightenment. You may *want* your soul to sit in your Message Center. You may *want* to be an enlightened being, but it is not your decision. The spiritual world decides where your soul can sit. The location of your soul, which reflects your soul standing, depends on your virtue. If you do not have enough virtue, your soul cannot sit in your Message Center. Only when you have enough virtue to meet the standard of enlightenment will the Divine send an order. Your soul will then jump up to sit in your Message Center.

To reach soul enlightenment takes lots of effort. It takes total service. Remember one important teaching: when you do good deeds, good things for people, it is better to keep quiet about it. Lots of people do good things, but they want people to know. They love to have their acts reported by the media and to have people talk about them. That's not very humble, but it's also not very smart.

Let me explain by sharing some secrets about how the Akashic Records work. When you do good things and you are acknowledged and publicly recognized, you will receive some red, gold, rainbow, or purple flowers from the Akashic Records, but those flowers will be limited in number. This is yang virtue. When you do good things, try to keep your actions secret. Better if nobody knows what you did. Do what you do quietly, from your soul and heart. You do not want people to know. You do not need people to know. You do not want or expect any acknowledgment, recognition, or return. You are offering *unconditional universal service.* The Akashic Records are open twenty-four hours a day, every day. They will record your service. For this yin virtue, they will give you ten times, even a hundred times more flowers than they would for yang virtue.

This secret wisdom tells you that if you do good service for the recognition, for the physical reward, for your good name, you will limit your spiritual benefits. In contrast, if you give unconditional universal service, which may be tremendously great good service, without anybody knowing, the Akashic Records will know. All of your service will be noted and recorded, and you will receive all the spiritual benefits that you have earned and deserve. You may not receive them in this lifetime. Your entire life could remain very difficult, even harsh. You may never see a significant change in this life. But know that in your next life, your next ten lives and beyond, you will receive incredible blessings for your health, your relationships, your business—for every aspect of life. Be farsighted. Look beyond this life. One life is brief. You have had, and you will have, many lifetimes. Consider your soul's journey, which is eternal.

I release these deep soul secrets so that everyone on the spiritual journey can understand the ultimate goal of the soul journey and how to achieve it. When you reach Tian Wai Tian, it can truly be said that you have accomplished your soul journey. Of course, it is not easy to reach this ultimate goal and destination. It could take hundreds, thousands of lifetimes. Patience. Offer total GOLD service. Climb Heaven's stairs one step at a time. Reach higher and higher levels of soul enlightenment. Persist. Remove all blockages in your spiritual journey. Finally, you *will* reach the ultimate destination.

The Divine is waiting for you in Tian Wai Tian. This is the greatest honor for every soul that is committed to moving closer and closer to the Divine. This *is* the direction for one's soul journey. This is the direction for one's enlightenment journey. This is the ultimate goal for *every* soul. Move forward! You *will* arrive in Tian Wai Tian.

Heaven Is Most Fair

Heaven is most fair. Some people may argue this point. You may note that there are many people who have lots of money and power, but who abuse their power and use their money selfishly. They may not be very nice people at all. You may wonder why they have so much money and power if Heaven is fair. You yourself, on the other hand, may be a very pure person. You may have served tirelessly for decades, giving your money to charitable causes, doing volunteer work, and so on. You may wonder why you are still struggling so much with money and many other issues. How is this fair?

The answer is simple. There is no contradiction here. People with great power and wealth did good service before, in their previous lives. If they misuse their power, if they do not offer good service in this life, they will learn lessons in their next life and all future lifetimes. You, who are so kind, so pure, and who offer great good service in this life, will receive great blessings in your next life and all future lives. To understand spiritual law and spiritual blessings, to appreciate spiritual law and spiritual blessings, do not consider only one life. See five lives, ten lives, one hundred lives. Do not be shortsighted. Better to be farsighted. You will deeply understand the spiritual journey. You will truly understand that Heaven is most fair.

Uplift Your Soul Further and Further

To reach soul enlightenment is not the end of your spiritual journey. Many people think, "Oh, I am an enlightened being. I've reached the pinnacle of my journey." This is a total mistake. To reach enlightenment is merely the beginning of your enlightenment journey. There are higher and higher levels of enlightenment—many levels, countless levels. In Jiu Tian alone, you can uplift your soul standing further until you reach level one, the highest saints' level in Jiu Tian. After, say, another thousand lifetimes, you could uplift your soul to Tian Wai Tian, the Heaven beyond Heaven. Within Tian Wai Tian, it may take you another thousand lifetimes to climb the stairs, to move higher and higher in Tian Wai Tian. Finally, if you can reach the level where you sit beside the Divine, you can say you have accomplished your spiritual journey. It takes a long, long, long time—many years, many lifetimes, many centuries, many eras. What adds to the difficulty is that it's very hard for even the most spiritual beings to move forward in their spiritual journeys all the time. There will always be many blockages. There will always be many tests. Remember a spiritual law: *Success and disaster happen at same time.* The more successful you are, the more blockages the spiritual world will give you. What can you do? Face the blockages and obstacles squarely and directly to remove them. Then, you *will* move further and further. When the difficulties and blockages come, do not be upset. Do not be disappointed. Be *grateful*. Without blockages, without conflict, there can be no progress. That is a universal spiritual law.

Think about all of history. Progress is always based on conflict. In every dynasty, in every period of history, there is always conflict, fighting, and war. Without conflict, there can be no progress. History will not move. When you understand this, you will not be disappointed or upset when confronted with blockages. Stay calm. Face the difficulties. Face the blockages. Remove them. Then you will progress further and further. You will uplift your soul further and further. The final destination is waiting for you. Remember, the higher you advance, the more humble you must be. The higher your soul stands, the more service you must offer. The higher you are, the more ability you are given. The higher you are, the more responsibility you have and the more tasks you are given. Be honored to have divine tasks and to offer divine service. Be honored to give universal service to humanity and souls in the universe. You will be blessed more and more. You will arrive at the final destination. You will accomplish your spiritual journey.

21

Soul Tapping Master Healers

In many religious and spiritual traditions—Buddhism, Taoism, Christianity, Judaism, Islam, Confucanism, and more—there are many stories of healing and other miracles. Best known in the West, of course, is the life of Jesus. Have you thought about what these great figures have in common? Have you thought about how these great teachers, great healers, great servants are able to create these stories and miracles?

Power is given. Their power was given to them by the Divine. You may not have realized this. You may have thought that Jesus, great buddhas, other great healers and servants were born with that kind of power. That could be possible, but in most cases they were given the power later in life. Why did they receive this high, divine power for healing and blessing? Because of their virtue. Because of their commitment to serve. The Divine gave the power to them.

As I explained in detail at the beginning of this book, I was chosen as a divine servant, vehicle, and channel on July 12, 2003. I was moved to tears. What an incredible honor, what an unimaginable blessing to be chosen as this servant—a servant of the Divine, a servant of humanity, a servant of all souls. From that day, I have offered Divine Downloads—permanent divine healing and blessing treasures—to humanity and to all souls. I'm extremely honored to be this servant. I cannot bow down to the Divine enough to be this servant. After I became a divine servant, miracles for healing, for blessing relationships, and for blessing business have been happening almost every day. But whenever anyone honors me or appreciates me, I always say: *Thank you, Divine. Give the honor and credit to the Divine.* I am a humble servant and vehicle. I cannot do these miracles or achieve these amazing results without the Divine. In fact, I didn't do this work. The Divine did these healings and blessings. I am a humble servant. I am extremely honored to be a chosen servant to offer Divine Downloads to humanity.

The Divine Downloads that I have been honored and blessed to offer include Soul Software, Soul Liquid, Soul Acupuncture, Soul Herbs, Soul Food, Soul Self-Massage, Soul Operation, and Soul Transplants. I cannot honor the Divine enough for the honor of the blessings that these divine gifts have brought to humanity.

I also was given a major task from the Divine to create Divine Healers, who are able to offer divine healing using a particular Divine Download of divine healing power. Of the thousand or so students who have applied to become a Divine Healer, I am honored and pleased that four hundred of them have received the special divine transmission of healing power. They are now using this permanent divine healing and blessing treasure to serve humanity with divine healing and blessing.

As I explained in the introduction, I received an inspiration in the morning of August 3, 2006, to flow this teaching on Soul Tapping. For that entire day, I was unable to offer any teaching at my workshop other than to flow this book. The Divine asked me to release this book quickly, so that millions of people can learn and use the sacred soul healing of Soul Tapping. Humanity and Mother Earth need as many people as possible to learn this advanced soul wisdom, along with its very simple and practical techniques, to serve.

After reading this book, I hope that you have already begun to offer Soul Tapping to serve others—generously and unconditionally. As you have learned, you will be able to serve according to your soul

standing and your soul abilities. In order to serve humanity even better, the Divine asked me on August 3, 2006, to transmit divine Soul
Tapping power to students who are interested in and ready for it. I
will create Divine Soul Tapping Master Healers worldwide, with
training and certification. Divine Soul Tapping Master Healers will
receive a Divine Download for Soul Tapping—a permanent Soul
Tapping healing and blessing treasure directly from the Divine.
When you do Soul Tapping with this treasure, it is no longer you
doing the Soul Tapping. The permanent divine healing and blessing
treasure is offering the Soul Tapping. Your Soul Tapping and Divine
Soul Tapping are completely different.

I am again extremely honored to be a servant and channel to create Divine Soul Tapping Master Healers as another major divine service. I hope you have benefited from these chapters on Soul Tapping.
Read them again and again. Apply the techniques to serve. Purify
your soul to serve better. Reach soul enlightenment. Uplift your soul.
When you are ready, consider transforming your Soul Tapping to
Divine Soul Tapping. When you hold a Divine Soul Tapping treasure to offer healing, blessing, and life transformation, you will be
able to serve better. Let me continue to be your pure servant. Let me
help you to move further in your spiritual journey. Allow me to offer
a permanent Divine Soul Tapping treasure to empower you to become a Divine Soul Tapping Master Healer. Let us join hearts and
souls together to spread Soul Tapping worldwide.

People need to heal. People need to prevent illness, rejuvenate,
and prolong healthy life. People need to transform their lives, including their relationships and their businesses. Let us become pure universal servants together. Let us join hearts and souls together to help
humanity and Mother Earth pass through a difficult transition
period.

I love my heart and soul
I love all humanity
Join hearts and souls together

Love, peace and harmony
Love, peace and harmony

Thank you, Divine, for your blessings, your teaching, your wisdom, your knowledge, your techniques, and your practice. Thank you, all the participants in my workshop for giving me the opportunity to flow this teaching in one day. It is my great honor. It is my love. It is my heart and soul. It is my service.

Thank you. Thank you. Thank you.

PART 5

Soul Dance

Soul Joy in Motion

Introduction

Soul Dance is another precious gift from the Divine. Soul Dance is a close companion to my teaching in this book on Soul Song. The two complement each other. Everything I wrote about Soul Song is also true for Soul Dance. The only teachings included in this section are those unique to Soul Dance.

Like Soul Song, Soul Dance is also the continuation and development of Soul Language. This may surprise you because superficially it seems the two are very different. While this is true, Soul Dance is definitely a development of your ability to do Soul Language. To help you understand this connection, it would be useful to refer to the Soul Language section in this book. Soul Language, Soul Song, and Soul Dance go together. They complete one another.

This section has many delightful teachings. As you read it, you may feel like getting up and dancing. Wonderful! Do it! Just ask your soul to guide you in dancing. As you have probably guessed, *Soul Dance is soul-guided dance*. Every time you are moved to dance, allow yourself to do just that, but let it be soul dancing. Consciously ask your soul to guide your body to dance. If you are in a public place, allow your soul itself to dance instead of your body. Allow the time that is needed for the dance to happen. If you have this experience throughout your reading of this book, it is part of the message.

It is part of the wisdom. It is part of the blessing. Allow yourself to benefit fully. When you follow this suggestion, you will be amazed at the extraordinary transformation that becomes possible.

You may discover that there are many times throughout the day when you feel like dancing. Allow that to happen also. It will make a definite difference in the way you go through your day. Your mindsets, attitudes, and beliefs will be transformed in a dramatic way. These are just some of the many gifts included in this section of the book.

Receive and delight in each teaching and each blessing here. The wisdom is new and the blessings are powerful. As you read, you will experience what I am introducing to you here. Some of you will read this section with a profound sense of recognition. You are truly blessed. Some of you will read this book with amazement at the teachings. You are also truly blessed. Some of you will have totally different responses. You, too, are truly blessed.

Keep openness in your body, mind, heart, and soul as you read this book. This flexibility is essential for the physical journey and the spiritual journey. This entire book is a very special blessing tool. Every sentence, every word, and every punctuation mark will assist you greatly in making these teachings present in your life. I am honored to serve you in this way.

22

What Is Soul Dance?

Soul Dance is a unique and special gift from the Divine at this time. It is especially important for this society, where many people move with a certain stiffness. Many people are embarrassed about allowing the dance that is within their souls to be released. This makes it difficult for energy and light to flow in a balanced and even way throughout the body. Releasing this stiffness and embarrassment is one of the great gifts of Soul Dance.

Soul Dance is directed completely by your soul. Your soul lets your body know what movements to make. It lets your body know the tempo and the rhythm of your dance. The movement, tempo, and rhythm will change from dance to dance and can change even within one dance. Your Soul Dance will also accompany your Soul Song even when you cannot dance physically. When you release your Soul Song, your Soul Dance is also released. The movement, tempo, and rhythm—every aspect of your Soul Dance—are determined at the soul level.

Significance of Soul Dance

Soul Dance is a connection with a very powerful aspect of the Divine and the entire Soul World. Soul dancing takes place in the Soul

World as well as in the physical world. It is an expression of the presence of the Divine. The most powerful and light-filled movement is the expression and manifestation of the divine dance and the dance of the Soul World.

The Divine dances. The highest saints and all those in the Soul World also dance. When you do your Soul Dance, you are connecting with all of them. The transformation you will experience is profound. The connection established through Soul Dance is crystal clear and pure. It is a high level of communication. Your Soul Dance can also be an expression of your gratitude, obedience, love, and devotion for the Divine and for the Soul World. Your Soul Dance occurs throughout your entire body. Every aspect of your being participates in and manifests the dance in its own way.

For some of you, the idea of the Divine, the highest saints, and the entire Soul World dancing may be shocking. For others, it may be quite familiar. Or this may be a new realization for you but one that you feel is familiar. The Divine expresses messages and teachings and reveals ancient wisdom through the vehicle of Soul Dance. All that is given to us through Soul Dance is of a very high quality. The messages, teachings, and wisdom have not been expressed in this way previously. Soul Dance is a powerful messenger of this first part of the Soul Light Era.

Soul Dance will make it possible for many to enter into aspects of the Soul Light Era that would otherwise be difficult to reach. Soul Dance is a special preparation of readiness for more and more people to enter into the significance and meaning of the Soul Light Era. Soul Dance can do this because it is a unique connection with the Divine and the Soul World. This connection is pure and uncluttered by logical thinking. Being given this precious gift at this time will also assist greatly in responding to the purification and transformation of Mother Earth.

The connection with the Divine through Soul Dance will help many throughout Mother Earth stay in the condition of total gratitude. Soul Dance will also provide the teachings that will be essential during this time of purification. Soul Dance will be given to many in all parts of Mother Earth. Of course, people have danced for thousands and thousands of years. Soul Dance is unique because it is directed by your own soul and by the soul of the dance itself. This gift is being given to hundreds, thousands, even millions at this time in the history of Mother Earth.

Soul Dance makes it possible for your entire body to respond in a way that is unique to your soul journey. Your response is a release of the message from your soul at the moment that you are doing soul dancing. The message is expressed in dance rather than words. Think of it as a form of physical language, like sign language. Your entire body is manifesting the message from your soul at that particular moment.

You may notice that your Soul Dance is almost the same every single time. That is quite all right. That simply means that you have been given a particular dance for this part of your soul journey. Think of it as your own unique personal logo. Your dance is the message the Divine has given you to express.

Because Soul Dance is a form of language, those who watch your dance will receive different interpretations. With a verbal language, this would be a "translation." It might be helpful to think of the responses of others to your dance as their translations. Each person who watches your Soul Dance will have a different understanding and will receive a different message because each message corresponds with the person's spiritual journey and soul standing.

By now, you already understand that soul dancing is much more than simply moving in a rhythmic way to your Soul Song or the Soul Song of others. Soul Dance is also a very special form of soul communication. The movements of your body and hands express the message that your soul is receiving at that particular moment. These movements are a manifestation of this message. Words are not used because words are not needed. Because this communication takes place through physical movement and without normal language, it is very pure. No logical thinking is involved.

It is important to avoid the tendency to allow logical thinking to enter into your soul dancing. Allow your body and hands to move in the way they desire to move. The message of your dance will be interrupted or even stopped if you think "I feel so foolish" or "I don't want anyone to watch me" or "I am afraid I will hurt myself."

When I spoke about Soul Language and Soul Song earlier in this book, I emphasized the need to allow your language and song to flow. This is equally true for Soul Dance. Just as you must avoid editing or censoring what comes out through your mouth with Soul Language and Soul Song, you must avoid editing or censoring what comes out through your body with Soul Dance. You must also avoid suggesting to your body how it should move. Pay attention to these important cautions and your Soul Dance will have the freedom it needs to manifest the message you are receiving.

Some of you may be concerned that you could injure yourself as you do Soul Dance. Let me assure you that there is no need to even think about this as a possibility. If you are truly connected to your Soul Dance, you will only move as much as your body is able to without being injured. You need only truly connect with your Soul Dance and allow your body to move as needed to express the message being received.

When you do this, it may be possible for your body to stretch more than it usually does. That is fine. Do not stop the natural, unforced movement of your Soul Dance. On the other hand, do not force the movement either. Absolutely avoid saying to yourself, "This is too much. I'm going to pull a muscle." You must also avoid saying, "Wonderful! I'm going to really stretch and get maximum benefit." The first statement will edit, censor, and limit your movements. The second statement may cause you to suffer an actual injury. Both statements allow your logical thinking to enter, which means you have left your soul dancing behind.

When you are doing authentic soul dancing, your body will move only as is appropriate to express the message of your Soul Dance (or someone else's). As you do your Soul Dance, you may be aware that your body is moving in ways it normally does not. That is fine. Having this awareness is different from editing or censoring the movements. Awareness will not interrupt or stop the soul's dancing. Awareness is part of the process. What needs to be avoided is moving from awareness to editing, or to worrying about injury.

It should be evident by now that your Soul Dance is much more than movement. It is a particular message from the Divine. If you can translate Soul Language and Soul Song, you will also be able to translate Soul Dance. Some of you will receive the gift of translating Soul Dance as a particular gift and ability.

As you are doing your Soul Dance, enjoy the experience. If you can translate your own dance as you do it, great! If you cannot do this simultaneous translation, wait until you are finished dancing and then try to do your translation. You will receive special messages, wisdom, and teachings from the Divine through your dance. Soul Dance is a particularly delightful way to receive these messages, teachings, and wisdom. Soul Dance is very important for humanity and Mother Earth at this time. The messages that will be received will assist greatly in this time of purification and transformation for humanity and Mother Earth. It is quite extraordinary, but no coincidence, that the Divine has given this particular gift to humanity at this time.

Benefits of Soul Dance

Soul Dance has numerous benefits. As you express your dance, you will become aware of some of those benefits. The more you dance, the more your awareness will increase. I will discuss several key benefits.

First, healing will take place as you express your Soul Dance. The movements of your body and hands are a response to the soul's song. These movements will be different from what you normally experience. They will allow your body a new flexibility. This flexibility will help remove some of the blockages that have been part of your physical being. The more you do soul dancing, and the more completely you do it, the more blockages will be removed.

Soul dancing also has the ability to boost your energy. The movements you receive to boost energy will be very different from the movements to remove blockages. The soul dancing that removes blockages will be gentle and slower. Sometimes there will also be what feels like shaking. All of these forms of soul dancing promote smoother and freer movement of light and energy in your body.

The soul dancing that boosts your energy may involve movements similar to those suggested in various meditations that I have taught. For example, your hands may focus on your Lower Dan Tian or Snow Mountain Area. This will help increase the energy in those two foundational energy centers. If you need your energy boosted for your spleen or liver, your hands may move to those areas.

I need to caution you at this moment to avoid being rigid in your thinking and to avoid analyzing what is happening. It is enough simply to be aware that your body will move in certain ways to help release blockages and in other ways to boost energy. It is also necessary to avoid directing your body to do one or the other, or to direct it at all. Allow the Soul Dance to flow. It will do what is needed in the healing process for your body. As your body moves, every part of your being is also participating in the Soul Dance. Your systems, organs, every cell, and every space are participating. Light and energy are moving throughout your entire being. Your being is experiencing this movement not only on the physical level but also on the mental, emotional, and spiritual levels. Soul dancing can definitely accelerate your healing process. The changes in your physical health may amaze you.

It is especially generous and compassionate of the Divine to give us this form of healing at this time in the history of Mother Earth. There is an urgent need for all the processes of transformation to be accelerated. Soul dancing is an especially delightful way to accelerate the healing process on the physical level. It is amazing to consider that something that is so enjoyable and fun has so many benefits attached to it. Very often those who are involved in their spiritual journey become overly serious. Many such people consider dancing to be frivolous, even something to be avoided because it is viewed as a distraction. If you are talking about ordinary dancing, those ideas can be correct, but they absolutely do not apply to soul dancing.

Those who have been very serious about their soul journey may find it difficult to begin to appreciate the difference between ordinary dancing and soul dancing. However, it is essential for those who truly desire transformation and especially an acceleration of their process of transformation to be open to receiving Soul Dance. This will be a stretch for some. Opening to receive and delight in soul dancing will touch long-held mind-sets, attitudes, and beliefs. Some will have great resistance to actually stand up and do soul dancing. However, it is absolutely necessary to do it. The mind-sets, attitudes, and beliefs that will be released are the ones that are most difficult to reach and transform. Soul dancing could be the only way for some to begin that releasing and thereby enter into the flexibility that is necessary for progress on the soul journey. Holding on to particular mind-sets, attitudes, and beliefs results in rigid thinking and this is manifested in a rigid body.

Many of those involved in the spiritual journey have resisted releasing what they consider to be sacred attitudes and ideas. To be given Soul Dance as the tool to accelerate the process of releasing is a delightful expression of divine humor. This humor can be experienced on many different levels. As those who feel resistance begin to release their Soul Dance, they will experience this quality of divine humor that has not been available to them before. This will assist greatly in accelerating their process of transformation and of healing on the physical, mental, emotional, and spiritual levels. They will become aware of a shift in their outlook. This shift will make it possible for them to manifest aspects of divine presence that they could not before. Every aspect of their being will benefit in ways that are impossible to put into human words. The more open they are to releasing their Soul Dance, the more they will understand and appreciate the benefits. Soul Dance is appropriate for everyone, no matter where they are on their soul journey. Some will find it easier to release than others. No matter what the degree of difficulty is, releasing your Soul Dance is essential at this point in the story of Mother Earth.

Another benefit of Soul Dance is the conscious connection that it establishes with the frequency and vibration of the Divine, the highest saints, and all creation. This vibration is one aspect of the manifestation of Soul Dance. At times everything within you is in "simple" vibration. At other times, that vibration has its own special rhythm and movement that make it so much more than "simple." Every system, every organ, every cell, every DNA and RNA has its own vibration. Each also has its own dance.

Think for a moment of dance scenes that you have seen in movies. Sometimes there are performers in the background who are all doing the same dance steps. Sometimes there are also performers in the foreground doing a special dance. All of the dancers are coordinated and moving to the same music. However, they are dancing different steps. Their movements may be entirely different. The Soul Dance that takes place within you is similar. The soul of an organ may be the featured performer at the front of the stage, while all the individual cells are in the background. This comparison will give you an idea of what the Soul Dance experience within you can be. At other times, every organ, every cell, and every space between the organs and cells dance exactly the same Soul Dance. Whatever takes place is correct for that moment.

Soul Dance is something that changes as your energy level and soul standing changes. It also changes throughout the day. The pattern and rhythm of Soul Dance are always in the process of transformation. Because of this, the benefits you receive through Soul Dance are also in the process of transformation. Soul Dance is a very powerful way to accelerate the healing process on all levels. When you are consciously aware of the gift of Soul Dance, you can connect with it and accelerate the healing process even more. The healing benefits can be extraordinary.

When you experience healing blessings, the benefits are manifest. Sometimes you are immediately aware of those benefits. Sometimes you must wait until the experience of healing has taken place. With Soul Dance you will be able to augment the benefits because you will have the conscious awareness of everything within you vibrating and dancing at a higher level and with an increased quality of light. Soul Dance brings about an increase in light in a most amazing way.

When you have this awareness, you will be able to connect in a powerful way with the Soul Dances of the Divine, the highest saints, and the entire Soul World. This awareness will make a great difference for you. When you are doing your Soul Dance, you are able to participate in a special way in the divine dance. You become the physical presence of that dance. Because there are countless ways for the divine dance to be present, your dance will be different from the dance given to someone else. Your own dance will also change according to what you are experiencing at the moment. Whatever happens is an expression and a manifestation that you have the privilege to make present at that moment. The great variety in the way that Soul Dance is expressed is part of the blessing and benefit of this gift. This variety also adds to the enjoyment and delight of this gift.

Participate in Soul Dance as often as you can throughout the day. The benefits for you, Mother Earth, and beyond will be amazing. You will participate in a light that is of a very high quality. You will also help to increase this light, which is sorely needed at this time of Mother Earth's purification. Being able to help bring and amplify the light is a very special service that will bring much transformation to you and to others.

Another benefit of Soul Dance is the possibility for bringing about a greater flow and coordination in the environments where you live and work. As you participate in your Soul Dance, what happens for you will radiate out to others. Others can become more in harmony with you or, to use the language of dance, more in step with you. As this happens, your surroundings and your entire environment begin to change. The vibrations and frequencies among your coworkers or your family members will be heightened and synchronized. It is as though there is an invisible director of the dance group that is your environment bringing all of the performers more and more in step with one another. As you participate in Soul Dance, your entire setting will begin to vibrate and dance in coordination with your Soul Dance. Some with whom you live or work will actually be aware of this change as it takes place. They may not be able to put their finger on this change or give it a name, but they will feel this greater coordination. Some will understand what is happening and some will only be aware of an improvement. This will be a great benefit to many. Having greater coordination within your family or your workplace is a very special aspect and benefit of Soul Dance. As you already know, the benefits are given with abundance.

Special Blessings Received Through Soul Dance

One of the special blessings of Soul Dance is improvement in relationships. If your relationships with family members or colleagues at work need to improve, Soul Dance is a special blessing. When you participate in Soul Dance, the souls of others recognize and are able to join the dance. In fact, they are happy to have this opportunity. Many souls have been waiting for this opportunity. When it becomes present, they join in the dance with great enthusiasm and delight. This very special blessing connected with Soul Dance is a wonderful way to help transform your relationships. For relationships that are already very good, Soul Dance will make them even better. This is a particular gift of the Divine at this time.

Many relationships are difficult to change. The usual approaches can be effective but are often slow and take a great deal of mutual effort. Shifting your efforts to participating in Soul Dance will have an amazing effect. How do you do it? Simply call the other person's soul to dance with you. (You can do this with two or two hundred other souls at the same time.) Offer love, forgiveness, peace, and harmony as you do so. As you dance, you may sing my Soul Song, "Love, Peace and Harmony." You may sing your own Soul Song. When you are done, thank and respectfully return the other's soul.

Transforming relationships through Soul Dance will be effortless for many. It will be a source of delight for many. Many will experience the humor connected with Soul Dance. All of these qualities will also be experienced by family members and coworkers. They may not know exactly why they are beginning to feel different or why their attitudes are changing. That is fine. What is important is to enter the process of divine dance and to make it present throughout your day. No matter what your occupation is, a conscious connection with Soul Dance will help bring about a transformation. Your Soul Dance will help manifest a higher quality of light, harmony, and peace.

Another special blessing from Soul Dance is financial blessings. When you are doing your Soul Dance, you can speak to the soul of the financial blessings. Ask it for special blessings so that your financial situation can improve. Visualize the ways in which you want those blessings to come to you. Then, begin to do the Soul Dance. As you do this and as you speak directly to the soul of the financial blessing, you are making a very special connection, one that is not possible in other ways. When you call upon the soul of the financial blessing you have requested, the possibility for connecting with that specific blessing increases significantly. If you use the name of the financial blessing you are requesting, even better. For example, if you would like a financial blessing for a business, calling the soul of the business by name makes everything more conscious.

This is similar to "saying hello" to the health issue before you begin a healing blessing. When you call upon the name of the particular healing blessing needed, the soul of that blessing will respond. Other souls will also respond, increasing the light and vibration. Calling upon the soul of the particular financial blessing requested will make a stronger response possible. It will open the possibility for the soul you have requested and your own soul to have a very powerful connection. You might say it becomes much more personal.

There is a great difference between making a request for financial blessings that is general and broad and making a request that is specific and focused. A specific request is like speaking to a friend by name. This personal connection strengthens the coordination and participation in the Soul Dance. This is one of the many blessings that you can request through your Soul Dance. You can also request healing blessings for yourself, for others, or for situations. The list could go on and on.

One of the blessings you might desire is a blessing for your soul journey and the soul journey of others. When you request this, the connection with the Divine and the entire Soul World is very powerful. The transformation that occurs is on a very high level. Your soul journey and the soul journey of others will benefit in a very powerful and accelerated way.

These examples give you an idea of some of the blessings you can receive through Soul Dance. There are many others, but this will give you an idea of the possibilities. These possibilities do not have limits.

23

The Heavens Delight in Soul Dance

All levels of Heaven—Jiu Tian, Tian Wai Tian, and beyond—delight in a special way in Soul Dance. What I teach in this book is connected to Jiu Tian because that is the realm that most people on Earth are connected with at this time. To talk about Heaven's delight in Soul Dance is to give teachings on an aspect of the heavens that many people have not thought about. The souls in the heavens participate in this divine rhythm and movement. Each level and each realm of the heavens has its own unique dance. There are also unique dances within each level and realm.

Consider, for example, the highest saints in Jiu Tian. You will know some of them. You will not recognize others. It does not matter. They include Jesus, Mary, Shi Jia Mo Ni Fuo (Shakyamuni Buddha), Ling Hui Sheng Shi (the Goddess of Compassion, called Guan Yin in the previous era), Tao Te Zhen Jun, Ling Tong Tian Zun, and Yuan Shi Tian Zun. These are only a few of the highest saints. There are many more. Each one has a distinctive dance. As you connect with each one, you will become aware of the different ways your body will move. You might even become aware of differences within your body.

As each of these highest saints and others participate in the divine dance, the quality of joy and light is unique to this particular activity. The depth and power to transform are not present in other blessings or healings. They touch the deepest levels of your being. They radiate throughout your entire being. The quality of joy that is present through soul dancing permeates and becomes part of you. It becomes part of your entire setting. As you connect with each of the highest saints, you are also bringing all the qualities of their particular dances to your environment. This is a most extraordinary blessing and gift.

Connecting Heaven and Earth

From what I have written, you will understand that Soul Dance is a very special way of connecting Heaven and Earth. The vibration that becomes present and increases through Soul Dance is unique to this form of connection. This quality of vibration creates special pathways of light. You could think of them as ribbons, rivers, or bridges of light. This imagery will help you understand the profound and numerous connections forged when you participate in soul dancing.

Your body has many organs and systems. Your brain alone has billions of cells. Each cell consists of many parts, including DNA and RNA. Use this example to consider how many cells there are within your body. The number is almost unfathomable. Now try to imagine how many parts there are within each cell. This will give you a small hint of the vast extent of the connections between Heaven and Earth when you participate in soul dancing.

What we have just considered are the connections within a single person. Now multiply this by hundreds, thousands, and eventually millions of people participating in soul dancing. Next, add all of creation, for it is not only human beings who have the ability to do soul dancing. All of creation is able to do soul dancing. (I will discuss this concept further in the next chapter.) The connections are not limited to human beings and Heaven. There are also all of the powerful ribbons, rivers, and bridges of light from Heaven's realms that extend to all of Earth.

All of these connections carry the light and blessings of transformation. When those connections are made, there is an extraordinary change in the matter and the space of all who are participating in soul dancing. Soul dancing is a powerful way to clear the spaces. It quite literally shakes loose the blockages. As blockages are loosened, they can be transformed. They can become the presence of divine light.

The connections between Heaven and Earth are also the unique connections of the highest saints. When you call upon a particular saint to ask for the blessings of that saint, all of the abilities, gifts, wisdom, and teachings of that saint become present. The movement, vibration, and frequency of that saint become present in the Soul Dance. When you participate in that Soul Dance, you become the physical presence of all of this. This is a most amazing blessing and gift.

Think of what it means to say that your Soul Dance connects with all of these qualities of the highest saint that you have asked to bless you. As you are doing this Soul Dance, go into the condition of that highest saint. You *are* that saint. This will give your Soul Dance an entirely different quality. The blessings of the saint become present in a very powerful way. You can radiate this presence to all around you. You can do this even if you do not actually dance physically in your surroundings. You might be in a public place. You might be at work. You may not be able to move because of illness or injury. You may not even be able to get out of bed. That does not mean you cannot do soul dancing. If you are physically limited in any of these ways, you can ask your soul to do the soul dancing. This is also very powerful.

What is important is to do soul dancing daily. Practice as often as you can throughout the day. Why? It should be clear from what you have learned so far. When you make these connections between Heaven and Earth, the blessings that become present and the transformation that takes place are very powerful. They will give extraordinary assistance to Mother Earth in her time of purification and transformation. This assistance is not only powerful, it is very gentle and full of delight and joy. As little children would say, "This is the funnest!" And it is a most fun way to bring about the transformation that is needed so very much at this time.

Being able to do all of this through soul dancing is a very special gift given by the Divine. It will assist all humanity and all of Mother Earth and beyond during this time of transition. Soul dancing will help to keep each one who participates grounded and centered. For many, it will be the most effective way to stay grounded and centered. Both of these qualities are very important and they will become even more important as Mother Earth continues her purification process. It is very kind, compassionate, and loving of the Divine to give us this gift at this time.

Soul Dance and Creation

All that has been said about your particular Soul Dance is also true for every aspect of creation. The various levels of creation will participate accordingly. Each aspect of creation has its own unique dance. For some aspects of creation, it is very easy to imagine that soul dancing is taking place. For other aspects of creation, it will be more difficult to imagine. However, Soul Dance is a possibility for all that exists. The light and the transformations that will take place through soul dancing are extraordinary.

Those parts of creation that are in motion have their type of Soul Dance. For example, the rhythm of ocean waves is an expression of soul dancing. The rotation of the planets around the sun is another expression of soul dancing. Those parts of creation that are more fixed, like mountains, also have their own unique dance. Those who have Third Eye abilities will see images of these various dances.

The movement and dance of creation have existed throughout time. However, in the Soul Light Era, the soul dancing of creation is being brought to a conscious level. It is connected with the soul dancing of each person and each entity. When you are doing your soul dancing, you could invite the various aspects of creation to join you in your dance. You could ask them to add their light, their frequency, and their vibration to your dance. You can also ask them to assist other aspects of creation. Bringing the Soul Dance of creation to a conscious level increases its power, light, and transformative abilities.

It is quite extraordinary to consider that all of creation can participate in soul dancing. When you are doing your Soul Dance, you could invite the rest of creation to join you, but it is important to include the phrase "if appropriate." You could say something like, "I invite all parts of creation that are appropriate to join in my soul dancing." Or you could say, "If it is appropriate, I ask creation to join me in my soul dancing." Adding one of these phrases is very important; in fact, it is necessary. Some aspects of creation may be in turmoil when you are doing your soul dancing. You do not want to invite that turmoil to be part of your dance. For example, you do not want to invite an aspect where there is a hurricane or tornado happening. You are not strong enough to try to transform the turmoil, so it is not appropriate to try to do so. Keep this teaching in your awareness when you invite creation to become part of your dance. If you are resisting this teaching, perhaps thinking it would be a wonderful service to calm the hurricane, I simply repeat, "You are not strong enough to do it." It requires huge amounts of virtue, and it is necessary to have been of a very high spiritual standing for hundreds and thousands of lifetimes. You would not have the ability without having the virtue.

Keep in mind that this is also a time of purification for Mother Earth. Do not do anything to interrupt that purification process. Always use the measured phrases "if it is appropriate" or "as appropriate," when you invite creation to do soul dancing with you. Many parts of creation will be able to join and benefit from the soul dancing. The resulting blessings that will go out to all creation will be exactly those needed at this time. They will be in harmony with divine wisdom and compassion. Keep this in your awareness so that you will respect what happens, which means that you respect divine wisdom and compassion.

The blessings you will receive by following these teachings are extraordinary and will transform you in a powerful way. Accepting these teachings will assist you in releasing mind-sets, attitudes, and beliefs that need to be released. Some of those mind-sets, attitudes, and beliefs could not be released in any other way. It is almost as if they have been waiting for this opportunity. However, some of them have also been resisting this opportunity. In any case, releasing the mind-sets, attitudes, and beliefs is necessary for continued progress in your soul journey.

Releasing the entrenched mind-sets, attitudes, and beliefs that are waiting or resisting will free you from what you have carried through many lifetimes. The lessons that you will learn as you release will make available wisdom that has been waiting for you through your many lifetimes. It is wisdom of great beauty as well as great antiquity. It carries with it profound teachings, blessings, and healing. The transformation that you will experience as you release is impossible to put into words. You will feel a lightness and freedom that you had no idea was possible.

As you do this releasing, not only do you benefit, but the benefits radiate out far beyond you. Those who interact with you directly will receive profound blessings simply because you radiate a higher quality of light. Your frequency and vibration will be very different. This is a great gift for you, and the gift is multiplied because it will radiate out beyond you to all of Mother Earth and beyond. In fact, all of creation will benefit by your willingness to follow these teachings. Your heart's desire to be able to help will be answered in a most generous and extraordinary way.

The dance of creation will participate in your releasing of mind-sets, attitudes, and beliefs. All of creation will participate in this process of releasing. This is a wonderful gift to be able to give. Just as you might experience some resistance and difficulty, parts of creation will also experience resistance and difficulties. As you do your releasing, the benefits and blessings will be available to all parts of creation. They will assist Mother Earth in her purification process. This is a wonderful gift to give to all of creation, and as this gift is given, it is multiplied.

All of humanity and all of creation will benefit from your willingness to participate in this process of releasing. It may seem amazing that your willingness to release has such far-reaching benefits, but this is just another example of the profound generosity of the Divine. The Soul Dance of creation is continuous. The connections are established and continue throughout the day. The benefits and blessings received and given are also continuous. No matter what time it is for you, creation is doing this exquisite dance somewhere. Some parts of creation, by their nature, continue day and night, such as the waves upon the shore. The blessings continue day and night.

Whether you are consciously participating in your Soul Dance or not, you are still able to benefit from what is happening throughout creation. This is a powerful and special gift. The next time you look at the enthusiastic play of a puppy, the gentle sway of the leaves on a tree or the rhythm of the wind as it blows through tall grass, realize that you are observing a particular aspect of soul dancing. When you begin to look at everything as an expression of soul dancing, you will be enveloped in joy and delight.

The movement of the leaves and the wind through the grass can be vigorous, full of strong energy. Seeing it as soul dancing will put it in a different light. You can experience these aspects of creation—any aspect of creation—to remind you to do your own Soul Dance. You can now look at everything around you in a different way throughout the day. For example, even your schedule can be looked at differently. The soul of your schedule is doing its own unique dance. When you look at it this way, you will be able to see a rhythm and a movement in your schedule. Many of you think of your schedules as being very full, but when you look at it as an expression of soul dancing your view will be very different. You will be able to appreciate the rhythm of your schedule. You, and the dance of your schedule, will be more grounded and centered.

Rather than seeing your schedule as crowded and scattered with many separate parts, you will see it as a unified whole from the perspective of rhythm and movement. Everything about your day will look very different. You will be able to appreciate the connections between one part of your day and the next. You will be able to appreciate the fact that your schedule is a dance. If you would like the dance of your schedule to be different, make that request to the soul of your daily schedule. Do a Soul Dance and request the soul of your daily schedule to join you in the dance. Ask the Soul World to bless you with calm, tranquillity, and peace as you do your Soul Dance with your daily schedule. You will receive many benefits.

This is an example of another aspect of creation. All of these examples illustrate how creation participates in soul dancing. As you do your Soul Dance, you will become more and more aware of the possibilities for the dance, for the blessings, and for the light. You are very blessed.

Soul Dance and Honoring the Divine

Since ancient times, people have expressed their respect and devotion to the Divine through movement and dance. Dance may have been humanity's first expression of devotion and honor to the Divine. Certainly, movement came before words. As humanity began to express itself through movement, it was natural to want to use that movement to give thanks to the Divine.

Thinking of dance as an expression of the sacred and as an expression of gratitude, obedience, loyalty, and devotion adds greatly to your appreciation of Soul Dance. In some traditions, it would be called prayer. In some traditions, it would be called ritual. In other traditions, it has no name. It does not matter what it is called; what is important is the realization that Soul Dance is a way to express devotion to the Divine.

To be able to express your devotion through Soul Dance adds a special quality and aspect to Soul Dance. It also removes some barriers in the form of limitations that some people place on expressions of devotion to the Divine. Some who have a limited idea of what is appropriate can be somewhat solemn. Their expressions can lack variety. Expressing devotion through Soul Dance is very important for those who have this solemn approach. They will begin to release long and deeply held mind-sets, attitudes, and beliefs.

When soul dancing is done as a means of honoring the Divine, the movements and rhythms will manifest great respect, appreciation, and gratitude. There is no need to be concerned that the Soul Dance may not be appropriate. When you have the conscious awareness and desire that this particular Soul Dance will be one to honor the Divine, the dance will do exactly that because the dance has its own wisdom. In fact, there is no need to be concerned about the appropriateness of any of your soul dancing. Your Soul Dance has its own wisdom. Your Soul Dance knows what is appropriate. It knows how to express gratitude and devotion. It knows how to express what is sacred. It knows how to connect with the Divine.

When you use Soul Dance to honor the Divine, you are joined by Heaven's realms. You are joined by the highest saints. You are joined by many parts of creation. What you express will be very powerful and the expression will be magnified far beyond you. It is a particular gift to be able to honor the Divine in this way. Soul Dance is fun. Bringing this aspect of fun, delight, and joy to the ways you honor the Divine is very important. Many people realize many aspects of respect. However, people are not as aware that joy and delight are also aspects of respect. When you do your Soul Dance as a way to honor the Divine, you are consciously presenting the aspects of joy and delight. As a result, this method of honoring the Divine is much more complete and balanced and very grounded and centered.

This method of expressing your devotion to the Divine is also a signal to others to do the same thing. When you honor the Divine in this way, the changes in your mind-sets, attitudes, and beliefs will benefit others who might be struggling with this teaching. The more you honor the Divine in this way, the more you help those who find this teaching challenging.

When you do soul dancing to honor the Divine, you have a very special connection with the Divine. Quite literally, you are in harmony with the Divine. Your frequency and vibration have been brought to a higher level, closer to the harmony and vibration of the Divine. You not only honor the Divine but you also become the physical presence of the movement of divine dance. This is yet another extraordinary example of divine generosity.

Your desire and effort to honor the Divine are received, multiplied, and returned to you in many different ways. You will become aware of profound changes on your spiritual, mental, emotional, and physical levels. The transformation will be profound, strong, and gentle. Your spiritual channels will open more and more. If you have Third Eye abilities, they will increase. Your abilities to release long-held mind-sets, attitudes, and beliefs will increase. Your physical health will improve.

All of this is possible simply because you use your Soul Dance to honor the Divine. It is amazing to realize that this happens for you as you dance. It is a special gift to be able to honor the Divine in this way. It is also a gift to all of creation. When you use your Soul Dance to honor the Divine, all of creation has the possibility of using their Soul Dance in the same way. Think about that for a moment. When you use your Soul Dance to honor the Divine and invite the appropriate parts of creation to join you, they, too, receive incredible blessings.

When you honor the Divine through Soul Dance, you are also joined by all of the highest saints. You are dancing in a very special chorus that is offering an extraordinary amount of gratitude, obedience, loyalty, and devotion to the Divine. Your Soul Dance becomes part of a very high form of respect and honor. You are able to connect with the sacred on very high levels. It is an extraordinary privilege and gift to realize that your Soul Dance is joined by the highest saints. This happens in a particular and unique way when you use your Soul Dance as an expression of honor to the Divine.

To say that the light is increased is an understatement. However, human words cannot adequately explain what happens for you when the highest saints join you in this type of Soul Dance. It is a dance in which the Soul World participates continuously. When you use your Soul Dance to honor the Divine, your dance becomes part of what already exists. You are quite literally invited to join their dance. This carries profound blessings. It is a powerful way to bring about transformation. The benefits are not limited to you. They radiate out far beyond you. They benefit Mother Earth and all of her creatures. The benefits extend beyond Mother Earth.

This transformation process initiated by participating in Soul Dance is heightened and accelerated beyond imagination when you use your dance to honor the Divine. Honoring the Divine through Soul Dance is a very special form of service. You are able to offer service and at the same time have blessings extended to you and others in extraordinary ways. Use your Soul Dance as often as you can and use it in this way throughout your day. Pay attention to all the changes you will begin to experience. As your awareness grows, you will be able to participate at higher and higher levels. Your Soul Dance will also be transformed. You are very blessed.

24

Soul Dance as a Manifestation of the Divine

Soul Dance is a unique and particular manifestation of the Divine. When you are doing your Soul Dance, you become a special presence of the Divine. Being the presence of the Divine through dance is a new way of approaching divine presence. Many of you could list the ways the Divine is present. Your lists might be quite long. However, I would guess that few of you would have included dance, at least before reading this book. Of course, I am not referring to just any "dance." It must be *soul* dance. It is a special delight to realize that soul dancing can be added to the list. It *needs* to be added. Soul Dance will bring the lightness that is so desperately needed during these times. When Soul Dance and Soul Song are manifested together, there is a special aspect of divine presence that is not available in other ways. To be able to manifest the Divine through Soul Dance is a wonderful gift, not only to you but to all those around you and beyond.

The lightness and the delight that accompany soul dancing are desperately needed. To know that the Divine has given us this gift at this time is to appreciate the generosity and compassion of the Divine in another way. The Divine is always making efforts to be present with us so that we can have a greater and greater connection. The Divine wants us to become more and more the pure presence of the

Divine here on Earth. There are many ways in which this has happened and continues to happen. At this time, Soul Dance is an extraordinarily powerful way for each of us to become the presence of the Divine here on Earth.

Soul Dance and Joy

There are many qualities that we think of as being part of the essence of the Divine or an expression of the Divine. Very often joy is overlooked as one of these qualities. As people make a commitment to their soul journey, they are usually more aware of the difficulties, the lessons, and the releasing that are part of that journey. They may overlook the fact that joy is also part of the essence of the journey. Joy is absolutely an expression of the essence of the Divine.

However, telling someone who is experiencing challenges that he needs to connect with divine joy is not the best approach. People have to be allowed to go through their process step by step. As it advances, the process itself will have a quality of joy. Having a full appreciation of the presence of divine joy requires attaining a certain level in your soul journey. That does not mean that the beginning or the challenging parts of the journey have no joy. It simply means that your experience of the joy will increase as your soul's standing increases.

Your awareness of the joy will increase as your participation in divine light increases. As you are doing Soul Dance, you will be able to enter into a fullness of divine joy. This will accelerate your soul journey and your soul standing. Participating in this aspect of the Divine brings many blessings and much healing. One of the very special blessings is a greater ability to release mind-sets, attitudes, and beliefs. This is a treasure, because being able to do this releasing will bring about great changes in your soul journey. It will bring much more purity to your soul standing. You will have greater clarity. It will also accelerate the healing and purification of all other levels of your being.

This is just one example of the blessings and healings that are available when you participate in this aspect of divine presence. You can receive so many benefits through your soul dancing that it is truly amazing. Soul dancing is such an easy thing to do. It is simple. It is enjoyable. That there are so many blessings and so much healing connected with soul dancing is extraordinary. You may be thinking, "This is too good to be true." Actually it *is* too good and it *is* true. The more you do soul dancing, the more you will experience the reality of what I am teaching. You will experience that it is this easy, this good, and this true.

To have Soul Dance as an expression and manifestation of divine joy is a special form of service. There is an absence of joy in many people, places, and situations. Instead of joy, there is heaviness, sadness, grief, and, in many cases, anger. The ability to bring divine joy to these people and situations is an honor and privilege. When you do your Soul Dance, you could ask for the joy that is within it to go to those people, places, and situations as appropriate. The ability to give these blessings to many who are desperate for them is a great honor. The ability to do this through soul dancing makes it easy and powerful. You can quite literally help bring divine joy to Earth.

You can become a manifestation of this aspect of divine presence. You can ask this aspect of divine presence to touch all the people and places for which it is appropriate at this time. You can literally dance away depression. You can dance away sorrow. You can dance away anger. As you do your Soul Dance, you can replace all of these emotions with light, love, forgiveness, peace, healing, and blessings. This is truly extraordinary. It is truly a privilege. As you do this, you will participate in and experience a greater and greater degree of divine joy.

The more you participate in your own process of transformation, and the more you become a being of light, the more you will be able to manifest divine joy. The more you are able to manifest divine joy, the more you will be able to connect with this aspect of the Divine. Divine joy will grow within you at an accelerated rate. As you do your Soul Dance, you will become more and more aware that you are connecting with this most precious aspect of divine essence, an aspect that is desperately needed on Mother Earth at this time. The ability to do this is a very special blessing and gift.

Soul Dance from Before Time

The vibration and frequency associated with the Divine come from before time. They have been the source of all that exists. They have been the source of nourishment. They have been expressed as vibration, sound, movement, and dance. They were the earliest and the most pure form of divine dance. As creation became manifest, this original Soul Dance from before time continued. It became present in all that came to exist.

In many aspects of creation, this original Soul Dance remained in its very pure form. However, in some aspects of creation, it was limited because of resistance. In some aspects of creation, the original Soul Dance had to adapt and change, and this affected its ability to be manifested. The original Soul Dance retained its original purity and strength; however, its manifestation was different. The Soul Dance from before time has kept a very special connection with the Divine and with the essence of all life. It has made that present throughout all time. It is almost as if this original Soul Dance has done many things simultaneously. It has remained pure. It has adapted its manifestation. It has continued on and been present in all of creation. It is with us and is being manifested at this time in a very special way.

In this era, the Soul Dance from before time will come into a fullness of expression. I will say more about this in the following pages. Knowing that Soul Dance has existed since before time, throughout time, and into what we call the future is important. When we connect with this original form, we are connecting with a very special presence of divine dance. To be able to do this, you must make a soul-to-soul connection. Very few on Earth at this time have made this connection. However, as more people participate in soul dancing, more people will have the possibility of connecting with the original Soul Dance.

As more individuals undergo the process of transformation that is the particular gift of soul dancing, it will be more possible for them to make the soul-to-soul connection with this magnificent dance from before time. As more people make this connection, the further possibilities are impossible to imagine. To help you appreciate how numerous the possibilities are, just think of the small part of creation that is familiar to you. It already holds infinite variety and possibilities. Multiply this by all creation on Mother Earth. Then, multiply that by all creation beyond Mother Earth and you will have a hint of what I mean when I say, "The possibilities are so numerous they cannot be imagined."

Connecting soul to soul with the dance that has existed from before time also makes present the most extraordinary blessings. It makes present the most extraordinary abilities, wisdom, teachings, and gifts. As I said, there are only a very few people at this time who have reached a high enough level to be able to make this soul-to-soul connection. However, as we continue through this Soul Light Century and Soul Light Era, more people will be able to make this connection. More people will be able to manifest the various aspects of this original Soul Dance.

To manifest even one aspect of this original Soul Dance is an extraordinary privilege, honor, and gift. It will make present such powerful transformation. The ability to make this type of connection will also be a most extraordinary form of service. Any single aspect of the original Soul Dance carries with it such power and abilities that the healing blessings will be profound. To be able to offer and manifest this for others is a service that will bring transformation and blessing on every level to countless souls on Earth and beyond.

The original Soul Dance is present whenever and wherever soul dancing takes place. However, only a few can connect with its presence at this time. Only a very few can manifest its presence. All others need to continue on their soul journeys and to advance their processes of transformation and releasing. As this happens, each one becomes more ready to manifest this extraordinary Soul Dance. Do not be in a hurry for this privilege and honor. Do not have an expectation or desire that you will make this kind of connection. Continue on your soul journey step by step. Continue your transformation process. Whatever is part of your process and journey is correct, for it is what has been decided and directed by the Divine. Respond with total gratitude for the gifts you are given and for the gifts you are not yet ready to receive.

The Soul Dance from before time sometimes disguises itself in the Soul Dance that is taking place. It will be present in the soul of the Soul Dance that is taking place. The original Soul Dance desires to be able to manifest. It wants to assist humanity and Mother Earth in its purification process, but it is also fully aware that it is not yet the appropriate time. Because of this, it chooses to disguise itself in some of the soul dancing that is now taking place on Mother Earth.

Of course, not every Soul Dance that is done is a disguise for the original Soul Dance. Avoid wondering if your Soul Dance is a disguise. Avoid trying to guess which ones are. Avoid any attachment to believing that any particular Soul Dance, yours or someone else's, is a disguise. You would be using logical thinking, which does not work. In fact, when you use logical thinking, more often than not you are creating huge barriers and blockages to your soul journey and your process of transformation. Put aside all of these thoughts that may come to you regarding your desire to recognize the original Soul Dance.

What is truly important is that you be completely committed and dedicated to your process of transformation. Do this and you will have the possibility of some day being able to connect soul to soul with the original Soul Dance. Focus on advancing your transformation and soul journey, and you will be assisting yourself in a wonderful way. Focus only on this. You will accelerate your transformation. You will increase your openness to divine light. You will help yourself become a being of light.

The Soul Dance from before time is a very special message. It is a very special soul. It is constantly influencing all that exists. In particular, it is influencing the presence of soul dancing at this time. It will continue to offer this service. It is a profound blessing for this original Soul Dance to be present in and with the soul of soul dancing. We are very blessed. We are very honored.

Soul Dance and the Soul Light Era

In this era there will be a greater manifestation of the original Soul Dance. There will be a fullness of all that is part of this original dance. In this beginning part of the Soul Light Era, there is the possibility of connecting with parts of the Soul World that have not been manifested before.

You should by now realize the power of soul dancing. You know that it is a special gift to assist humanity in the days of purification and transformation of Mother Earth. When this process of purification reaches the stage at which there is broad awareness of the need for huge changes and transformation, the power of Soul Dance will become more and more evident. As Mother Earth goes through her purification and transformation process, and as all who dwell upon her go through this same process, the presence of light will be most extraordinary. People will gain a most extraordinary awareness. There will be great clarity in thoughts and behavior.

The process of purification will reach a particular point that could be called a "high point" or an "apex of great intensity." When that point is reached, divine healing, divine light, and divine transformation will manifest for thousands of people at the same time. These simultaneous manifestations will be global. As this happens, the significance and benefits of soul dancing will become obvious, because they will be manifested in many ways.

The Soul Light Century is itself an introduction to all that I have said about soul dancing. Not only is soul dancing the preparation for what is to come, it is also the *process* to accelerate what is to come.

This is quite amazing. Special gifts and abilities often are either part of the process or part of the preparation. Very rarely are special gifts, abilities, or blessings part of *both* the process and the preparation. We could say that the Soul Light Century will be danced into a fuller manifestation. Although it is not the only way that the Soul Light Century will become more present, soul dancing is a significant part of that process. It is wonderful to realize that something as joyful and delightful as soul dancing will be able to help all of humanity, Mother Earth, and beyond in such a powerful way.

As Mother Earth goes through her purification and transformation, Soul Dance will assist in numerous ways. It will help humanity, Mother Earth, and all who dwell upon the Earth go through the process and reach the other side. Doing Soul Dance during the most difficult times will help you in ways that are impossible to describe. The ribbons, rivers, and bridges of light that I mentioned earlier exist for the time and the process of purification and transformation. Soul Dance helps you to connect with these ribbons, rivers, and bridges, helps you and others to pass through this time of purification and to come to what will be on the other side. This is a very powerful aspect of Soul Dance.

Soul Dance is a wonderful way to better understand the extraordinary generosity, compassion, and kindness of the Divine. To be given this gift at this time is so very special. Make use of the gift of Soul Dance as often as you can. Use it in a focused way when you are experiencing challenges. Remember that it is a ribbon, a river, a bridge to help you through whatever it is you are experiencing. It helps you reach the other side where there is much more light, a higher frequency, and a higher vibration.

As we get closer and closer to the other side of Mother Earth's purification, what will be is beyond our ability to imagine. At this moment, it is enough to know that what will be will be extraordinary. It is not a good use of your time and energy to try to imagine what it will be like. That is like trying to do tomorrow's work today. Keep your awareness on what is taking place at the present time. Know simply that there will be great changes and that the changes will be of light and divine presence. What that will look like and how it will be experienced have not yet been manifested. What we are experiencing now is what is important for this moment.

Focusing on what will come causes you to neglect or avoid being really attentive to what is actually happening. It is absolutely necessary to give your attention to the present process, to *now*. I have talked about what will come just to provide an anchor for you if you begin to feel stressed and overwhelmed by the purification process of Mother Earth. Soul Dance is a wonderful gift to transform feelings of stress and being overwhelmed. It is also a wonderful gift to express your joy, gratitude, and devotion.

Soul Dance will have many different forms of expression in the Soul Light Century and Soul Light Era. The connection with the highest saints and with all the heavenly realms will be powerful and profound. Soul Dance will help bring about a new creation on Mother Earth. It will assist you as this new creation is coming into existence. There are many possibilities connected with Soul Dance and its gifts. As you experience your Soul Dance, you will begin to understand and appreciate some of these possibilities. Soul Dance is a special gift and blessing for humanity, Mother Earth, and beyond. It is a special kindness from the Divine to give us this gift at this time. We are very blessed.

Conclusion

From all that I have taught in this book, it is easy to appreciate Soul Dance as a very special gift. It is easy to understand it as a powerful tool for transformation. Soul Dance is also a very significant part of each person's healing process, as well as of the process of transformation for Mother Earth. This process of transformation and purification of Mother Earth can also be considered a healing process. The ability to participate in and contribute to this process through Soul Dance is very special. As a soul dancer, you can help to accelerate what is happening and you can also participate in aspects of the Divine, the highest saints, and the highest realms in ways that are not possible through other activities.

Soul Dance is a unique gift. It is a unique key that opens treasures that are desperately needed at this time. These treasures are not available in other ways. I encourage you to use your gift of Soul Dance as often as you can. I would also encourage you to ask your Soul Dance to continue on the soul level even when you are preoccupied with the tasks of your daily life.

It is a particular kindness of the Divine to make this gift available even to those who are not able to move freely because of illness or other physical limitations. Knowing that anyone can fully participate in soul dancing regardless of physical condition is very special. Anyone can make an extraordinary contribution to the transformation process of Mother Earth. Anyone can offer the profound service available through soul dancing.

Regardless of your physical condition, you can also experience all of the benefit connected with soul dancing. If your body cannot dance, your soul still can. All of your inner souls—of your organs, systems, cells, cell units, DNA, and RNA; of the spaces in your body; of your mind and emotions—can join the dance. The joy, the delight, the greater flexibility, the ability to release mind-sets, attitudes, and beliefs, and the increase in the frequency and vibration of divine light are all available to you.

All of these gifts are waiting for you. All you need to do is open yourself to receive and release them. When you do that, your process of transformation and your soul journey will change profoundly.

The service that you offer to Mother Earth, to all of her creatures, and to all that exists beyond is extraordinary. It has been my greatest honor and privilege to offer these teachings and to offer the blessings to accompany the teachings. I am very honored to serve you, all of humanity, and beyond in this way.

Acknowledgments

I cannot give enough thanks to my most beloved teacher and adoptive father, Master Zhi Chen Guo. Without his blessings and teachings, I would not be able to give these teachings to you. He has been an extraordinary gift of the Divine. He is also much more. It is not possible to state in two brief paragraphs how extraordinary he is and what a privilege it is for me to be his disciple and lineage holder.

I am deeply grateful and appreciative for everything I have received from him and that I continue to receive. He is always with me. I always benefit from his blessings and teachings. Since I pass along what I receive, you have also benefited more than you can imagine from my dear father and master's teachings and blessings.

I am deeply grateful to the Divine. There are no words to express my gratitude. To have been chosen as a direct divine servant, vehicle, and channel is a special and extraordinary blessing and gift. To receive special authority to transmit many gifts from the Divine to you is an extraordinary honor. Through this book, I have passed to you gifts of Soul Language, Soul Song, Soul Movement, Soul Tapping, Soul Dance, and Divine Downloads. The Divine also teaches me and blesses me continually. I cannot express my gratitude to the Divine enough. I cannot honor the Divine enough. I cannot thank the Divine enough.

My Shi Fus are also continually present, teaching and blessing me. My gratitude to all of them and especially to my first Shi Fus, Yun Zhong Zi and Shi Jia Mo Ni Fuo, is beyond words. Their teachings, their blessings, and their help are most powerful. I am deeply grateful. I cannot honor them enough.

I am also very grateful to all my beloved students, Assistant Teachers, and Divine Direct Soul Communicators. They have made a strong commitment to following my teachings, to doing the practices I have suggested, and to living their lives in complete gratitude, obedience, loyalty, and devotion to the Divine. Many of them have heart-touching stories about their life transformation. Some of these can be found on my website, where you can benefit by reading them. I am grateful that they have performed this service and that they are so dedicated to the Divine.

I also give very special thanks to my dear parents and to my dear wife and children. Their love and support help me to be able to continue spreading my mission.

I am deeply grateful for the opportunity and privilege to be a divine unconditional universal healer, teacher, and servant. It is my greatest honor to serve you. Thank you. Thank you. Thank you.

Master Zhi Gang Sha

A Special Gift

In early 2008, the Divine guided me as follows: "Zhi Gang, this is the time for you to sing Soul Songs for healing and rejuvenation for humanity. Because you are my servant, vehicle, and channel, your Soul Song carries my love, light, and compassion. I will also download many divine souls to your soul. When you sing a Soul Song, these souls will come out to serve humanity and other souls."

I was deeply touched and moved. After receiving transmissions of new divine souls from the Divine every day for a week, I invoked these new Divine Downloads and recorded a number of Soul Songs for Healing and Rejuvenation of various organs, systems, parts of the body, and emotional imbalances.

The Divine guided me to offer Soul Songs for Healing and Rejuvenation to all humanity. You can sample them at www.master shasoulsong.com. People have already reported hundreds of heart-touching stories of remarkable healing and life transformation that they have received by listening to my Soul Songs. My heart is deeply moved. I cannot honor the Divine enough for his guidance, blessing, and Soul Power.

As a special gift for you, I am offering you a download of my Soul Song for Healing and Rejuvenation of Brain and Spinal Column. It is available on my website: www.drsha.com. I recommend you listen to this often, even repeatedly. You could have it playing constantly at low volume in your home or office. This Soul Song offers you healing for many health challenges, particularly because the brain and spinal column include the central nervous system, which connects with every system, every organ, and every cell of the body.

When you listen to this Soul Song, do not forget to say *hello* first:

> *Dear Soul Song for Healing and Rejuvenation of Brain and Spinal Column, I love you, honor you, and appreciate you. Please give me a healing and a blessing for* (state your health challenges or the blessings you wish to receive). *Thank you.*

A soul healing wave of divine love, light, compassion, vibration, and frequency will pour into your body and soul to serve you. My Soul Song is your servant. I hope you will receive great healing results from this Soul Song.

Thank you. Thank you. Thank you.

Dr. Sha's Teachings and Services

Books

Body Space Medicine by Dr. Zhi Chen Guo (Foreword by Dr. Sha). Heaven's Library,® 2007.

Living Divine Relationships. Heaven's Library, 2006.

Power Healing: The Four Keys to Energizing Your Body, Mind & Spirit. HarperSanFrancisco, 2002.

Soul Communication: Opening Your Spiritual Channels for Success and Fulfillment (revised edition). Atria Books/Heaven's Library, coming October 2008.

Soul Mind Body Medicine: A Complete Soul Healing System for Optimum Health and Vitality. New World Library, 2006.

Soul Wisdom: Practical Soul Treasures to Transform Your Life (revised edition). Atria Books/Heaven's Library, 2008.

Multimedia

Soul Mind Body Medicine: A Complete Soul Healing System for Optimum Health and Vitality. Heaven's Library/Alive! eBooks Network, 2008; www.heavenslibrary.com. Includes one hour of new audio content and one hour of new video content with Dr. Sha.

Healing, Blessing, and Life Transformation

Free Remote Healing Teleconference, Tuesdays, 5:30–6:30 p.m. Pacific Time. Register one time at www.drsha.com for this ongoing weekly healing service.

Divine Remote Group Healing, Rejuvenation, and Transformation Session with Master Sha, Sundays, 5:00–6:00 p.m. Pacific Time.

Divine Downloads and Blessings (www.drsha.com)

CDs and DVDs

Blessings from Heaven. Institute of Soul Mind Body Medicine, 2007. Divine Soul Music by Divine Composer Chun-Yen Chiang and Dr. Sha.

God Gives His Heart to Me. Institute of Soul Mind Body Medicine, 2008. The second Soul Song given by the Divine to Dr. Sha and humanity.

Love, Peace and Harmony. Institute of Soul Mind Body Medicine, 2007. The first Soul Song given by the Divine to Dr. Sha and humanity.

The Music of Soul Dance. Institute of Soul Mind Body Medicine®, 2007. A ten-CD boxed set of Heaven's music to inspire and help guide your Soul Dance.

Power Healing with Master Zhi Gang Sha: Learn Four Power Techniques to Heal Yourself. Institute of Soul Mind Body Medicine, 2006. This four-DVD set offers a comprehensive teaching of the wisdom, knowledge, and practice of Power Healing and Soul Mind Body Medicine. All aspects of Body Power, Sound Power, Mind Power, and Soul Power are covered in depth. Dr. Sha reveals and explains many secret teachings and leads you in practice.

Power Healing to Self-Heal Ten Common Conditions. Institute of Soul Mind Body Medicine, 2004. On this DVD, Dr. Sha teaches the Four Power Techniques® to self-heal:

- Anxiety
- Back pain
- Carpal tunnel syndrome
- Common cold
- Constipation
- Energy boosting
- Headache
- Knee pain
- Menopause
- Weight loss

Dr. Sha also offers personal blessings for each condition.

Soul Songs for Healing and Rejuvenation. www.mastershasoulsong.com, 2008. Divine Soul songs for various organs, systems, parts of the body, and emotions.

The Voice of the Universe: Power Healing Music. Qi Records, 2002. Four powerful new universal mantras for the Soul Light Era recorded by Dr. Sha:

- God's Light
- Universal Light
- Shining Soul Light
- Follow Nature's Way

www.drsha.com
www.heavenslibrary.com
1-888-3396815